THE WIND
IN MY WHEELS

THE WIND IN MY WHEELS

Josie Dew

WARNER BOOKS

A *Warner* Book

First published in the United Kingdom in 1922
by Little, Brown and Company
This edition published by Warner in 1993

A CIP catalogue for this book
is available from the British Library

ISBN 0 7515 0249 9

Printed in England by Clays Ltd, St Ives plc

Warner
A Division of
Little, Brown and Company (UK) Limited
165 Great Dover Street
London SE1 4YA

FOR CHRIS AND
FOR EVERYTHING
THAT HE WAS

Contents

Acknowledgements

Many thanks are due to the following who have helped and encouraged me on my way:

My father for refusing to buy me a horse for my tenth birthday and for buying me a bicycle instead; my mother for letting me go out to explore on it without too much fuss and for all the other touching things that mothers do, like sending out emergency supplies of cycling shorts to far-flung destinations; to Melanie for foolishly agreeing to cycle to Morocco with me and for turning her hand to the chapter heading illustrations; to Ward for a memorable up-and-down three years of togetherness; to Peter-Panty'osed-Wilson for drawing the maps and for a memorable hot and steamy few weeks in a Delhi hospital; to Jimmy Holmes for stimulating evenings of hob-top gossip; to Mrs Serena Churchill (alias 'Block'ed') for sending back my manuscript untouched and unread; to Makl Thomson (alias 'Red'ed') for not hitting me when I burnt his porridge pan, for teaching me everything I know about bottom brackets and for his unrivalled expertise in building me a bike when he didn't know what he was doing; to my rock-clambering editor Hilary Foakes for pulling me out of the pile; to Val Porter for sifting through a fat wodge of illegible manuscript in record time and for teaching me a thing or two about ferrets and keeping a cow; to Jane Hawkins for use of her hut during a summer of two-fingered typing; to Jim and Barbara Gavin for use of their granary over an autumn of two-and-a-half-fingered typing; to Jim and Jean Saunders in Nova Scotia for 'pampering' me and for managing to cram so many edible gifts into my panniers; to Maeve McGuiness for her ceaseless and typically touching Irish hospitality; to Robin Elsdale of Heathmount for early morning swims; to Nick Crane and John Pilkington for the Hand and Shears; to Ian Hibell for inspiration; to Lucinda Boyle and Sally Newman at The Traveller's Bookshop for indispensable tips, books and maps; to Cotswold Camping and Pam Fulton for indispensable advice; to Richard Dale at Smuggled Goods for indispensable and bottom-saving 'short liners'; to Jim McGurn at *New Cyclist* for all sorts of things; to Stuart Cycles and Condor Cycles for being bicycle shops that you wish there were more of; to Adrian Lowe for teaching me how to avoid being jettisoned out of a hammock; to James-Surecraft-Shaw for introducing me to Campagnolo and teaching me how to mend a puncture; to Kermit and Ursula Bartlett for letting me live in their nut-drawer; to all the people I cook for who never know where I am and yet still put in their multi-coursed menu orders; for my other brother Ant (alias 'Fiendish Warrior') who threatened not to give me a Christmas present if I didn't mention his name somewhere; and to all the many other people I've met far and near, whose names I will never know but whose help and heart-warming friendliness have made my past fifteen years of bicycle touring so memorable and such fun.

Maps by Peter Wilson
Sketches by Melanie Dew

THE WIND IN MY WHEELS

The Wheels Start Turning

AN INTRODUCTION

I started bicycle touring when I was eleven. At about the same time Ian Hibell (bicycle tourist extraordinaire) was halfway across the world dragging his bicycle waist-deep through the swamps of the South American jungles for fun. Meanwhile I would set out on day trips to explore new people and places, filling my bicycle basket with banana sandwiches and an inspirational Enid Blyton. Bicycle touring means different things to different people.

Although my adventures were comparatively tame, they still roused in me an excited anticipation of the unknown — that addictive feeling familiar to all cycle tourists. To be allowed out alone on my bike and to be able to decide simple things like when and where I could eat my lunch was immensely exciting. I bought a little plastic container for my packed food and an Ordnance Survey map with a bright pink cover so that I could embark upon some serious exploration of the local environs on my two small wheels.

Before setting out on my cycle-training missions, I would have to receive the go-ahead from my father. On my map he marked out an exclusion zone which, along with busy main roads, was forbidden territory for me, and he insisted on knowing my intended route in advance so that, in case of mishap, he would have a better idea of where to start searching. I found all this restraint most tiresome!

It was only when I decided to take a short-cut home one day that I discovered something even more invigorating: cross-country biking. Tearing down Titty Hill (its real name), through the beechwood, over the cattle grid, into the back woods and past the Lightning Tree before arriving home was indescribably wonderful and I began to make a habit of it. Had my father known what I was up to he would certainly have been shocked, but I meticulously cleaned all rough-riding evidence from my machine so that he was none the wiser.

All went well until the day I took the Dunner Hill route, a particularly bumpy and rutted descent, which was hilarious fun — while it lasted. Unfortunately my small-wheeled King Pin bicycle was far from boasting the robust sturdiness of today's mountain bikes. Hurtling downhill at full speed, I received no response whatsoever when I applied my brakes. Wondering why I was not stopping, I glanced down and realized (far too late) that the only problem with the back brake was that it did not exist. Almost simultaneously, my front axle snapped and I lost all control. I shot swiftly through the air and narrowly missed impaling myself on a heap of stakes before coming to rest on a large mound of bracken.

Picking myself up, I was dismayed to discover the damage I had inflicted on the King Pin. My immediate reaction was to kick the bike and pelt it with a barrage of stones — which was slightly unreasonable, considering the circumstances, but I was a little upset.

When I had composed myself after this outburst, I was alarmed to hear some stifled sniggering. Furtive investigation revealed one of my brothers (a budding ornithologist) perched precariously up a tree. He had witnessed the whole incident through binoculars and still relishes the memory to this day.

This was only the first of many dramatic tumbles and did not put me off bicycles in the least. My appetite for adventure was well and truly whetted and I was already on the road to a lifelong addiction for two-wheeled touring, wherever it might lead.

1

Itchy Feet and Bicycle Wheels

HARWICH TO THE SAHARA

'One of the main troubles about going to Europe is that no one wants to hear about your trip when you get back home. Your friends and relatives are not only sorry you went to Europe, but deeply regret that you came back!'

ART BUCHWALD

The plan was to cycle to Africa, a continent that had always seemed a million miles away. I conjured up images of Zulus running around with spears in their hands chasing man-eating lions, or of David Attenborough crouched low in wild shrubbery extolling the virtues of some evil-looking insect that could kill you in seconds.

Cycling to Africa sounded a lot more daunting than it actually was. On the map, it looked easy — downhill all the way. Also it did not look very far. It was only six-and-a-half thumbnails in my Philips School Atlas.

The previous year, I had cycled around Ireland with my boyfriend, Ward, a tall Scouse journalist, before continuing alone round the coast of Britain. Ward and I had originally met on bicycles while I was cycling around the Isle of Wight for fun and he was there for work. The tourist board was promoting it as the Bicycling Island and he was finding out, for the *Bournemouth Evening Echo*, whether it really was and, if so, why.

At first I did not like Ward at all. He chased me up one of the island's vertical hillsides on a single-speed, rusty boneshaker; then he chased me down the other side. Although it was a steep descent laced with hairpin bends, he attempted to carry out his chat-up routine as if we were standing sedately at a drinks party.

We screeched to a halt in Ventnor town centre. I managed to decipher only a handful of his heavily accented words and was rather shocked to realize that he had asked for my address. I kept my head and showed enough foresight to give him a false one but it was not false enough. A week later he had tracked me down and stood on my doorstep with a silly smirk on his face. After the initial shock, I allowed him in and was pleasantly surprised to discover that he held potential as a cycling companion. Over a bowlful of curried carrot soup, we decided to cycle around Ireland together.

At Dun Laoghaire we rolled off the Holyhead ferry into thick mist. It was very wet and very cold. Tired, hungry and with legs of jelly, we finally found a farmer's marshy field where we pitched the tent inconspicuously at the foot of a dense hawthorn hedge. Covered in mud and cow dung and with tent poles protruding at dangerously inappropriate angles, we clambered inside out of the rain.

I had failed to test Ward inside my tent before departure and somehow I had overlooked the fact that he was almost twice my length. To fit inside, he had to undergo a series of painful contortions. Having reached an ungainly degree of compaction, he had little choice other than to remain prostrate, able only to turn from his stomach to his back. Should he attempt any movement without consulting me, there was a very real possibility of the tent collapsing.

For me, though, fitting into tents was no problem. It was as if my small-scale body had been specifically designed for them. Even with Ward obstructing the main gangway like some beached whale, I was still able to wander around quite happily (albeit stooping) despite the roof standing at little more than three feet high. Tents are to me what marquees are to others.

After the events of the day we were looking forward to a good night's sleep. I slumbered soundly until about midnight, when I was woken abruptly by Ward's elbow in my side.

'Ow!' I said, slightly peeved. 'What are you playing at?'

'Ssssh,' hissed Ward nervously, 'there's something outside.'

I listened, ears straining into the night.

'I can't hear anything,' I told him. 'I'm going back to sleep.'

Suddenly a torch beam flashed erratically across the tent. Ward yelped and practically leapt into my arms. I thought he was overdoing it and was on the point of telling him so when merely feet away, but on the other side of the hedge, a couple of cars pulled up.

We heard the sound of car doors opening and banging and heavy-booted footsteps scuffing across the gravel. Rough Irish voices started arguing angrily and obscenities flew thick and fast. A scuffle broke out: we could hear a man pleading for his life. I suspected the whole incident was nothing more than an out-of-hand pub brawl but Ward, his journalistic mind working furiously, was adamant that it was the IRA; we were close to the border, after all.

'If we get discovered,' he whimpered, 'we'll be knee-capped — maybe even murdered!'

What seemed like hours was probably no more than minutes but to lie in a field only inches away from a bunch of IRA suspects was not pleasant. Finally the vociferations abated. Car doors slammed, engines revved impatiently and then the vehicles disappeared into the night as eerily as they had arrived.

'We're safe!' we cried. And then something brushed past the tent.

That was the last straw. I could take no more. Someone was prowling around outside the tent. I ordered Ward to venture outside and investigate — a request that sent him recoiling even further into his sleeping-bag. I was in no mood for any cowardly behaviour.

'Go on,' I said encouragingly, 'have a look.'

I extracted him forcefully from his bag and pushed him towards the mouth of the tent. Cautiously, he stuck his head through the zip door and immediately withdrew it with a yowl.

'What is it?' I asked, alarmed. 'What did you see?'

Before he had a chance to reply, a muzzle protruded through the tent opening. It was not a shotgun; it was a very inquisitive cow.

Africa, according to our measurements with a piece of thread wiggled down the map, lay roughly a 2,000-mile cycle ride away. We had felt high-spirited and confident until the moment the boat slowly eased out of Harwich, but moods rapidly turned sour when Ward asked me, 'Have you got the tea-bags?'

I swallowed hard, felt a little sick and admitted I had not. This might not sound a particularly serious misdemeanour — after all I had remembered passports, money and spare under-pants — but to Ward it was truly tragic. He happened to be from the north where, he told me, the tea-drinking ritual was performed with even more religious fervour than in the south. A cup of tea was not good enough for Ward, either; he had to have it by the pint mugful. He was also a habitual dunker and needed a ready supply of digestive biscuits, bits of which would break off and disappear into the murky depths of his mug.

Whilst list-making in preparation for our two-wheeled trek, Ward had seriously contemplated taking four months' supply of Tetley's to see him to Africa and back. I managed to talk him down to just a 'supply-load' which, as I was now being reminded, I had left behind.

It did not take long to reach Holland where, having disembarked, it did not take long to realize that we were lost. Leaving tea-bags behind may have been my fault, as I was in charge of food supplies, but getting lost was definitely Ward's, he was in charge of navigation.

Everywhere there were signs to a place called Dorgand Verkeer but no amount of searching revealed it on our map. We ended up going round and round in circles.

'Ward,' I said, feeling a little giddy, 'we're going round and round in circles.'

There are two things which make Ward feel like headbutting his handlebars. One is the thought of no Tetley's tea, the other is being lost, and both had occurred on the first day of our epic voyage to Africa. It was not a promising start.

Passing over the same bridge for the tenth time and seeing that my navigational expert was fast losing his temper, I took it upon myself to wave down a native approaching speedily on a traditional Dutch cycle. It turned out to be a woman, a genial one at that, with her son attached to an impressive construction on the rear rack. This was my first foreign cycling trip and this would be my first attempt at asking directions in a foreign tongue. I fumbled nervously in my handlebar bag for my handy pocket-sized but irrelevant phrase-book.

'*Goedendag, Mevrouw*,' I ventured. '*Wat is de beste weg naar Dorgand Verkeer?*'

'Aaah, British! How delightful!' she exclaimed in perfect English. 'Now, tell me, what is it you were trying to say?'

Rather taken aback, I finally stammered, 'Ooooh! I was just wondering if you knew which is the way to Dorgand Verkeer. We seem to be having a bit of trouble finding it on our map.'

The way the woman laughed was a touch disconcerting. After all, locating this elusive place was becoming a serious problem.

'Dorgand Verkeer,' she hooted, clutching her ample midriff, 'means "on-going traffic"!'

'Ah, yes, of course,' we said, sheepishly wondering how we could have been so dim. By way of compensation for such an inauspicious start, the woman kindly invited us to follow her back to her house for orange squash and a sit-down. We felt a lot better after that and started much refreshed on the road to Amsterdam.

Nearly half the population of the Netherlands rides a bike daily. They treat the bicycle as the obvious and sensible alternative to anything motorized and bounce along on their humble vehicles over a vast nationwide network of more than 6,000 miles of cycle paths.

The Dutch favour the sturdy and traditional sit-up-and-beg type of bike for their commuting, shopping and business needs and for getting to and from school; but most of those who like to cycle longer distances for pure enjoyment keep a light-weight, multi-geared model behind the scenes, ready and raring to go.

The number of dismembered bone-shakers chained to railings, lamp-posts and even boats or barges was truly staggering. I had never seen so many bicycles with so many bits missing. I could not understand why this should be until the day I stayed with my Dutch friend, Maarten.

We had arrived by bicycle to see a local band and had left our machines locked together. When we emerged around midnight onto the still busy streets of Nijmegen, we discovered that Maarten was now one front wheel and saddle worse off. This struck me as a blow and I felt nonplussed that someone could just come along and whisk away these vital necessities. I was equally perplexed as to why my own bicycle remained intact and I was just on the point of asking Maarten whether we should inform the police when he strode across to the nearest cycle (of similar design to not only his own but everybody else's), extracted a spanner from his knapsack and removed the wheel and saddle, returning to place them on his own bike.

I was shocked. My immediate reaction was to disown him but none of the people who passed him by in mid-theft batted an eyelid.

'Maarten!' I cried. 'What are you playing at?'

Maarten was disconcertingly unruffled about the whole business and even expressed amusement over my concern.

'It's all right,' he reassured me, 'this is quite normal and is the advantage of all owning similar bicycles. We all take bits off each other's. That's why nobody has touched yours — it's different so nothing will fit. Our method not only works well, it also saves going to the shops.'

Although the Netherlands caters for cyclists better than any other country in the world, it can take a while for a newcomer to come to grips with the system. The first feature I noticed was that a map is almost superfluous if you have long-distance cycling in mind. This is because maps mark roads — and to travel on these on a bicycle is forbidden in Holland. You are given your own roads and, by golly, motorists certainly do their utmost to make sure you stick to them. Should you dare place even so much as one wheel on their rightful territory, you find yourself at the end of a rapid stream of native abuse and frantic gesticulations.

So you find yourself being channelled and diverted off on to a specially-designed track in the opposite direction from which you intended to go. I am not saying it is unpleasant to be whisked away from thundering vehicles and to have your own special little traffic lights and signs. Far from it: it is lovely. In fact, it is stupendous. However, these special signposts rarely tally with the places marked on your map. Strangely, fellow cyclists seemed to have no problems and I put it all down to Ward's suspect navigational skills.

It also takes time to master the art of cycling *en masse*, a problem rarely encountered in Britain where the infrequency of passing a fellow pedaller is so exciting that you either wave, bid good day or end up having tea together. In Holland, however, you are one in a pedalling crowd and cycling in convoy can be quite an unnerving experience. You are swept up amongst the throngs and whisked away in a forest of whirling wheels and the shrill cacophony of a million bicycle bells. In places it feels like being on a motorway and attempting to overtake can be a hazardous affair. Mirror, signal, manœuvre — that is the routine and even then things can go worryingly wrong. Multiple pile-ups are not uncommon.

When we finally arrived in Amsterdam we immediately headed for Pizzaland. Ward might have been missing his English tea and dunkable digestives but I was missing my baked potatoes — and Pizzaland does surprisingly good ones. Then, well fuelled, we swivelled round 180 degrees and started on the long journey south.

At first, Ward and I positively bowled along. We raced past windmills, tulip fields, gabled houses and dykes; we crossed canals, rivers and waterways; we saw clogs, cheeses, sand dunes and seas of glass under which salad vegetables, fruits and flowers flourished. It was a wonderful feeling to be on our way at last, with no commitments and no time schedule. This was not a two-week package tour: we had four months or more of fanciful freedom.

Ward had left his job on the *Evening Echo* and I had put my bicycle-delivery catering business on hold, at least until our funds ran out. Our bicycles were our mobile homes. Packed on them was everything we needed (except Tetley's tea-bags) for the next few months of life on the road. Ahead of us lay an adventure into the unknown and we embarked on it with an unsuppressible surge of excitement.

It is amazing how quickly you can adapt to a completely different lifestyle. By the second day, Ward had almost forgiven me for leaving his Tetley's behind and was quite happy with a peculiar coloured fruit tea as a substitute. On the third day, as I distinctly remember, he extracted himself from the tent, stretched in the fresh morning sunshine and exclaimed, 'This is the life! Feels as natural as if I've been doing it for years.' He rapidly changed his attitude when a steady drizzle set in.

It did not take long to cross Holland — or, as my Dutch friend continuously corrects me, the Netherlands. Holland is the name more accurately applied to its two wealthiest provinces, Noord Holland and Zuid Holland. Whatever they call it, most people think of it as the ideal country for cycling, mainly because of its flatness and suitability for cyclists. However, it is also a country beset by insistent winds; and winds, as every cyclist knows, invariably blow head on, no matter how many times you change direction to avoid them.

The advantages of living in continental Europe are that it is both varied and compact. America, China, Australia and Russia, for example, are so *big*. European countries are much less daunting: if you happen to have had enough of one country, it only takes a quick burst of pedal-power to find yourself in a new one with a new culture.

Sometimes we found the countries so small that we had crossed them before we knew it. Belgium just passed us by. It tends to be a country that you visit only if you must — on the way to somewhere else, perhaps, or because you work for the EEC or have a boat to catch. As a nation, Belgium has not really had long to get its feet on the ground: it is only about 160 years old. It is as though it could not decide what sort of a country it wanted to be when it grew up and so it has become a cultural soup with ingredients from France, Holland and Germany. It was born of a revolution within the larger kingdom of the Netherlands and had to import a king from

Germany since it had no royalty of its own.

I did not know that it was possible to import kings. It makes you wonder. Here in Britain we have a large assortment of royals in all shapes, sizes and sexes. Perhaps we could export a royal or two in exchange for something useful like a crate of kumquats or some precious metal.

Belgium's population is divided into Flemish-speakers, who speak in a phlegmy sort of way, and French-speakers who, to confuse matters further, are known as Walloons although hardly any of them speak that language. The Flemish outnumber the Walloons by about three to two and they say that no other fact about modern Belgium is so important . . .

It is not entirely true to say that we passed through Belgium scarcely aware of having done so. I remember cycling along on a very hot day on a very flat road when I was overtaken by two racy cyclists dressed in body-hugging lycra. They slowed down and waited until I pulled broadside before squirting me with the contents of their water-bottles. Then they accelerated off, laughing. I thought: how curious.

I also remember sleeping in a Belgian rose garden. We had plunged down a steep hill into Liège (Belgium's chief industrial town) and were ever so slowly labouring back out again up an equally steep hill when it got dark. Just like that. When we had started up the hill it had been sunny and bright but by the time we reached the top it was black. It was not a particularly long hill. Maybe it had something to do with our two-hour rest halfway up for light refreshments at a bar. Anyway, there we were at the top of the hill in the dark, with nowhere to spend the night. We carried on cautiously until we came to a house.

Until now, Ward and I had slept in campsites. This was our first opportunity to knock on a native door and request permission to camp in the garden. When it came to something like this, Ward would urge me to venture forth and for the first time in the whole day he would become uncharacteristically complimentary. 'Go on,' he would say, pushing me houseward, 'you're much better than me at this sort of thing and I'm sure no one with a heart would turn you away. Anyway, your

French is so much better than mine.' That was true.

Thus I found myself knocking hesitantly on that Belgian front door as Ward cowered out of sight in the shadows. Finally the door opened and a little wispy man with fluffy hair stood there in his wishy-washy pyjamas, looking a little unsure of himself. I wondered if that was what a Walloon looked like.

Down the hallway I caught a glimpse of a lurking, witchlike character with wild black hair and a long, flowing cloak.

The man said, '*Oui?*'

Rather awkwardly, I said, 'Oh!' and then, as an afterthought, '*Bonsoir, Monsieur.*'

I was not getting a good feeling about the whole affair, especially when I caught sight of the witch again — this time spying through a door left ajar. I felt like turning tail but instead I decided to say something else.

'*Excusez-moi, mais avez-vous une petite place pour notre tente? Nous sommes en velos.*'

Monsieur Fluffy Head failed to answer but I heard a distinct hiss from the direction of the witch. It sounded like the French equivalent of: 'Albert, if you dare let them two put so much as one foot inside our garden, I swear you won't hear the end of it!'

Then I saw her hand. It slithered round the side of the door and the hairs on my neck went all bristly. Those grotesquely long fingernails looked like clawed tentacles . . .

Albert then said something that I did not understand but which, surprisingly, sounded kindly and almost welcoming. I felt he was acting in complete disregard of the witch's wishes. Indeed, after he had been speaking in this benevolent manner I heard a rather shocked and disapproving hiss — and I am pretty sure it was not the kettle.

Albert then said something else that I failed to understand but I pretended I did and nodded and smiled accordingly. When, in his amicable way, he muttered something about '*tente*' and '*jardin*' and led us round the back, I thought: I like you, Albert, even if you are a Walloon.

And that is how we found ourselves setting up camp

amongst Monsieur and Madame Langlois's roses. Every now and then I would look up towards the house and catch a sinister glimpse of the witch slinking stealthily behind a crack in the curtains. Presently Albert, still in his pyjamas, shuffled across the lawn and indicated that we could use the toilet in the basement of the garage.

He was about to return to the house when suddenly, bounding across the garden towards us, came his big, buxom daughter, Fabienne. As she bubbled forth in boisterous gabble, I stood bemused. Could this really be a descendant of the witch? She seemed a most unlikely daughter. Thanks to her, we were in a moment transported to their balcony where a candlelit table was set and food and drink placed before us. There followed much roisterous merrymaking into the night, though the witch still lurked ominously behind the scenes. Finally, in Franglais, I asked Fabienne why her mother did not join us.'

'*Oh là, là!*' she said. '*Ma maman*, she eeze ver-ee, ver-ee worry. She saze you 'ave much madness. No one, she saze, rides a *bicyclette* for fun!'

What a strange woman. But she was not alone, it seemed. During the next few weeks I was amazed at the number of people we met who expressed a similar opinion. And I thought: what a shame.

Rolling over the Ardennes, we found ourselves in Luxembourg, a country no bigger than Hampshire. All I knew about the place was that it was small and was home to Europe's first commercial radio station, Radio Luxembourg, which went on the air in 1934.

Luxembourg is Europe's last independent grand duchy and some say the country was formed as a sort of buffer zone to keep France and Germany from each other's throats. To help preserve their identity, the people have devised Letzeburgesch, a language based on old Teutonic, which nobody can understand. It was a nice idea but not very practical and the majority of the population speak perfect English.

The capital, also called Luxembourg, sits above sheer cliffs with impressive vistas over the Alzette and Petruse valleys. As we moseyed with our mounts into the Place d'Armes, a band was playing enthusiastically in the bandstand and big, bright flags adorned the sides of ancient buildings. Crowds of happy drinkers sat chatting beneath colourful umbrellas at the many bars that surrounded the square. In the long shadows of the warm evening sun, it was a cheerful and bustling scene and it seemed a friendly place — until I tried to make my first phone-call home.

The operator told me she was unable to connect me because a bomb had gone off in the city, destroying the lines. How strange! Were we talking about the same place? I had heard no bang and, from the looks of things, nor had any one else in this peaceful main square. Maybe the operator was just having one of those days at work and was longing to get home to put her feet up in front of the television instead of talking to an infuri-ating foreigner who could not even speak the language. I didn't blame her — and at least it was an excuse with a difference. Anyway, she told me to go away, brush up my French and try again later.

We spent that night in a campsite at the foot of the city. For our bicycling tour I had bought a hooped tunnel tent supported by lightweight, flexible graphite poles that slotted together. To erect the tent, you simply fed the poles through an outer sleeve, hence bending them round into an almost endless curve, and pegged it out. That sounds impossible but it was so easy that even Ward could do it.

That night we found ourselves camped next to a York-shireman who had a conventional A-frame tent. He ambled over to our designated plot (number 471) and commented on the design of our tent.

'Eeh, lass,' he said, 'that's a raat fan tent you've goot yerselves there. You never fand yerselves with problems with them poles laak — you nor, what with breakin' and sooche-laak?'

'Oh no,' I said confidently, adding like some old hand, 'we've had no trouble since we've been on the road and I don't think we will. They seem pretty sturdy. Anyway, the shop where I bought them said because they're graphite they won't break unless an elephant falls on them.'

The Yorkshireman seemed suitably impressed and looked as though he was about to say so when we were startled by an ominous cracking noise. We turned to see the back pole of our tent no longer bent but broken. The two fractured pieces pointed skywards in an inverted V-shape that looked as if our tent was trying its utmost to imitate the conventional A-frame on plot 470.

''Ere, luuv,' said our friend, 'cum an' 'ave a naz coopa tea.'

In Europe there is a route where it is possible to cycle through five countries in a day without too much effort. The distance is about 103 miles and links the Netherlands, Germany, Belgium, Luxembourg and France. Attempting this ride tickled our fancy and by the time we arrived in Luxembourg we already had three countries under our belt. That, though, was as far as we got. Somehow our one-hour lunch break turned into a three-hour siesta, by the end of which I declared my legs were feeling tired. Sun, snooze and sustenance can have an overwhelmingly soporific effect. Ward feigned disappointment but was secretly rather relieved when he discovered his own limbs were not quite the powerhouses he had believed. Instead, we lay flaked out on the grass, practising the traditional English art of snoozing in the sun. Jerome K. Jerome's words in *Three Men on the Bummel* seemed particularly apt: 'We did not succeed in carrying out our programme in its entirety, for the reason that human performance lags ever behind human intention.'

We pedalled on in due course to Strasbourg, the capital of Alsace. By this stage I was suffering seriously from the one thing that puts most people rapidly off bicycles: sitting on them. Saddles are a sore point with cyclists. As we bumped our way over the cobbles towards Strasbourg's impressive Gothic cathedral, I felt as though I had a sheet of coarse-grade sand-paper down my shorts. ('Smuggled Goods' and their padded shorts-liners had yet to be invented.)

The sight of the red sandstone cathedral reflecting the deep, rosy hues of the setting sun momentarily took my mind off any posterior problems, as did the discovery of a Marks & Spencer food department. But remounting brought me back to painful reality.

Campers seem to think that, once zipped into their tents, they are insulated from the outside world. It is not so. Tents may screen their occupants from neighbouring eyes but not from neighbouring ears. The most private conversation whisks straight through the canvas. Lying in such close proximity to other tents on a campsite is aurally as good as all being in the same tent. You hear a lot of rude noises. Then there are the sounds made by doting couples ...

Ward and I found ourselves housed next to such a pair that night in Strasbourg. The campsite literally reverberated with their passion — and that was not all. Tent-dwellers also appear unaware that inner tent illumination reveals silhouettes of immense interest to outside observers and our Strasbourg couple put on an impressive and explicit *son et lumière*.

Switzerland would be a huge country if it were ironed out. Instead, the land lies in lofty concertina folds which rise into the skies. These are mountains. The usual advice from people who have never cycled over such barriers is: don't. Stick to Holland, they say, nice flat Holland. For us, this was not prac-tical. After all, we had just come from there and were heading for Italy. Before we reached the land of Pisa and pasta, a lumpy obstacle lay in our path: the Alps.

Until you have cycled over a mountain, it is hard to imagine what to expect. Of course a lot of effort is involved and —

depending on your state of fitness — a degree of pain, a pain which situates itself not only in the legs but also in the stomach. Cycling uphill for hour after hour can produce alarmingly frequent hunger pangs and, ironically, mountains are the least likely places to find food, especially lots of it.

So far, my initiation into cycling uphill for any distance had proved far from encouraging. The previous week, when riding in the mountains of the Black Forest on a hot and humid day, I had overheated. Jelly-legged and furiously panting, I had collapsed into a supine stupor and it was a while before I had sufficiently recovered to continue. It was not a good rehearsal.

I need not have worried. The Alps did indeed reduce me to a quivering wreck but it was with a feeling of conquest (and thanks to the numerous vehicles that passed waving and cheering encouragement on the way) that I made it to the summit. At the top there was a family having a snowball fight. 'Bravo!' they shouted as we eased to a halt. The view, though, was nothing to write home about and it was cold; we did not linger for long but, hastily wrapping up, embarked upon the descent.

Here we were greeted with the spectacular sight of neighbouring peaks, grassy valleys and the corkscrew road which curled ahead of us — but careering over cobbles and round hairpin bends down steep gradients does not give much chance to soak in the scenery. As your bike surges forwards, the wind whistling through your hair, it is tempting to release the brakes and fly, in imitation of those Tour de France boys, but plunging into a bend at breakneck speed is far too risky. You might meet a car, or hit loose gravel, or realize too late that your brakes are not so good and simply plummet over the edge. Hannibal had experienced similar problems when he marched his army over the Alps in 218 BC. After an elephant overshot a bend, the general was heard to say: 'At least he won't do *that* again.'

We felt wary about Italy. It was only a month since the terrible disaster at Heysel Stadium in Brussels when Liverpudlian football fans had gone on a rampage at the European Cup Final. Forty-one Italian and Belgian supporters had died and at least 350 had been injured, and many violent reprisals were carried out by the Italians against the British in the following weeks. That Ward was a Scouser would not help matters. We therefore approached the border with some trepidation and prepared ourselves for an icy, intimidating reception. Our mouths went dry as the Customs officials flicked through our passports.

'Liverpool!' cried one, spotting Ward's place of birth. '*Fantastico!*' Then they saw his christian name. 'Trevor!' they shouted gleefully. 'You are Trevor Francis, no?' They slapped him on the back in jest.

For five weeks in Italy we had no trouble at all, and arrived at Lake Como in a spectacular thunderstorm. Palm trees were bent double, waves lashed the shore and people shouted excitedly as they ran for cover. Beneath an awning, an old man with a creased face was sitting on a bench, hunched over his stick. He wore a large black hat and gazed knowingly out over the choppy waters. I asked him for directions but when he replied his false teeth fell out. I shall always associate him with Lake Como.

We should have avoided Milan, Italy's leading industrial and commercial city. As we approached the centre, after passing miles of high-rise blocks and factories belching out evil smoke, Ward's brake cable snapped and he collided with a taxi.

Italy is one of those rare European countries in which bicycle-racing can actually be called a national sport. Despite this, a bike-shop mechanic either treats a bicycle with the love and respect it deserves — or he does not. The stocky little Signore who attempted to tend Ward's machine did not. With hammer in hand, he embarked upon the delicate operation with a violent, unmechanical air. Bang! Thwack! Crunch! Luckily we salvaged Ward's steed before further mutilation, preferring a bodged DIY job.

The Piazza Duomo made up for any misgivings about Milan. Here in the middle of the city stands the third largest cathedral in the world, a building of Gothic splendour that explodes skywards in a riot of pinnacles and spires. However, our last two Milanese hours were spent cycling round in infuriating circles. We tried desperately to leave the city but every person and every signpost directed us towards the motorway, on which bicycles were prohibited. Finally, in desperation, we had to ride along it anyway, ignoring the blaring horns and waving fists of kamikaze drivers as best we could.

A couple of days later we were crossing the Alpi Apuane — a small, twisting mountain range that hugs the Gulf of Genova. The deep blue sea of the Mediterranean came into view but our moods turned sour as we arrived in Chiavari. The town appeared dead to the world and its restaurants and shops were closed for their endless siesta (the time, it is said, that is most favoured for extramarital affairs). The streets were empty. It was a ghost town and, as far as our stomachs were concerned, an unwelcome initiation to the Italian afternoon.

Once again we became lost as Ward experimented with an alternative to the traffic-laden main road. At last, after a very long short-cut, we plunged down a vertical mountainside and arrived in a small seaside village at its foot. We were tired, hot and hungry. It was still siesta time. Nothing stirred. The only road out led back up the mountain again. Hunger pangs led us to take the train a few miles down the coast to Pisa — a simple enough journey in theory ...

After we had bought our tickets in La Spezia, we discovered that there were delays owing to industrial action. No one knew what time the train to Pisa would leave and so we sat it out amongst the chaotic throngs on the platform. Five-and-a-half hours later we were still there, but word had it that a train would soon be leaving.

We found the train and clambered on board. Our bikes had been left with the baggage handlers who had assured us they would be travelling on our train. Ward had his doubts about this and, shortly before the train was due to depart, he told me he was just going to check that the bikes had been put in the guard's van. 'Watch the bags,' he said, 'and don't let the train go without me.'

Minutes passed and still there was no sign of him. People were frantically rushing, waving, kissing and slamming doors in last-minute haste. A big, burly guard with a thicket of black moustache started signalling to the driver and blowing his whistle. Apparently we were about to leave. With still no sign of Ward, I started to panic.

'Hey, *uno momento*, Signore!' I said. '*Mi scusi*. We can't leave yet. We must wait for my *amigo, per favore*.'

But this train had waited long enough and it was not going to wait any longer for a typical tourist making an unintelligible fuss. Annoyed with the delay, passengers leaning out of the window started impatiently shouting and gesticulating. I thought: I suppose I had better wait for Ward.

Hastily I started to remove our ridiculously large mound of eleven bags from the train. I had three panniers on the platform when the train started to move. Panic prevailed. I had a split second to decide whether I wanted to stay with Ward and lose our luggage, or stay with our luggage and lose Ward. The decision was easy: our possessions were far more precious and I frantically hurled them, along with myself, back on to the slowly moving train.

By now I had attracted considerable interest from fellow passengers and was being observed with bemusement. I could see them wondering: what on earth is a little girl like her doing leaping on and off a moving train with all that luggage? It was a good question.

Then I realized that Ward had the tickets. Hiding in the toilet to avoid the guard, I pondered on my next move. Would Ward be waiting for me back in La Spezia or should I continue to Pisa with the hope of meeting him there? I decided to jump off the train at the next station and return to La Spezia, an operation which involved staggering numerous times across the track with my luggage. The friendly stationmaster told me there would be a train shortly; an hour later I was still there.

Then the fast train for Pisa approached. I was just wondering whether Ward might be on it when suddenly I caught sight of his blurred form dangling out of the window, semaphoring towards Pisa. And then he was gone.

I thought: well, that's just great. He has all the money and I have all the luggage.

Hours later, I arrived at Pisa and trudged wearily across the platform, laden with bags that stretched my arms down to my ankles. There was no sign of Ward. Had I imagined seeing him on that train? Had he gone back to La Spezia? I staggered around the station looking for him, growing progressively more desperate. Finally I found him at the restaurant across the way, casually shovelling in mouthfuls of *spaghetti alla marinara*. He looked up and grinned.

'What took you so long?'

I felt like hitting him. And I believe I did.

The next day, all had been forgiven (our bikes had been on the train all along) and nearly forgotten. We were in Pisa and, although we were no great lovers of major tourist attractions, a visit to the Leaning Tower was high on our agenda.

This toppling construction, built as a bell tower for the nearby cathedral, is nearly seventeen feet out of true at the top, its ten-foot foundations being inadequate for a tower 179 feet tall. I knew that it leaned, of course, but not *that* much. As I climbed around the vertiginous open arches on a polished floor as smooth as an ice rink and with no safety barriers to prevent you skidding off, it struck me as decidedly dangerous. I kept getting wheelspin. The more desperately I tried to clamber away from potential danger, the further I slipped back towards potential death.

Some years later, in October 1989, the Ministry of Public Works declared the tower unsafe but there was uproar from the locals, arguing that the tower's revenues amounted to over a million pounds a year.

By now we had been riding for several weeks and we had

enjoyed almost every moment. It had been an easy ride, despite people's words of warning before leaving. It's madness, some had said, you'll be robbed or run over; the Alps will be hell; you might be murdered by the Monster of Florence — a psychotic serial killer who was at large in Italy after more than two decades of carrying out the sexually macabre murders of canoodling couples in remote areas of Tuscany.

I was pleasantly relieved that none of these hazards had yet befallen us but Ward wanted an adventure and expressed disillusionment at just how easy the going had been.

'Don't worry,' I said, 'we've hardly started; anything could still happen.'

Ward was not satisfied. As nothing of significance had so far occurred, he decided to fabricate his own excitement; after all, he had been a reporter on the *Bournemouth Evening Echo*. Scribbling in his diary in elaborate detail, he described how he had stumbled across a grotesquely mutilated body in a campsite 'Gents' and how we unwittingly became involved with a clandestine gang of murderers. Being innocent cycle tourists, we were used as the perfect decoy.

Acting as Little Miss Sensible, I told Ward that I would disown him if the diary was discovered. Worryingly, such threats only encouraged him.

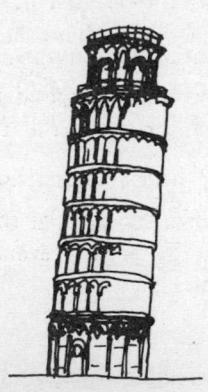

I had first heard of Siena in a dark, seedy cinema on the outskirts of Liverpool, where it had featured in a trailer film. As Ward and I sunk into our seats, we became aware that the murky gloom was alive with missiles, some of which were evidently children. The scene was one of mayhem. Scouse youngsters were clambering over seats, falling over each other, fighting, farting, guffawing. Then the curtain lifted and the trailer began. In direct contrast to the cinema's bedlam, the serene Italian city of Siena appeared on the screen in a documentary about the famous Corsa del Palio, a dangerously thrilling city-centre horse race which has been held since the Middle Ages between teams in costume representing the city's mediaeval quarters. This race, which inspired Daphne du Maurier's *The Flight of the Falcon*, is held in honour of the Virgin (the city's patron) and to commemorate ancient victories.

Hours before the race begins, the square is packed with people and every available viewing space, window and rooftop is taken. The excitement of anticipation rises to a sweaty crescendo as the start of the race approaches. Each of the town's fifteen parishes enters a horse and a jockey and the crowd breaks into a frenzy of shouts and cheers as they career around the piazza. The winner earns the much prized Palio, a banner bearing the effigy of the Virgin, and the right to celebrate in true Italian style for weeks afterwards.

Although we were too early in the year for the races, we still paid Siena a visit and sat at a restaurant on the piazza's 'racetrack', refuelling with pesca-pasta salad and vino. On a hot, sleepy afternoon, the rumpus of that Liverpudlian cinema seemed another age away. With stomachs and senses well satisfied, we wandered over to the stripy Gothic cathedral, delineated by bands of black and white marble like a vast Liquorice Allsort.

As we neared Rome, I began to suffer from backache. It grew worse until one night I woke up and had trouble moving. Even breathing hurt. For a few days I lay flat out in the shade at our fly-ridden campsite on the outskirts of the city. Things did not improve and so Ward escorted me to hospital. After much queuing, waiting and form-filling, I finally found myself on Dr Feo's couch.

Dr Feo was small, bald and sweaty-headed. As he leant over my lower back, poking and prodding, little beads of perspiration dripped off his forehead and some splashed on me. He may not have been a romantically macho Italian but he was nice and spoke excellent English (the only one in the hospital who did) with a distinct American drawl.

'Hey! How're ya doin'?' he asked as he pummelled and tapped and stretched various parts of my anatomy.

'Not so good, thanks,' I replied.

He suspected that I had pulled a muscle or something (I admitted that I had been giving thirteen-stone Ward piggyback rides), and gave me some pills.

'Now, take it easy,' he said, and I left.

Our campsite was not an ideal place for a speedy recovery. Because of the heat, I could not lie in the tent to escape the incessant flies and the only shade was down near the stench of the overflowing toilet block. There were ants, too, of a small but particularly vicious biting variety. They were everywhere: in our tent, our sleeping-bags, our bread, our jam and, yes, even in our pants.

The pain grew worse. I had never been ill abroad before and I was not enjoying it. I pined for my own bed with cool, clean sheets and my own mother tending lovingly to my every need. The thought of cold, wet, drizzly England had never been so appealing.

As Ward busied himself with sleeping and eating (giant butties of Emmental and mortadella — a sliced pork sausage flavoured with garlic, coriander seeds and pistachio nuts), I studied our fellow campers.

Shaun and 'Tray-ceeee', two big blubber-balls, had cycled from Southend. Apparently they hated every moment. 'It's been awful, ain't it, Trace — such bleedin' 'ard work. We're only doin' it for the paper. We're trainee journalists, ya know. Never want to see another bleedin' bicycle. We're flying home, thank Gawd.'

Simon the Economy Backpacker was another distraction. I watched him set up and dismantle his tent six times. 'I lak to gettit joost rhat,' he said. He was from Yorkshire and 'training it' around Europe on Interrail. 'It's the travelling I lak,' he said, 'and not the saat-seeing. That costs mooney. Sor I spend most ma time on the train lak, yer knor. Joost cum from Barcelona I 'ave and slept most of the ware. Tear-ken a good two days and I've spent nowt.'

Most curious of all was a wizardly man of unidentifiable nationality. He never spoke except to his parrot, Dennis, which, judging from its replies, possessed an impressive vocabulary. All day long the wizard would sit by his tent hunched over his handiwork: he was meticulously stitching together an enormous pair of snakeskin trousers. As dusk approached, he would mount his moped and disappear off down the road with squawking Dennis obediently following overhead.

My backache was worse and I paid another visit to Dr Feo, who sent me to have an X-ray. He appeared encouraged by the results.

'You have a kidney infection!' he announced triumphantly. 'A possible kidney stone. This explains your backache. I put it down to dehydration. Where did you say you were heading?'

'Africa,' I said.

'No way! No way! You'd be a fool to try,' he admonished, giving me a bottle of large green pills. He told me to drink at least five litres of water a day and, above all, to rest. 'Leave off that bike!' he advised.

For the first week I obeyed Dr Feo's instructions to 'take it easy'. I had little other choice as even moving hurt and peeing was a painful problem. Luckily I improved and, encouraged, we packed up and cycled south, albeit slowly. I felt very weak, became easily exhausted and suffered sporadic stabs of backache. Apart from that, I felt fine and was raring to go.

We rode on down the coast to Anzio where, so I had been

informed by Dad, who thought of himself as a potential war correspondent, one of the most bitterly contested operations of the Second World War had taken place.

Down at the sea-front, bronzed fishermen were rhythmically thrashing octopuses upon the rocks. Black clouds lowered in the sky and it felt hot and muggy. As we ran into the sea to cool off, there was such a violent hailstorm that we had to keep diving under the water to avoid being knocked out by the colossal hailstones.

On the outskirts of Naples, I ran across the road to buy Ward a giant cornetto ice-cream from a streetside stall. The woman, a Big Mama, told me to remove my neck-chain and earrings before a thief did. 'Napoli,' she said, '*molto pericoloso!*' It was dangerous, she said, because of the Mafia — there was on average four murders a week.

Just down the road we passed a hearse. Sobbing and wailing women veiled in black dabbed lace handkerchiefs to tearful eyes.

The Bay of Naples resembles a vast, cavernous mouth ready to engulf whatever floats or falls in its way. Looming behind is the watchful, ominous mound of Mount Vesuvius and it is this mighty volcano to which the mouth belongs. In AD 79 it erupted and swallowed up three flourishing towns; in Pompeii alone more than two thousand people died beneath a blanket of ash and dust twenty feet deep. After that, Vesuvius exploded a further nine times until 1036 and then lay dormant until 1631 when, as though awakening full of energy from a long and satisfying hibernation, it cleared its throat again and killed more than three thousand people. Lava flowed down to the bay and Naples (about ten miles away) was left knee-deep in ash. Vesuvius had remained intermittently alive until fairly recently, erupting another nineteen times.

As Ward and I camped at the foot of Vesuvius, I lay on the dusty, black ash soil and thought about the horrific scenes of destruction and death those eruptions had caused — the screams and lives that had been muffled and buried by this vast, voracious volcano. And still it is not dead yet. Today, with more than two million people living in its shadow, Vesuvius remains the only active volcano on mainland Europe and the prospect of another catastrophe is never far away.

Early next morning we followed the well-worn tourist trail to Pompeii, hoping to beat the crowds, but we had no such luck. As we skidded to a stop in the gravelled tourist park, monstrous coaches with gaping exhaust pipes, like colossal colons, were spewing forth their noxious waste. Phalanxes of lard-white sightseers spilled out of their air-conditioned capsules through tinted double doors, all of them skimpily clad even though it was not yet hot.

It was easy to guess their nationality. The men wore baggy shorts, dark knee-length socks and Jesus sandals; the women wore towelling shorts two sizes too tight. A rotund lady, endeavouring to conceal her pneumatic body, was draped in baggy wraps and clung to two books, a Michelin guide to Italy and a copy of *The F-Plan Diet*. And of course there was a spotty-faced youth wearing a shimmering pair of acrylic Union Jack shorts.

As these British coach tourists were taking a while to regroup, we scurried past — careful to keep our eyes averted and English mouths firmly shut. Quickly, to beat the hordes, we plunged into the ruins of Pompeii.

They had lain hidden for a good sixteen centuries. The first findings of a subterranean town came in 1738, when some peasants discovered several statues. For these they were able to demand high prices, and considerable enthusiasm was stirred.

The massive layer of ash had preserved much of the detail of town life. I tagged on to the end of a tourist party (they have their uses) and was intrigued to discover what forward thinkers those Romans had been. Central heating, one-way streets and take-aways were just three of their inventions.

The most astonishing revelation of all was that the bodies of the volcano's victims had left moulds in the solid ash before the flesh had decayed. Fiorelli, the chief archaeologist, had poured plaster of Paris into the moulds and then removed the ash once the plaster had set. Thus he had recreated dozens of motionless scenes filled with the postures and even facial expressions of the terrified, fleeing citizens captured at the very moment of death. It was grim but compulsive viewing.

Before the heat and the crowds became overpowering, we scuttled back to our bikes and headed out through the modern town of Pompeii. It lies just to the east of the ruins and, as well as catering for tourists, it manufactures macaroni and packing-boxes. We saw no reason to stop but ventured southwards in leisurely style until we reached Sapri. Here, over our habitual bowl of morning porridge, navigator Ward suddenly realized that we had precious little time left to catch our booked passage to Africa. What with malfunctioning kidneys and finding the relaxed Italian lifestyle of sun and siesta rather agreeable, we were now behind schedule.

It was serious pedal-pushing time and we shot down the ankle and into the foot of Italy. So furious was our pace that Roberto, an under-twenty-five hill-climbing champion, ex-pressed amazement.

'*Mama mia!*' he exclaimed. '*Inglese — si? Troppo in fretta!*'

As he pulled alongside on his dazzling featherweight racer, I saw that he epitomised Italy's national sport. On his head of raven-black hair perched a Campagnolo cap, its peak upturned. He was dark and attractive, with a pure power-pack of solid muscle rippling beneath a tanned, sun-soaked skin. He cast a knowing and critical eye over our trusty steeds, dismissing Ward's British-built Revell Romany with a wave of the hand. My mount fared better. Spotting Cinelli handlebars and various Campagnolo components, he threw his arms triumphantly in the air.

'*Italiano! Molto buono!*'

The towns and villages flew by in a blur: Paola, Pizzo, Rosarno, Palmi. And it was hot. With sweat-soaked backs we cycled. In the mountains a constant salty stream of perspir-ation ran down my cheeks, leaving white-dried wakes. I thought: for my kidneys' sake, I must keep drinking.

The land became scorched — hard, brittle, dry and dusty. The sun always shone and I had become blasé about it. At first so many sunny days had been a novelty — 'Isn't it hot! Lovely day! Isn't it blue! Aren't we lucky!' But you cannot keep exclaiming. The sun was soon taken for granted and our rain-capes lay redundant.

In more wild and rocky areas, tyre-squashed snakes were a frequent sight. Their bodies would shrivel up and desiccate in the fierce heat, leaving just weightless shells of scales to blow across the road. Lizards were everywhere — fast, darting and scared, or slow, basking and lazily unaware of us. The brittle-leaved and stony roadside would crackle and crunch and move as they scampered away.

Where the traffic was heavy there were dead dogs, too; lots of them, the four-legged victims of hit 'n' runs, sprawled in various states of rigor mortis and decay. Their unbelievable stench, when blowing downwind, could be smelt long before you saw the hapless corpse.

From Reggio, the toe-tip of Italy, we caught the ferry across the Straits of Messina to its football, Sicily. The largest island in the Mediterranean, Sicily has a complicated history: it has been ruled by the Greeks, the Romans, the Bourbons, the Saracens and the Moors as well as the Normans. All left some kind of cultural or architectural heritage and were largely responsible for the development of the resilient Sicilian character. Sicilians are tied closely to their families and to their land; they also have a certain genius for *sistemazione*, or the ability to give order to chaos. They are particularly adroit at inventing ways out of intricate tangles and grasping the essence of a situation. The bitter joke about the Italian boot kicking the Sicilian football dates from the time of unification with Italy in 1860, which brought few benefits to the island.

The heat there was enervating. The scorching wind hit the face like a furnace blast and filled my lungs with fire. Yet Sicily was not a burnt desert and agriculture was rich and flour-ishing. There were vines and olives on the slopes, with a profusion of orange and lemon groves; and, high up among the rocks, the eucalyptus forests were full of swooping birds.

Such was the heat during early afternoon that it was wise to lie low. As we rested beneath the spiky shade of a palm tree near Cefalù one day, we watched bemused and then bewitched as a corpulent fisherman, with trousers rolled up, waded surreptitiously into the sea. Crouching low with net in hand, he moved stealthily around the shallows. Every now and then his meaty frame would freeze motionless. Then, in one sudden deft movement, he would fling his net into the water and catch a slippery handful of tiny silver fish. He never failed.

In the north-west corner of the island are the tightly packed, traffic-jammed streets of Palermo, the Mafia capital. Only a minority of Sicilians are members of the Mafia and today its activities are largely hidden within the confines of many legal and respectable businesses. Tourism being one of the most important of these, we were told that we would be safer in Palermo than in the streets of Milan, where muggings and violence ran rife. However, thoughts of *The Godfather* made us wary and the possibility of being mown down by stray machine-gun fire seemed not an unlikely one as we cycled past dark, seedy bars. With such a film scenario in mind, we might have given Palermo a miss altogether had we not met the effusive Franco and Antonietta in the campsite at Villafranca Tirrena. They were both students at the end of a week's camping holiday. Treating us to one of their barbecue specialities, they had said, 'If you go to Palermo, you must of course stay with us.' With such offers of native hospitality, how could we skirt round the Sicilian capital?

If some places in Italy are noted for their particular modes of transport (the gondola in Venice, the Vespa in Rome, the tram in Milan), then Palermo is the town of the motor car. We jostled apprehensively for space on the roads with a morass of squabbling Fiats that skidded and sped around the streets as if competing in the Lombard Rally, but using horns instead of brakes.

Sweat-soaked and grimy, we arrived at Franco and Antonietta's early in the evening. A refreshing shower would have gone down a treat but the water was turned on only between 5 AM and 2 PM. We sloshed ourselves with recycled dregs from a bucket instead.

There was no time to relax. We were whisked back out on to the streets as it was the *passagiata* — the most important time of day in Sicily. Just before dinner the town woke up after a long siesta and all the citizens sauntered up and down the Via Roma in the 'cool' of the evening. (Such is the ferocity of the sun during the day that even by midnight the walls still radiate absorbed heat and feel almost too hot to touch.) Young and old parade the street eating ice-cream, shelling pumpkin seeds, scrutinizing each other and gossiping with emphatic gesticulations.

The next day Franco and Antonietta took us to the Convento dei Capuccini — an intriguing but macabre chamber of horrors where, beneath the monastery, the Capuchin friars have hung their customers along the rough-cut stone walls of the catacombs. Originally these burial grounds had been reserved for the convent's deceased (many of whom died during a plague in the sixteenth century) but later the idea caught on amongst the Palermitians to such an extent that the catacombs became a sought-after preserve for the wealthy, and until 1881 it was fashionable for the dead members of rich families to be laid to rest here. The grotesque skeletal remains of some eight thousand of Palermo's most prestigious citizens now line the long, chilly, and fusty subterranean corridors.

The bodies were preserved by various chemical and drying processes: they were either soaked in vinegar, arsenic and quick lime, or placed in earthen driers to drain off their fluids, or simply left out in the sun to dry. Then they were dressed in their Sunday best (presumably to give them reasonably lifelike proportions) and suspended in individual niches, segregated according to sex, status and past professions such as lawyer, soldier, surgeon, professor, philosopher or clergyman. The bodies were pinned with identifying tags and relatives could visit and renew the acquaintance of their dear departed.

Most of the mummies were now in a pretty bad way and

some of the contorted, grinning figures were decomposed beyond recognition. Others, still complete with skin and hair, looked so real that I kept glancing behind me to check that one had not sprung down from its perch. Even those that had lost their glass eyes (most were removed by American soldiers as souvenirs during the Second World War) appeared to watch me with a chilling stare. Other corpses lay in stacked glass coffins.

The priests were the best preserved and in times of calamity they were regarded with superstitious dread. One bishop was reading a recent copy of the local newspaper — maybe a sympathetic relative was helping to keep his boredom at bay. After all, it is a long time to be hanging around doing nothing.

With not a moment to spare, we at last found ourselves on the boat crossing the Sicilian Channel. Next stop: Africa! The deep, pellucid blue sea was so transparent that we momentarily spotted a shark swimming just off the bow, skimming along like a silver-glinting, phosphorescent torpedo. Things were hotting up.

The idea was to cycle along the coast of North Africa to Morocco before heading home through Europe. As we spread the map out on the salt-dried deck, we noticed a vast expanse of nothingness — the Sahara. Suddenly, we changed our plans. We would head south, away from the tourists on the busy coastline, for a taster of the desert sands. Why hadn't we thought of it before? Ward became quite excited and fashioned himself a headcloth from his towel in keen preparation as a modern Lawrence of Arabia. (Our desert geography was a little vague.)

As the hazy outline of the massive African continent appeared on the horizon, we settled down to some serious planning. What would we need for such an expedition? Water. Yes, water. Very important. So 'water-bottles' topped our list. What else?

'Sterilizing tablets!' enthused an eager Ward.

Rummaging deep into my bags, I emerged with a squashed box of Puritabs.

'There's a lot here,' I said triumphantly, 'we'll be fine.'

We could not think of anything else to aid our desert survival: 'water-bottles' remained the sole entry on the list and we scuttled off towards Tunis in search of such life-sustaining equipment as soon as we had disembarked.

Having touched down on African soil, I felt a trifle perturbed. With a suspect navigator and a dicky kidney, I was journeying into unknown territory: a new continent with new and totally alien cultures. To be standing on the north-eastern tip of such a gigantic landmass made me feel even smaller than usual.

Tunisia is the Arab world's most liberal nation and recognisably Mediterranean in character, but it still has the limitations and restrictions of an Islamic and essentially Third World country. However, it is not a fanatical Muslim country and it has liberated its women from the veil since independence in 1956. Polygamy was also abolished then (as Mohammed's stipulation that each wife was to be treated equally was held to be impossible if a man had several) and Tunisian men and women eat together, which is not the case in many other Arab countries. Yet the women still take a back seat and Western women need to be wary of the men: Western films have done an excellent job in persuading them that all Western women are 'fair game'. Having Ward around reduced this problem for me but, to prevent any misunderstandings, we decided to tell those who enquired that we were married — heaven forbid such a calamity!

Shanty towns lined the rutted, dusty road to Tunis. Half-naked ragamuffins played or cried or screamed in squalor. I was shocked. I had never seen such poverty before. I felt embarrassingly rich in comparison — and actually scared.

Our first port of call in Tunis was the Post Office, where I hoped to pick up a new set of tent poles dispatched from England. Amazingly, they were there and Mum had even sent the right ones. Our tent could now resume the shape of a hoop — but for how long?

Feeling peckish, we sniffed out a source for our first taste of

African cuisine. The best we could find was an open-fronted restaurant with a grimy floor, full of flies and staring men. I had a salad (the first mistake) and omelette; Ward's meal was an unidentifiable lump of gristle. My salad was awash with olive oil; olives and olive-related products are to be found everywhere in Tunis and the oil brings in fifteen per cent of the country's export earnings — half as much as the petroleum revenue.

The salad was also dressed with a liberal splattering of flies. Dead ones. Being a novice at this rough-stuff travelling lark, I felt that I had the right to complain, in typically British fashion.

'Waiter! Waiter!' I squawked. 'There are flies in my salad.'

The waiter, quite rightly, appeared nonplussed at my outburst. Naively, I was half expecting him to apologize and exchange my salad for another one. Instead he said, '*Madame, pas de problème,*' and proceeded to pick out the offending insects with the dirty-nailed forefinger which, only moments before, had been earnestly ensconced up his nose. My appetite vanished.

We dived into the glorious chaos of the medina — a labyrinth of tunnel-like alleyways in winding coils. Traders were selling their wares in vaulted souks (ghetto-like markets) and ceramic-tiled courtyards. I was in my element: I was surrounded by endless tantalizing merchandise and curious characters and the whole place smelled mysteriously exotic. With Ward following in my slipstream, we ended up in an apothecary's multi-coloured, jar-laden cave of potions and perfumes and witches' brews.

Having purchased plastic water-bottles as our sole aid for Saharan survival, we went in search of an hotel. '*Complet! Complet!*' said a stream of people and signs. The idea was aborted and, instead, we wove our way out of the city amongst a crowd of moth-eaten vehicles and donkey-carts and their respective dangerous emissions of suffocating fumes and skiddy droppings. We headed south, with the fiery red sun slipping away to our right. The time was nigh to call it a day but where would we sleep? Cycling on into the approaching dusk, we spotted a small, dilapidated abode.

As we wheeled our mounts up a dusty track leading towards it, a handful of scraggy chickens scuttled away in clucking commotion. Inquisitive faces peered at us with suspicious curiosity. As usual, Ward urged me forwards to break the ice and ask permission to pitch our tent — a request which was all very well if you shared a common tongue or culture but less easy if you did not.

I approached, grinning inanely (smiles are useful in any language) and, hoping to win favour with animals and owners, threw encouraging compliments to the chickens as if they were dogs — 'Here, boy, here! Who's a lovely hen, then?' Miraculously, this ploy worked. The father, with a bevy of mucky-faced offspring, emerged from a doorway and returned my smiles.

'Hello,' I greeted him, first in French, then in English and then, evidently incomprehensibly, in Arabic. This decidedly one-sided conversation seemed none too successful, however, and I tried a new approach: vivid gesticulation. That did the trick and with copious laughter on both sides we were shown a small clearing in the olive orchard where we could pitch our tent. Later, one of the small daughters shyly handed us a saucerful of freshly boiled eggs before scampering off in a fit of giggles.

Passing through a sparse village the next day, Ward punctured. Within moments we were engulfed by a crowd of boisterous, bare-footed youngsters dressed in clothes that people back home would use only for wiping oily hands. Many had open sores (a magnet for flies) and filthy faces, with noses that had never been wiped. They laughed and shouted excitedly, pushing and jabbing our bodies and bikes and falling over each other to get a better look. A noble school-teacher ran to our rescue, angrily scattering the boys in all directions.

'Please, I apologize,' he said, 'they have no manners. Now, follow me!'

He led us into the safe haven of the school compound and then disappeared indoors. Ward occupied himself with puncture-mending, cursing furiously — he was no mechanic and a simple operation turned into a bicycle blood-bath, with nuts and bolts and limbs and obscenities flying wildly in all directions. As he worked, a few cheeky scoundrels climbed on to the schoolground wall and dropped their shorts. Ward explosively told me not to laugh as it was only encouraging them.

When these budding perverts were joined by equally eager reinforcements, Ward, by now apoplectic, flung his tyre at them. This provided an even better game than revealing their chipolatas and they danced off merrily down the road rolling their new rubber hoop.

'Never mind,' I said consolingly, 'at least you've got a spare. And just think how much weight you'll be saving.'

The teacher, having missed the excitement, reappeared with an earthenware jug of cold water and a plate loaded with grapes, tomatoes and prickly pears. We had noticed that Tunisia was well supplied with these barbaric cactus-like fruits. They are about three inches long, ovoid in shape and covered in minute hairs which protrude from their skins like small, sharp needles and which (as Ward had already discovered) can become painfully embedded in your hands. The tweezers of a Swiss Army knife are handy for their removal.

In Tunis, carts were piled high with these dangerous but delicious fruits and Ward had learnt to leave any pear preparations to the professionals: deft-handed vendors split, skinned and sliced them in one dextrous move and then offered the yellowy-apricot flesh from the tip of the knife. Out in the countryside, boys waited by the road with bucketloads of pricklies, ready to hawk them or, for fun, hurl them at passersby.

We ventured through Kairouan, where the ninth-century Grand Mosque is one of the holiest of Muslim places in the world; to visit it seven times is an act of piety equal to a visit to Mecca.

It was mid-morning when we had our first encounter with the Tunisian police. They appeared on motorbikes which sounded (and moved) as if each was attached to a couple of outboard engines. White-gloved, they motioned us to stop and we did so obediently, thinking with an inkling of consternation: now what?

Our confrontation was not what we had expected. They dismounted, shook our hands, slapped our backs, felt our tyres, exchanged names and addresses and handed us their own packed lunches before put-putting off down the road.

The further we cycled south, the more daringly rumbustious became the roadside youngsters. Their idea of a welcome was to pelt us with a barrage of the first things that came to hand — usually stones, wood and hunks of watermelon, with the occasional prickly pear for good measure. Such missile-hurling was not aggressively hostile but simply an entertaining way (for them) of giving vent to their feelings of intense curiosity. We also offered unusually mobile targets. And who could blame them? A pair of shiny-cycled Westerners provided a welcome distraction from lengthy hours of goat-herding or fruit-foraging. For us, however, it could be frightening — and painful, especially when a small boulder hit you squarely and forcefully on the back of the head.

The children were not the only mischief-makers. We could sometimes avoid their stone-throwing tribes but we could not escape the nuisance of the flies. They were everywhere; in, on and around everything — food, faces, faeces. There was no respite. They drove us to despair and we would flap our limbs and leap around in wild, sporadic bursts like a couple of demented chimpanzees. We were surprised that the natives completely ignored such infernal insects and I would stare incredulously as flies freely perambulated over an apparently unconcerned native's legs, arms, eyes, nose and mouth. Some flies were so confident they would not be slapped or swatted or whisked aside that they even took the liberty of administering the leg-raised business of their meticulous hindquarter hygiene. And I saw one winged couple hitting it off together on an old man's neck.

One morning, we dived into the midst of an olive grove to

give a particularly persistent gang of missile-throwers the slip. The torrid heat and the headwind of the Sirocco (the oven-blast that blows off the Sahara) were so exhausting that we decided to make this our lunch break.

While eating sun-stale bread, Kraft cheese triangles and gelantinous cold tinned chickpeas — food in one hand and fly-swishing olive branch in the other — we were interrupted by a mischievous imp crouching behind a tree and excitedly signalling to his back-up flock of shepherds to advance with their prickly pears. We thought: uh-oh! All we wanted was half an hour's rest free from pests and pestering.

Ever eager to let peace prevail, I was quite prepared to pack up and retreat — it was their territory, after all. But such an act of surrender was not for Ward and he had other ideas. Emulating Tarzan, he released a desperate, death-defying war-cry and charged after our hapless entourage like a crazed bull. Plumes of dust, squeals of terror and roars of a tourist fit to explode dwindled into the distance.

Then silence. Suddenly I was alone. Wonderful! Making the most of what little peace I had, I hastily covered my body with olive branches as a fly-deterrent and caught forty winks.

Ward returned battle-scarred, sweat-gritted but jubilant.

'They won't be coming back!' he said triumphantly.

The statement caused me concern. What had he done to them? Before I had a chance to enquire, he was flat on his back and asleep. With him in such battling mood, I thought: best not to wake him. Peace prevailed — for ten luxurious minutes.

I heard him first, a-whistling and a-warbling: a young man topped with a straw hat was bearing down on us, fast. I assessed the situation through slitted eyes.

'Approaching rapidly at two o'clock,' I reported.

'Whatever you do, ignore him,' snapped Ward, who commenced to feign sleep. I obeyed orders and did likewise. Then he was upon us.

'Bonjour, Monsieur et Madame. Ça va? Français? Anglais? Allemands? Ah! English book! My friends, you speak English? Hey! Hallo! Hallo!'

Making such a din, he must have thought we were either zombies or dead. Surely no one could sleep through such a racket? He continued in this insistent, demanding style and was obviously not going to give up until he received some acknowledgement. His staying power was remarkable. I felt like laughing at how absurd we must look — Ward apparently dead to the world and me attempting concealment beneath a cloak of olive leaves — but the thought of Ward in such a dangerously unpredictable mood deterred me.

The last straw came when our inquisitive visitor picked up my leg and dropped it.

'Hey, easy!' I said. 'That's my leg!'

We had come to life! He was exuberant. There was no going back now. Once surrendered, we were whisked up and led proudly back to meet his 'fam-ill-ee' ... all thirty-seven members. They put on a display, made a great fuss over us and dressed us up in traditional costume. (This was to become a regular feature of native-meeting for us.) With me looking like Mata Hari and fez-hatted Ward like Tommy Cooper, I was led off to the women's quarters, where I watched, fascinated, the preparations for our evening meal of stuffed sheep's intestines. The fillings were of meat, coriander, chickpeas, tomatoes, onions, herbs, spices and home-grown almonds.

Afternoon turned to evening and still we were introduced to an endless stream of excitable, loquacious relations and friends. Being at the hub of attention hour after hour can be as exhausting as cycling sixty miles into a ferociously hot headwind; and a continuous smile turns into a painful, muscle-bound grimace. Being an honoured guest has its obligations — you have to be entertaining as well as appearing to be entertained — but, as we were to discover over and over again, it seemed that the greatest honour and pleasure we could give to the people was to accept their invitation and visit their homes.

After being forced to feast ourselves silly, I became acutely aware of a need to relieve myself. I made enquiries and a troop of family enthusiastically led me behind a mud hut to an odorous expanse of ground. Performing in such a latrine caused me no concern whatsoever but I was surprised that my audience insisted on watching — all seventeen of them. I tried in vain to encourage them to leave. I was so nervous and desperate that in the end I decided just to get on with it.

Shockingly, nothing happened. My bladder was bashful. Embarrassing as it was, I called the mission off as abortive while pretending to my transfixed audience that the whole operation had run according to plan. Apparently this only added to their bewilderment. I could see them thinking: how can Western woman go to the toilet and not produce anything? Later, in danger of exploding, I escaped into the glorious privacy of darkness. What a relief!

The next morning, after a breakfast of hard-boiled eggs and watermelon, Ward was presented with a large straw sun-hat and I was given a foulard 'It's a traditional Arab headscarf,' they said, though later in the day I noticed its 'Made in Japan' label. Our new friends were embarrassingly generous and they were so poor in comparison with ourselves that we were unsure how to repay them for their kindness. They wanted nothing more than our Echo and the Bunnymen tapes, which sent them into rapturous delight. They had good taste.

With a change of wind, we sped into Gafsa and saw our first oasis. Founded by the Romans, it was a picturesque town of solid brick buildings decorated in bold geometric designs and enclosed by protective rose-pink walls.

Wandering around, we came across some old Roman baths still in use. As we leant over the side looking down into the tempting cool waters, a lithe-bodied Arab boy was upon us.

'Hey my friends! You watch me climb tree and I jump. Yes?'

Before we had a chance to reply, he had shot off and shinned with breath-taking ability up a formidable palm tree which towered over the baths. Alarmed, we did not know if he was out to impress, out to get money, or out to commit suicide. The water did not look deep enough for such a stunt. Eighty feet high, he turned round on the overhanging tree, gripped it tightly with his legs and stood momentarily swaying in the breeze.

'Don't do it! Don't do it! Don't jump!' we shouted.

It was too late. He flung himself off the palm and plunged downwards in a terrifying but highly spectacular dive. Splash! Down, under and up he came, his glistening features smiling radiantly.

'You like?' he called.

'Yes,' we said breathlessly, 'very good.'

Venturing into the lush green oasis, we were accosted by a chirpy black boy holding a giant, stalk-eyed lizard. With saurian example in one hand and me in the other, he led us deep into the fertile oasis to a cornucopia of delights. Everywhere exotic fruits grew in profusion — oranges, figs, pomegranates and hanging clusters of fresh dates — and he eagerly scurried up the trees to pick up copious amounts of each. Laden with these tantalizing offerings, we retraced our steps back out of the oasis where (once Ward's back was turned) our escort attempted a momentary grope amongst the foliage of a fig tree. Saucy little devil, I thought, and we returned to our hotel for a feast of fruit.

Entering the sparser and less inhabited lands of the desert, it dawned on us what the second item on our Saharan survival list should have been: toilet paper, a superfluous commodity for Third World inhabitants. Some Westerners, I know, adapt with ease to the less wasteful and arguably more hygienic method of a thorough sluicing with an adept left hand — but old habits die hard and on that distressing day when the last of our Italian *carta igienica* had run out we were forced to turn to pages 1–47 of *Birdy*. It was an unfitting end for a wonderful book.

Apart from these minor sanitation problems, we adapted quickly to our African way of life. Rising at dawn to beat the heat, we would cycle along roads free of traffic (save for the occasional heavily laden taxi, truck or camel) which inevitably disappeared into the shimmering, hazy distance. Whenever we stopped in a village, we were besieged by smiling, rotten-toothed locals. '*Monsieur! Monsieur! Bonjour!* You have *bonbons?* You — my friend, I show you souk.' We slept in mud huts with the natives, sharing big communal bowls of rich spicy stews, and with some families we were proudly treated to a demonstration of their most prized possession: an antiquated wireless plugged into a beaten-up car battery and emitting a stream of ear-splitting distortion.

Sometimes we pitched our tent in an oasis, shaded by date palms and fig trees, with not a soul for miles. Here, of course, finding water was no problem and we would drink from gushing pipes and wash and swim to our heart's content in the hot, sparkling pools. It was only later that we learnt about bilharzia, a disease caused by the parasitic worms which infest the fresh water of oases. The flukes enter the body by burrowing into the soles of your feet. After dental decay, it is the second most common disease in the world (some 200 million people suffer from it, including about ninety per cent of Egypt's population) and it can be fatal.

It was hard to get used to the way the Arabs treated their livestock, especially the sheep. Life for these creatures was certainly no holiday, shuffling around under the relentless sun in such thick woolly coats while dodging crop-thwacking shepherds. They could find precious little shade apart from the occasional cactus or spindly tree. And what did they eat? There were no succulent, grassy meadows for grazing here — just parched, rocky, sun-scorched earth.

As we sat revitalizing ourselves at a small village café, a battered old car pulled up. The driver, clad in voluminous flowing cloaks, opened the small boot. I saw what I thought at first was a large collection of moth-eaten fleeces crammed into the dark confines. Slowly, they came to life — five extremely sheepish sheep. These poor, forlorn creatures were then dragged roughly across the dirt to the rear of a neighbouring building and there followed a cacophony of desperate baaings and other unpleasant sounds. Moments later, a blood-spattered youth appeared wheeling a cart full of butchered bits of sheep. Whistling, he trundled off towards a small wooden hut where the edible contents of his load were left to hang in the dusty, flyblown heat.

On another occasion, an overladen lorry slowly spluttered past with a supercilious sheep strapped into its passenger seat. It had a more comfortable ride than its boot-packing colleagues, but no doubt its fate was similar.

Our next stop was Nefta where, legend has it, the first spring of fresh water to issue from the earth after the Flood was discovered by Kostel, one of Noah's grandsons. From that spring developed the fertile oasis of today surrounded by ochre-coloured hills — a vivid patch of green amidst an endless sea of sand. Fed by more than 150 springs, it not only provides a handy stop-off point for camel caravans but is also a religious centre for the mystical Sufi pilgrims and a welcome respite for migrating birds.

It was in Nefta that we decided to swop our two-wheeled transport temporarily for the native four-legged version and booked a tour of the oasis on a couple of unpredictable and mean-tempered camels. Unlike their Bactrian counterparts in Asia, these Arabian dromedaries have only one hump and the majority are now almost entirely domesticated (herds of wild camels still exist in Asia). They are used as riding and pack animals and to supply milk, meat, wool and hides.

Contrary to my childish belief, these Ships of the Desert do not store water in their humps but fat reserves; the hump shrinks noticeably when food is scarce and is a good indication of a camel's health. Having such a concentrated lump of fat allows the animal to lose heat more freely from the rest of its lean body, and the reason that camels do not suffer from sunstroke is not only because of an insulating layer of air within their hairy coats but also because of their ability to avoid dehydration by not starting to sweat until their body temperature reaches 115 degrees Fahrenheit, a temperature that would kill almost any other mammal. After a lengthy period without water (two weeks in summer or three months in winter), they can drink an incredible 180 litres in one go and swell visibly as they do so.

We arranged to meet our guide at three o'clock. He turned up but the camels did not.

'Where are our camels?' we demanded.

'They've been held up,' he said, which made it sound as though they were stuck in a contraflow system on the North Circular.

We waited and waited, and would have gone on waiting had the guide had his way. Finally, fed up, we said, 'Okay, you be our camel and lead us through the oasis.' So we ventured forth into the luxuriant greenery, not by delayed dromedary but by less exotic Shanks's Pony.

Even in the cool of evening, it was still hot — the shade temperature in summer can often be within a degree or two of a camel's boiling point. Once we had forgiven our guide for the camel mix-up, he turned into a chatty and informative young soul and gave us a good run for our money, plying us with details such as the fact that the oasis is home to some 350,000 date palms (one of the world's oldest cultivated plants) which can grow up to a hundred feet tall. They belonged, he told us, to the Deglas variety and the dates, known as 'fingers of light and honey', were reputed to be the finest in the world. They certainly tasted like it.

We were led through hot, ankle-deep irrigation ditches of clear, bubbling water to a little hut of palm fronds. Here we were treated to the juicy fruits of the oasis and a small cupful of *lagmi*, a sickly-sweet wine made from date sap. Not one bit of these date palms goes to waste: the stones are ground and fed to livestock; leaves are cut into strips, dried and woven into baskets; and when the palms have finally stopped producing fruit (after two centuries) their wood is used for timber.

In the morning, standing atop the hill beside the grandiose five-star Saharan Palace Hotel (reputed to be Brigitte Bardot's favourite), we looked out over Nefta's tawny brick buildings with their pristine white cupolas shimmering in the sun, and beyond to the notorious desolate expanse of the Chott Djerid. In winter this is a vast shallow lake which is transformed during summer into a parched, salt-encrusted plain. The seasonal flooding of the Chott results not from the sparse local rainfall but from a rise in the underlying watertable. In spring, when the water level drops, the lake becomes an immense muddy swamp and in the past unwary travellers who strayed from a prescribed path of solid ground, marked with palm trunks, came to a sticky end. A twelfth-century Arabian writer reported how a caravan of a thousand camels was swallowed up by the desolate wastes:

> Unfortunately one of the beasts strayed from the path, and all the others followed it. Nothing in the world could be swifter than the manner in which the crust yielded and engulfed them; then it became like what it was before, as if the thousand baggage camels had never existed.

Entering Algeria, the second largest country in Africa after Sudan, was easy. After all the rumours about hostility to foreigners, lengthy searches and mind-boggling bureaucracy, we only had to endure a two-hour border wait in the heat. The liveliest things were the flies.

Then we followed the gently undulating road that carved a dead-straight slice through the barren desert. I had never seen so much of nothing — our only distractions were an infinite number of telegraph poles, red-topped roadside kilometre stones, the occasional camel-hazard warning sign — and Ward's potentially dangerous riding techniques. There we were, two solitary cyclists wheeling along a deserted desert road. I was ahead and Ward was bringing up the rear when suddenly, for no apparent reason, CRUNCH! He had crash-collided into me and we landed in a heavy-heaped mesh of bodies and bikes — a desertway pile-up. Momentarily stunned, we lay amongst a tangle of metal frames, escaped panniers, broken mudguards and bruised limbs as the silence of the sands settled around us.

Taking stock of the situation, Ward suddenly burst into an

apoplectic fit, most unreasonably blaming the whole unfortunate incident on me and likening my riding technique to a
'snail in labour'. I retaliated with an equal show of insults and
invective and reminded him just who had piled into whom. In
enraged silence we brushed ourselves off, straightened forks
and assessed injuries (mine were far worse) before I tore away
into the heat-haze to let off steam, sincerely hoping never to set
eyes on my cycling companion again.

A few hours later I reached the town of El Oued, the 'oasis
of a thousand domes'. By then Ward had unfortunately caught
up, with effort.

'We need to find a bank,' he puffed. 'We need to get some
dinars.'

We dragged our tired steeds across the sand-strewn streets.
It was market day: the small square was bustling with activity
and hooded heads turned to stop and stare — and then
followed, shouting excitedly in our wake. Just one eye was all
we could see of the veiled, thickly robed women who, intri-
gued with the sudden arrival of two flush-faced foreigners,
shuffled like daleks among the rapidly increasing crowds.

The bank was little more than a cramped corrugated iron
shed packed with Arabs (sheik by jowl) in a heady smell of
sweat and smoke. The temperature within would have put a
sauna in the shade — it was an airless, enervating heat.
Fighting our way through a sea of bodies, we finally surfaced
at the desk and I began to write out a traveller's cheque.
Knowing the trouble I have with calculating exchange rates,
Ward turned to me and asked if I was all right.

'No,' I said, referring to my current state of health rather
than currency problems. The pile-up, the strenuous pedalling,
the heat, the lack of sustenance and now this smoke-filled
scrum were suddenly too much. For the first time in my life I
fainted, keeling over into the arms of an Arab.

We found a small hotel but it provided no respite from the
clamouring crowds. It was full of noisy and continuously
hawking locals who banged relentlessly on our door and
shouted and shrieked through the broken window. The

ablution facilities were non-existent — the squat toilets over-flowed with effluent which seeped down the stairs into the corridor and worked its way perilously close to our room. The smell was nauseating. Luckily I found an old bucket under the bed and used that instead.

As dawn approached, the shouting and screaming of our noisy neighbours abated and at last we fell into an exhausted slumber. But not for long. Five times a day, from the minarets of the mosques, the muezzin calls the faithful to prayer. Until fairly recently this was a romantic vocal calling but with the advent of the Tannoy it has become an ear-splitting screech.

Bleary-eyed, we dragged ourselves awake, ate half a mouldy melon and then left, cycling into the glorious tranquillity of the desert.

We had chanced upon the Great Eastern Erg ('erg' means 'great area of sand'). Although these lazy, ever-shifting, crescent-shaped dunes symbolize the Sahara, they only cover a fifth of its surface: the bulk of the world's largest desert is composed of vast, monotonous gravel plains, arid mountain peaks and mirage-filled salt plateaux. The formidable Sahara appears to be stable but the surface sand is in constant motion and massive dunes, as high as 400 feet, creep slowly across the desert in towering pyramids or huge U-shaped groups like earthbound flocks of geese.

It was early and these long, cool-shadowed dunes resembled a sea of petrified waves. As the sun climbed slowly over the horizon in a blazing fireball, the razor-edged crests were set aglow; the heat rose and the sun bleached all colour from the finely sculptured sands, burning the very blue from the sky. Only towards evening, when the sun hung low, did the radiant colours return to the delicately rippling surfaces.

Ward was ill; of that there was no doubt. Usually his appetite was insatiable and he was capable of consuming awesome amounts of food but now he only pecked at bird-size portions and what little he did eat rapidly re-emerged at one end or the other. He was losing weight and energy fast.

We rode deeper into the dunes but it was no way to convalesce because we ran out of water. Three of our life-saving water-bottles had simultaneously sprung leaks. Dehydration was bad enough on its own but on top of that Ward had to keep diving urgently into the dunes to answer Nature's frequent calls. The day became a mesmerizing heat-haze; at one stage we rested at the base of a telegraph pole and slowly rotated as our heads followed its shade — the only respite for miles.

Our tongues were as dry as sandpaper when we saw it: a well! With a surge of energy, we hot-footed it across the sand and threw the thick-skinned receptacle down into the cool, murky depths. Splosh! It was a glorious sound and the water had a glorious taste, even if it was moss-coloured.

Later that day we came across a small awning of palm fronds leaning against a telegraph pole. Heaving our mounts across the sand, we collapsed exhausted into its shade and promptly fell asleep, despite the incessant whirring and buzzing and ticklish pestering of the flies.

I awoke in the comparative cool of evening and found myself covered in sand, which had stuck to my sweaty skin. My mouth was full of the stuff and so was my hair: for days afterwards, a cascade of sand would shower forth whenever I shook my head. I left Ward sprawled asleep in the shelter while I went and marvelled at the many pieces of *rose de sable* (naturally petal-shaped lumps of sand rock) that littered the ground.

We made it to Touggourt — just — but it did not look as though we would make it to Morocco. Ward had had enough of feeling unwell, enough of Arabs, enough of Africa. He wanted to leave, and fast.

Touggourt had a railway station and we decided to take the train to Algiers. As we cycled through the market with its displays of gory, fly-ridden sheep-heads, their eyeballs piled high on dishes beside them, we suddenly found the prospect of being homeward bound an enticing one. I thought: Algiers! We'll be there soon. And then the boat to France.

That, though, was wishful thinking. The train journey can only be described as 'an experience'. At 2 AM, after a delay of eleven hours, we piled into the crush of an overloaded carriage. Burrowing down through a sea of concertina'd bodies, we elbowed a space for ourselves on the filthy, phlegm-covered floor. I found myself straddled across the gaping join between the coaches, with a chill wind blasting up through the opening; one portion of my body was being pitched one way with one coach while the rest of me disconcertingly rolled another with the other. It was when I spotted a pile of fresh vomit dribbling menacingly towards me that I forced Ward up: we had to move.

Somehow I managed to become wedged among the bodies on an already jam-packed bench. Ward, however, had to confine his long body into a wire-ribbed luggage rack and there he had to remain, still suffering from spasms of violent diarrhoea and clenching both teeth and buttocks for the entire nine-hour journey. I felt not only for him but also for those hapless souls directly beneath. I prayed that disaster be averted and, thankfully, it was.

At Biskra we were disgorged on to the platform for a connection to Algiers. A guard brusquely informed us that the next train was unable to take both us and our bikes. If there was room, the following one would take us. We had a twelve-hour wait. We were both feeling tired, stiff and disgruntled but a conductor sprang to our rescue.

'My friends!' he announced. 'Please, my country welcomes you. I show you my house, my family, and we feast — yes?'

It sounded like a nice idea. Leaving our cumbersome cycles at the station, we followed him to a rambling complex of white-washed buildings where, true to his word, a feast was served. For the first time in weeks, Ward did more than just pick at his meal and I suspect this recovery had something to do with the incongruous appearance of chips among the traditional spicy foods. His eyes lit up; with relish, he made himself a chip buttie and devoured it within seconds.

We caught fleeting glances of Conductor Ali's wife and small entourage of daughters but they did not join us. It was the custom, said Ali; they busied themselves in the kitchen instead, all for us, chattering excitedly. Whenever I caught one's eye, she would smile shyly and then turn away in a fit of giggles.

The room where we ate was sparsely furnished — a thickly woven *kelim* on the floor, a low table, some rough shelves — and I was surprised to see a television set. I asked Ali what he watched.

'Mainly Algerian television,' he said. 'Our government, it does not show your Western films, but we see *Dallas*. This we like very much.' (Later, back in England, an Algerian student told me the government actively resisted Western cultural influences but *Dallas* was a firm favourite because of its extended family.)

Before our train left, Ali insisted on showing us the sights of Biskra. Exhausted from the previous night's journey, all we really wanted to do was to sleep, but after such kindness the least we could do was comply. We traipsed into the afternoon heat and tried to express enthusiasm. Biskra is famous for its oasis (one of Algeria's finest), its Roman spa (the hottest in the world after Iceland) and its prehistoric stone tombs — but none of these was on Ali's agenda. His idea of interesting sights included a modern complex of concrete and a couple of hideous new tourist hotels, designed by the French and an eyesore in any language.

In theory, the train journey to Algiers should have been a simple affair; in practice, of course, it was not. I lost count of the number of times we had to change trains and of the hours of delay. It was the kind of journey where patience was of far more use than a valid train ticket. On one locomotive, however, we were treated like Allah: the staff invited us into their carriage, where we met the rotund and jolly driver, who spent more time dressing us up in the conductor's uniform than at his controls. He took a note of our addresses and said he would send us a hamper of dates for Christmas.

But at last we reached Algiers. The first thing I noticed was not the French colonial architecture but the traffic lights — the first we had seen for weeks. There was no time to stand and gawp; we had to buy boat tickets to France.

Down at the ferry office the assistant said impassively, 'The boat is booked up for three months.' Three *months*! Surely he was joking. But, no, we visited every ticket agency and incredibly it was the same story. Reluctantly we entered the Air France building. Flying would be far more expensive and far more trouble; we had never flown with our bikes before and it would involve complicated dismantlings of the machines.

Incredulously, we learnt that no flights were available for two weeks. Ward was not happy. His mind was set on leaving Algeria within a couple of days and he was determined to stick by it. We walked from agency to agency, pestering and checking for cancellations, but the answer was always the same — a definite No! As a boat was leaving that night for Marseilles, we finally decided to buy a legal ticket for a crossing in three months but illegally change the date and try our luck on the night boat.

Then we were told that we could not buy a ticket until we had our money exchange forms stamped at the bank as proof that we were not illegally taking any dinars out of the country. However, the bank told us it was impossible to stamp our forms and give us the necessary papers unless we possessed a valid airline or ferry ticket. Catch 22! We ran round in vicious circles until finally we persuaded the ferry man to sell us a ticket. We returned to the bank, only to be told that they did not stamp money exchange forms at that branch.

When we finally found the address of one that did, it was closed for lunch. We waited, we fidgeted, we fretted. Hours later we entered the bank. Hours after that we were served. We exchanged our money, filled out a ream of nonsensical papers and at last had our exchange forms officially stamped.

The only trouble was that the bank official retained them. I did not like the look of this at all.

'Hang on,' I said, 'aren't we supposed to keep our forms for Customs?'

'Hey! No problem, *Monsieur-Dame*,' he said, much too casually. 'We keep for our records.'

There was no persuading him otherwise. The bank was closing and we had little choice other than to leave and sincerely hope that luck would be with us.

Arriving at the docks early, we joined the crowds and waited. There were no other Westerners to be seen: the bustling masses consisted of a convivial army of Arab families clutching an assortment of offspring. From what we gathered, most were emigrating to France; they were surrounded by mountains of possessions, mostly tied up in battered cardboard boxes or black dustbin bags. Apparently we were not the only people intent on leaving Algeria.

Passing through the main gates was easy: the officials scarcely glanced at our tickets as they waved us through. Our problems began at Customs. We needed boarding cards.

'The date. It is no good!' declared the sullen official as he stared questioningly from the tickets to us.

I gulped, felt sick and sweaty-palmed, and prayed that Ward would spring to the rescue — but I should have known better.

'Deal with it,' he muttered and slunk back into the crowds.

I whinged, I whined, then I jested and joked and reeled off a stream of unbelievable stories. 'No, no, no,' I was told, and then ... 'Wait!' Wait? Was there hope? I waited, for over an hour. Nothing happened. From time to time Ward would appear from the chaos for an update on events. Just as swiftly, he would make himself scarce again, saying that a damsel in distress had a much better chance of bending the rules alone than if he joined me. I did not complain, believing by now that Ward would only hamper progress.

I remained waiting, ever hopeful. Time was running out. The boat would soon leave. When it had become obvious that nothing would happen, I sniffed out the Chief Official's office and marched in. I was emphatically told to leave. I stayed.

'Get out!' he bellowed.

'I can't,' I said, 'I must see you.'

I proceeded to gush forth a torrent of inconsequential trivialities. Surprisingly he listened. He mellowed.

'Wait!' he said, and marched from the office. I waited. Finally he returned.

'Okay,' he said in a matter-of-fact tone, 'I give you tickets. But first I must see money exchange forms.'

Elation was hit on the head by deflation.

'You can't,' I said. 'The bank has them.'

'Then I'm sorry. You cannot leave my country.'

I did not like the sound of that at all.

'Monsieur,' I whimpered, 'the bank said they must keep them.' It was about the only truthful thing I had said all night. Monsieur, quite rightly, looked far from happy.

'Wait!' he snapped and stomped from the room. Once again I waited, by now in some agitation. Ten minutes before the boat was due to depart, he returned with a ship steward and handed me two boarding cards.

'Go,' he said, 'but quickly. The steward will show you the way.'

We went.

Marseilles! Apart from the prices, it was paradise — and a welcome relief that we were no longer the centre of attention; we blended with the crowds instead of sticking out like a sore thumb. But what a shock to the system! A few days earlier we had been cycling amongst camels and carts and discreetly-robed bodies. Now it was flashy cars and fleshy buttock-revealing swimwear.

Everywhere oozed money. Scenes that used to seem normal I now saw with different eyes. It all struck me as obscene and yet I knew I was part of it. This monetary world was my world, the familiar world. The African world across the water was an alien one but I had tasted it and felt it and the contrast between the two made me distinctly unsettled. With the mad rush to leave Algeria, I had not stopped to think. Now, in the south of France, away from hassle and hardship, there was time and peace to do so and I thought: I want to go back to Africa.

We paid for our drinks at a harbourside café (they cost more than a night in an Algerian hotel) and made our way down to a shingle beach to sleep. During the night I awoke as something brushed past my face and, wide-eyed, stared into that of a cat.

In the morning Ward said, 'I think I saw a rat run past me in the night.'

'No you didn't,' I said. 'It was a cat.'

As darkness encroached that evening, we were on the same beach polishing off our supper when, out of the corner of my eye, I saw something move among the rocks behind Ward's back — a faint shape, darting and fast and sinister. Then there was another, and another and another. So much for cats. They were rats the *size* of cats. As the darkness deepened, the beach became alive with these audacious, bickering beasts. The shingle stirred into life as a beefy battalion of belligerent rodents scarpered and raced across the stones inches from our cowering forms. The thought of having slept oblivious to such rattish antics was not pleasant and we were not going to do it again. High-tailing it down the road, we spent the night in a campsite — extortionately priced but it was better than Rat Beach. For the next two weeks we slept in a sandy, rat-free cove where Ward convalesced on a steady intake of huge Danish pastries.

Our route home through the centre of France was in theory straightforward. However, the day we left Marseilles coincided with a massive taxi-driver's strike and the city was in turmoil as hundreds of taxis blocked the streets. In some areas shop windows were smashed, some drivers set fire to huge piles of rubbish, others to cars, and vicious scuffles broke out. Typically we found ourselves in the wrong place at the wrong time and became surrounded by the infamous CRS riot police who fired tear gas into the crowd. Spluttering and with streaming eyes, we escaped into the suburbs and headed for Avignon.

It was in Avignon that we were nearly arrested over a lavatorial dispute which was entirely Ward's fault. The trouble started when we were paying for some drinks at a café. As a result of our imperfect French, we had misunderstood the prices. The *garçon* was demanding a total which struck us as steep but, liking to think that we were law-abiding types, we paid up, disgruntled and without ceremony. Feeling he might as well get a run for his money, Ward disappeared to visit *la toilette*. Moments later I heard a kerfuffle from within and Ward emerged, looking far from happy.

'Now what?' I asked.

'They're trying to charge me three francs for a pee.'

'Let's go,' I said. 'You can go in the bushes for free.'

'I know, but that's not the point.'

The point was that Ward objected to paying what he considered an outrageous price to use the toilet after having paid so much for the drinks. He stomped back inside and I sensed trouble. A stormy linguistic exchange commenced between him and the toilet attendant, an ample-chested, cherry-lipped old hag with a peroxided carpet of curls on her head. In no mood for a scene, I tried gently to coax Ward back to his saddle but I was fighting a losing battle. By now every head in the café had turned to watch the furious fray. I knew what they were thinking: bloody tourists! And quite rightly, too. Catching a few eyes, I smiled sheepishly, trying to convey that he was nothing to do with me. Some exchanged a commiserating look but the majority were too deeply engrossed in the show.

From a spectator's point of view I have to admit I was actually quite enjoying this Franglais fracas, until Madame, close to bursting point and with a face the colour of her lips, got on the hot line to the gendarmes. Then I felt it was high time for us to beat a hasty retreat.

Again I tried to lure Ward away, but in vain. In retrospect, I should have made a solo escape but I could not bring myself to do so: Ward needed me, if not for support then for my limited translating abilities when the police arrived.

They came in a great plume of dust and a battered blue Renault 4 van. For a moment I mistook them for postmen, until they swaggered into the café with gun-holstered hips and a Deputy Dawg demeanour.

As anticipated, my services as interpreter were required and in worse than O-level French I struggled to relay the events of the past hour. Either the gendarmes misinterpreted my ramblings or else they did not take kindly to Madame Cherry-lips. They simply mumbled something which I did not under-stand (though I pretended to, grinning inanely and saying, '*Oui, oui*'), scribbled down our passport details and told us to '*Allez! Allez!*' Ward never did have a chance to relieve himself but at least we were not arrested.

A few days later, we found ourselves in a campsite which turned out to be a nudist camp. This came as something of a shock especially when, in order to stay, one was naturally required to go natural.

Of course I had read and heard about such establishments but I never thought for a moment I would end up in one. Whereas Ward the Exhibitionist was delighted with such a find and flung off his clothes with great gusto, I was decidedly more demure and removed my protective coverings in slow motion, casting surreptitious glances as if all eyes were upon me.

I was not opposed to such antics in principle; it was just that, having spent the nineteen years of my life fully clad, I felt that suddenly dispensing with the reassurance of clothing to strut around starkers required a little careful conditioning.

Shopping was a joke. Men and women would stalk up and down the supermarket aisles wearing nothing more than sandals, hat or handbag. The meat counter was a dangerous place for a male and I noticed many a wary man standing well back from that lethal cleaver.

Living in a commune of nudists, one was expected to treat

the situation as normal and not go around gawping and leering at other people's shapes. Refraining from casting a lustful look in our camp was easy: the majority of the bodies would undoubtedly have been more appealing had they been clothed. But it was impossible not to stare; bared bits and pieces were dingling and dangling wherever you looked. Passing the time of day or acquainting yourself with a neighbour took on quite a different air. Introductions and formal niceties were the most difficult and it took all the willpower in the world not to lower an investigatory glance to nether regions while shaking hands.

It was October and a beautiful time to be cycling. The trees were resplendent with leaves dripping the colours of mustard and rust and the road-clogging caravan tourists had long ago headed for home. We came to the Ardèche river, situated in the wondrous Cévennes mountains and running its course through deep limestone gorges before joining the Rhône. Stopping to look over the edge, we noticed a few bright orange blobs floating past downstream and we realized they were canoes. We promptly cycled to the top of the gorge, found a kayak and began to paddle eighteen miles down river.

We had never travelled by such means before and at first our excursion was frought with difficulties, disputes and dangers. Ward took up position in the aft of the craft and automatically assumed the domineering rank of Cap'n. This was a bad start. I felt that my position up front was potentially more risky (I would hit or fend off the rocks first) and deserved a proper title of command.

It took us a while to master the art of propulsion. For a long time we either drifted round in hopeless circles or veered off in the opposite direction to the one intended. Then there were the rapids. We had not bargained for their size. They were of course minor compared with the likes of the Amazon or Congo but to us it was like plunging over the thundering waters of Niagara Falls. Being passed by empty, upturned canoes did little to boost our confidence but, with blisters and aching forearms, we made it without capsizing and thus, with

an air of contented complacency, felt suitably qualified to tackle the angry white waters of the advanced kayaker.

Camping in the famous Fontainebleau forest, we celebrated our arrival in the environs of Paris by treating ourselves to an avocado pear. That evening, in fast fading light, I took my Kitchen Devil serrated knife and cut not only the avocado in half but also my finger. The devilish blade had slip-slid across the pear's stone and skidded into my index finger, severing the nerves. Being nigh on dark, Ward failed to realize the extent of my injury and as I howled he hooted, 'At least you've made me sarnies!'

We were almost home — just the last leg to Le Havre and that was it, back to the familiar, the routine and work. We hoped to make it in time for my friend's twenty-first birthday. She was having a big party at which we pompously imagined we would be heralded as heroes. On the cross-Channel boat we whimsically jested that perhaps a 'We Conquered the Sahara' expedition stand would be set up for us; there would be desert sand (from Bournemouth beach) and we, the transglobal, weather-rugged cyclists, would proudly pose by dirt-dusty steeds and faded panniers amongst an impressive display of travel-weary equipment. Yes, we would be only too happy to answer questions, demonstrate survival techniques and injuries (my finger) and sign autographs.

Our heads and visions grew to absurd proportions. Perhaps tension was already mounting as gathering crowds eagerly awaited our arrival at Portsmouth docks. 'Welcome Home' banners and flags would be flying, trumpets trumpeting, and people waving and cheering us as glorious, victorious heroes.

In reality, Mum and Dad were held up in a traffic jam and were late to meet us; and at my friend's party no one was even aware we had been out of the country. We realized then that there was nothing worse than the Travel Bore and so kept our mouths firmly shut.

2

From Flying Stoves to Deadheads

ST MALO TO MALAGA

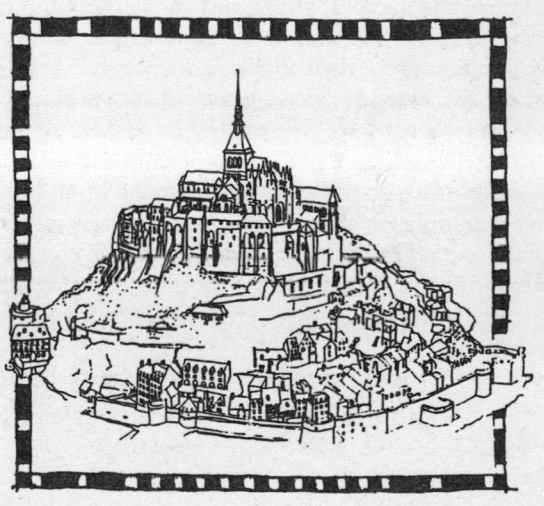

'He travels best that knows when to return.'
THOMAS MIDDLETON

The plan was to cycle to Morocco. Ward and I both wanted to revisit Africa and Morocco was a country we had planned, but failed, to visit the year before and it seemed a nice idea to try again.

For me, travel is based around three things: schedules, plans and ideas, but it is the latter which is most essential to enjoyment. Schedules involve statements like: 'We must leave at once to catch the bus,' or: 'We've exactly two hours to visit this town,' or: 'There's no time to stay with you — our flight leaves tomorrow.' I cannot cope with schedules. They are fine for a package holiday, fine for a coach tour, but if you really want to see a country and visit people and places as the fancy takes you — forget schedules. They pressurize and everything is one big rush.

Plans are useful but easily fly out of the window. Flexibility is the name of the game. If your plans can be bent and adapted and changed at the last minute without leading to any major mess-up or altercation, then so much the better.

Ideas are the best idea. You leave for somewhere with the idea that you want to see this or that or go here or there but have absolutely no idea what will happen in between or when you get there. Indeed, you may not get there at all because as you travel you may get the idea that you do not want to see the place that you had originally planned to visit as you have now been struck by the idea that you would far rather divert to somewhere which, before you left home, you had absolutely no idea existed.

The nicest idea of all is to be unburdened by schedules and rigid plans. Venturing forth into the unknown, it is best to be adaptable, flexible and fancy-free.

Lifting Ward's bike into the boot of my parents' car for transportation to Portsmouth docks, we noticed with dismay two broken spokes on the rear wheel — before it had even embarked on its Moroccan quest. Naturally Ward blamed me for this inconvenience and I should have heeded this omen.

We rolled off the roll-on, roll-off ferry at St Malo into bucketing rain. Ward promptly collided with an American tourist and broke his watch as well as another spoke. I have implied before that Ward is not mechanically minded but he ignored my warnings and attempted cack-handedly to replace the broken spokes himself. Another one snapped as he did so. So far he had managed to tot up four broken spokes without cycling a yard. Things were going well.

On the previous year's ride to Africa, we had taken a small calor gas stove which was not only cheap but had never given us a moment's trouble. Inexplicably, Ward had decided that we should purchase an expensive petrol-burning stove before we had left for St Malo. Perhaps he had imagined we had reached the 'experienced expeditionist' stage and should progress to more advanced equipment. He wanted that stove badly. I said it was messy, fiddly, complicated and heavy, but there was no dissuading him and we now ended up on a campsite outside St Malo with a stove that failed to function — just as I, the cautious one, had predicted. I saw the funny side but Ward saw blue and I left him to tamper and test his patience trying to get the thing to work. Heat was not being produced by the stove but it was certainly emanating from Ward: steam hissed from his angry ears and the temperature radiating from his face was so great it could have boiled a kettle in seconds. I said as much, which was a mistake. I found myself the target of an airborne stove which hit me full frontal with force. I was no longer amused. I hurled it back with equal vigour and it landed with a satisfying clunk on his head.

By now fellow campers had gathered to watch this novel tennis match and cheered enthusiastically from the side lines. Heads swivelled from side to side as Ward delivered a vilifying backhand, only to have the missile returned by my swift and forceful smash. In attacking mode I accelerated in for the kill, but there was no need: it was game, set and match. The stove's days were over before they had even begun.

*

Set amid sandbanks just off the Normandy coast is a vast and impressive granite rock 256 feet high. It is Mont St Michel, and perched on top is a Benedictine monastery on the site where St Michael the Archangel was said to have appeared in the year 708. More than 700,000 visitors flock there annually and we added to the many nationalities to mingle and jostle our way around this beautiful but tourist-trodden mount.

We spent the night at a campsite down the road, strategically placed to provide us with a vista of the exalted rock. Early the next morning, as my fellow campers lay in slumber, I paid a visit to the *Dames* as urgency demanded. The toilets were of the hole-in-the-floor variety and as I set about normal procedures I heard the arrival of a pair of booted feet. They were boots with a purpose but not a purpose for which the *Dames* was designed. They stopped, then they started again and then they shuffled closer towards the decrepit, peeling door of my cubicle. There was a six-inch gap between the bottom of the door and the floor and, in my crouched position, I could see the concrete floor outside. Then I saw the boots — old, scuffed boots. Men's boots. Then I saw a face. It was that of an unshaven, crooked-mouthed man who was bending down and leering under my door. At that crucial stage of my procedures, there was not a lot I could do — I had literally been caught with my pants down. Disgusted, I hissed and spat out a stream of abuse, which only seemed to add to his perverse enjoyment. He broke into a dirty, twisty-faced grin and then he shuffled off. There was no one else around. Feeling rattled and a trifle shaken, I scurried back to the safety of the tent.

Outside Nantes we stopped on a quiet country road and waited for the most physically self-punishing cycle race in the world — the Tour de France. In three breathtaking weeks about 200 riders attempt to spin 2,000 miles around France in this gruelling whirlwind competition. Many never make it and even those who do all suffer as fatigue eats into mind and body. It is too bad if your legs feel wobbly: there is no time to take a breather nor even to dismount for a pee — you urinate on the ride, although not within town limits (the rules say), and woe betide the unlucky souls who find themselves downwind. Feet remain firmly fixed to the pedals as you eat and drink and have your gears or derailleur adjusted *en route* by acrobatic mechanics who dangle out of the windows of cars that run alongside. First aid to an injury or buttock boil (one of the competitors' biggest problems, which can often be remedied by cutting a hole in the saddle where it rubs) can also be applied on the move. However, if you puncture you are forced to stop, although not for long. A dab-handed mechanic can change the front wheel in ten seconds, the back in fifteen. It takes me half an hour.

All the riders have their sights set on the Arc de Triomphe at the end of this annual madness. They may not have acquired the winner's yellow jersey but they will be cheered and filmed and watched by millions as they roll gloriously across the finishing line, hailed as indisputable heroes. Those who fall by the wayside, however, are swept up like stray dust by a small blue van known as the broom wagon.

We were in for a long wait before we would see so much as one rider, but that was the fun of being a spectator at the greatest bike race in the world. For hours the crowds swelled and the tension mounted as Tour vehicles of every description passed in a massive, colourful, horn-blaring cavalcade. Giant inflated Michelin men tottered on motorbike pillions; a van's roof was moulded to the shape of a Coke bottle; cars and wagons and people were covered in colours and streamers; and, bearing the name of sponsors, free gifts like caps, pens, stickers, leaflets and endless other paraphernalia were flung into the growing crowds of onlookers, who pounced eagerly to claim a memento of this momentous occasion.

When all the games and gimmicky vehicles had passed, the serious business began. Ears were pressed against radios to catch the running commentary. The leading race car arrived, the megaphones, the motorbikes whose backward-facing pillion riders carried television cameras strapped to their shoulders. At last came the leader, the pack, the speed. In a sweaty, multihued mass the sight we had come to see, the sight we had awaited with bated breath for hours, sped past in an instant whirring blur of lycra and glistening muscle and the swoosh of a swarm of humming bicycle spokes. No rider was even faintly aware of us — their pained features were set in steely concentration, eyes focused and never flickering from the wheel in front. And then, just as suddenly as they had arrived, they were gone. We picked up our tacky but much cherished memorabilia and cycled away.

Once upon a time I had longed for a horse but my father had bought me a bicycle instead. In retrospect, I think he regretted this decision at times because at least horses have their limits as to how frequently they can be ridden, and where. Those limitations can prevent a pleasurable pastime from escalating out of all proportion.

It is different with a bike. Bikes are convenient. Unlike horses, they can be swiftly dismantled and forced into the confines of a car boot, driven 200 miles and still be able to function in fully operational order. Horses cannot be lugged on to trains, harnessed bungie-fashion in the guard's van, transported for eight hours and then be prepared to tear up Snowdon and back without so much as a whinny. Horses are not practical for riding to and from school, or for weaving through London's rush-hour traffic, or for soaring across the Sahara or, for that matter (unlikely as it might sound), for riding underwater along the bottom of a swimming pool. But with a bicycle none of this is any trouble. Bikes are useful, versatile and fun.

When I was eleven and went on my first cycle-camping excursion around the Isle of Wight, weight of equipment was of no concern. I took a tent the size of a house, enough cooking utensils to fill a kitchen and a huge assortment of footwear. So fastidious was I about cleaning the tent's interior that I even strapped a dustpan and brush to my panniers.

Several bike tours later, I had managed to cut down considerably on superfluous equipment. If I thought something might be useful but did not want to carry it because of its weight, I would sneak it into Ward's panniers when he was not looking. When it was eventually discovered, I would adamantly plead my innocence and generally won. Ward had little idea what lurked in the depths of his bags.

The more camping we did, the more disillusioned Ward became with the length of his legs. Unlike me, who possessed Lilliputian legs which could conveniently be retracted out of the way, Ward could find no comfortable stowage position for his limbs. Sitting on the ground for every meal became a painful and dead-legged affair for him. So he bought a collapsible chair and tied it to his rear rack. Carting around such ungainly and weighty apparatus did not worry him at all (even though he was breaking spokes faster than he could eat Danish pastries) and at the end of each day he would rig up his cumbersome contraption and recline like a complacent king.

The Loire was teeming with cycle tourists. It seemed that following France's longest river and visiting the glorious châteaux on two wheels was in fashion. The region was almost as busy as the cycle tracks of Holland.

We stopped at Saumur for lunch. When we asked for the bill, the surly waitress barked at us to wait. We waited for a while and then tried again. As she steamed out of the kitchen, Ward tried to attract her attention. She cast us a glowering look and accelerated past. When she clumsily knocked our table on her return journey, we once again asked for the bill and once again she curtly hissed at us to *attendez*.

Ward had had enough. 'Go and unlock the bikes,' he told me imperiously. 'I'm going to pay at the bar.'

Obediently, I unharnessed our steeds. While I waited for him, I composed a suitable photograph in which Ward would be the subject against an impressive backdrop of the neighbouring château. Yes, I could see it now. All I needed was Ward and the camera.

Ward appeared but the camera did not. Before I had a chance to ask for it, he slung his leg over his crossbar and tore off down the hill. I followed suit, not quite so briskly and totally nonplussed. I finally caught up with him five miles down the road.

'Crikey!' I panted. 'Talk about the wind up your bottom. What's got into you?'

'It was imperative we left that restaurant at speed,' he said, tight-jawed. 'There was no time for small talk.'

'What are you going on about? Did you forget to leave a tip or something?'

'I didn't leave a tip and I didn't leave something.' He laughed sardonically. 'No, I didn't leave anything at all — we had a free meal.'

'Really? That was nice of the waitress,' I said with genuine innocence, thinking perhaps we should cycle back and thank her. 'And there we were thinking she was the most ungracious waitress in the world.'

'No, you clothead! The waitress didn't give us a free meal. I went to the bar and handed her some money but she roughly pushed it aside and told me to sit down and wait. I'd have been there all day. So I tried once more to pay, received the same response, thought "stuff that for a lark" and walked out. I was sure that would get her attention. Well, it didn't, and here we are now — in a right mess.'

I lapsed into brooding silence as I absorbed this arresting news. I felt like saying, '*We're* in a mess? It's nothing to do with me. Don't bank on me to scurry to your rescue when you're thrown into gaol.' But I restrained myself, sensing that Ward was beginning to panic.

'Quick,' he said, in shaky tones, 'we've got to act fast. As soon as they've realized what's happened, the place will be running with police. The waitress will give them our description so the first thing to do is put them off the scent by changing clothes.'

The whole affair suddenly struck me as faintly ludicrous.

'What, change clothes? I can't. I'm saving my clean T-shirt and shorts until wash day.'

Ward was not amused. 'Don't mess around,' he retorted. 'This isn't a joke.'

He hastily dived into some shrubbery with a bundle of clothes. Apart from a cycling cap and different coloured shorts, he emerged looking remarkably similar. I laughed, out of nervousness perhaps, and promptly regretted it.

'Luckily,' said Ward, 'there are plenty of cyclists around so we don't stick out immediately.'

Suddenly, at a junction down the road, we both saw a police van shoot past. Ward's jaw dropped.

'Oh my God! They're after us already. Quick! We've got to move. We'll ride along the river, crossing bridges from bank to bank. If we keep changing directions, we might give them the slip.'

I felt such actions were more appropriate to a fox shaking the hounds off its scent and would only draw attention. However, Ward's mood was volatile and I decided to keep my views to myself.

We cycled off, oblivious to the glories of the Garden of France and submerged in gloomy, guilty thought. Occasionally, though, a thrilling shiver would shudder down my spine and I would think: this is pretty exciting stuff. Then we saw them. Waiting down the road were two gendarmes. A hasty retreat was out of the question. They both stood rigidly, arms folded, glaring at us.

'Act normal!' ordered Ward who, ashen faced and shaking like a leaf, looked far from normal himself. Through clenched teeth this hero motioned for me to lead the way into our imminent and uncertain encounter with the law. Dutifully I did so.

With knotted stomachs, we crossed the junction opposite the boys in blue. A flat-palmed hand was raised, which I rightly interpreted as '*Arrêtez*!'

I could hear Ward's knee-caps rattling in terror as he pulled over just in front of me. He said nothing but fixed me earnestly with that familiar pleading look which said, 'Deal with it.'

I dealt with it by first bidding a suspiciously over-chirpy '*Bonjour*'. Just as I was expecting a pair of handcuffs to snap on to the scene, they sternly reprimanded us for having crossed the road without looking for oncoming traffic. This indeed was true but was not quite the confrontation I had expected.

And that was it. We were briskly waved on and the encounter was over. As we cycled off, I wondered if it was a cruel ploy — perhaps we were being lured into a trap. I sensed that we were being observed. We stopped at a café and concealed our bikes round the back. Moments later, a rickety police van shot past with its siren wailing. I emitted a nervous titter but for Ward it was a sure sign that we were being hunted.

We waited until dusk to find a camping place. For two days we lay low but on the third day we rose again and descended at speed down the road *en route* for the Dordogne.

It was in some loos in Toulouse that a further nasty experience occurred. While brushing my teeth in a campsite *Dames*, I looked up and saw in the mirror (reflecting the mirror opposite) a bearded and swarthy face ogling at me. Embarrassed, I immediately presumed I was in the *Hommes* by mistake. I hurriedly rinsed my mouth but when I next looked up I saw the man's reflected face again, only this time he was in the cubicle beside me.

He was obviously up to something and I had a pretty good idea what it might be. Trapped in the corner, I waited with growing alarm, sincerely hoping someone else would come in. No one did and I decided to make a run for it. As I accelerated out of my cubicle he blocked my escape route and, with trousers undone, exposed the inevitable. Kicking out viciously, I managed to dart past and scarpered at speed back to the tent. I was not having much luck in French toilets.

High up in the eastern Pyrenees, we ventured into the tiny semi-autonomous republic of Andorra. Situated in a beautiful valley among spectacular mountain peaks, the ancient capital Andorra la Vella is incongruously surrounded by a hideous array of duty-free supermarkets. It has merged with the neighbouring and larger town of Escaldes to form one gigantic zonal shopping centre.

Tourism has had fundamental social and economic consequences here. About six million tourists (mainly French and Spanish) flock to this shoppers' paradise each year. A constant stream of cars descends upon the narrow streets, which are lined with ugly displays of hi-fi and electrical shops. Into these gadgetry oases pile floods of hungry-eyed bargain hunters. Laden with booty, they crowd into the hotels and restaurants to refuel on an abundance of absurdly cheap alcohol. Then, fuddle-headed, they sway back to their vehicles to join the queue for absurdly cheap petrol before joining the queue to leave. We passed an endless traffic jam as we freewheeled down the mountains into Spain.

Standing high like a row of jagged teeth is the isolated mountain of Montserrat, so called because its uneven rocky outline resembles the serrated teeth of a saw. We clambered eagerly into an aerial cable car, which swayed unsteadily as it ascended the jutting rockface in the middle of a dramatic and violent thunderstorm. Higher and higher we creakily climbed, up to the huge Benedictine monastery that dominated the imposing, pinnacled mountainside. It is the home of the Black Virgin, a much venerated icon blackened by the smoke of countless candles.

A hot, stormy tailwind blasted us on to Barcelona, capital of Catalonia — the most fiercely independent of Spain's provinces. The Catalans, living within an autonomous region with their own language and culture, belong to two nations: political Spain and the cultural nation which has no physical borders. The Catalans' pride in their separate heritage and identity is most clearly seen in the language; they have their own newspapers, theatres, schools, radio networks and television stations. Catalan also takes precedence over Castilian Spanish for street names and signs. The language was forbidden for over thirty years during Franco's dictatorship but it survived behind closed doors and staged a dramatic comeback after his death.

Talking to some locals at the market, I was amazed at their passionate belief that Barcelona (not Madrid) was the capital of Spain. The rivalry between these two cities is probably as strong as ever, though less violent than in the days when capitalists in Madrid sent secret policemen to murder capitalists in Barcelona. In those days, Barcelona's inhabitants claimed that the sea beside their city had been filled with sharks imported by Madrid from the West Indies. Today Barcelona, ancient port of the Mediterranean and modern powerhouse of Spanish industry and commerce, has reclaimed its former position as one of the great metropolitan centres of Europe.

Ward and I set up base in a packed campsite on the outskirts of the city and soon found that it was impossible to say or do anything without someone seeing or intervening. One evening, when talking to some neighbouring Dutch friends, Ward aired his mostly favourable views on Spain's controversial national 'sport' — bullfighting. This evoked a fervent response from an unseen soul in a neighbouring tent. Loud and clear on the still night air came the exclamation: 'Fascist!'

We roamed the city streets for five days — streets of low houses that seemed to be linked by a mesh of washing lines running above our heads from one window to another. Big Mamas stood on ornately wrought balconies, flapping their arms in animated discussion with neighbours across the street. In the more commercial areas I immediately noticed the shoe-shiners doing the rounds of the pavement cafés. In England I know of only one shoe-cleaner, an elderly gentleman who has firmly established his territory on a hectic spot in London's Regent Street. Most people in northern Europe would rather be run over in dirty boots than have their shoes cleaned in public but in southern cities it is hot business. Trying to shun shoe-shiners in Spain can be as tedious as evading windscreen-washing touts in London.

Down the famous, well-trodden route of Las Ramblas we rambled. This broad central pavement, lined with massive plane trees, runs from the enormous Plaza Catalunya down to the seafront and is the social heart of the city. A hive of activity, it is the boulevard described by the great Andalusian poet Lorca as 'the only street in the world which I wish would never end'.

This pedestrianized artery of crazy-paving is Barcelona at its most extrovert. The central 'aisle' is a clamour of kiosks selling flowers, European newspapers, domestic pets (gerbils, goldfish, finches, parrots) and guides to the brothels. Further along buskers, mime artists, fortune-tellers, fire-eaters, palmists, tarot-card readers and lottery-ticket sellers compete enthusiastically for business.

Las Ramblas cuts right through the heart of the notorious red-light district and streets at the port end are crammed with sleazy clubs and sex shops. Prostitutes loiter by twenty-four-hour newspaper stands, soliciting passers-by. The street never goes to sleep. All day and all night people sit in cafés or bars watching the parade of fashionable crowds, peddlers and prostitutes.

To one side of the boulevard is one of Spain's great covered markets. The high-vaulted glass roof traps the aromas of fresh fruit, herbs and vegetables; the air is cool in the dairy section, salty in the fish section. There are stalls selling only eggs, or cheese, or bread, or freshly plucked chickens. Customers sniff and pick and prod the produce — there are no 'Don't squeeze me till I'm yours' labels here. These people are connoisseurs; they know what they want. Earnest discussions prevail about the source, the quality, the freshness. There is no haste to buy

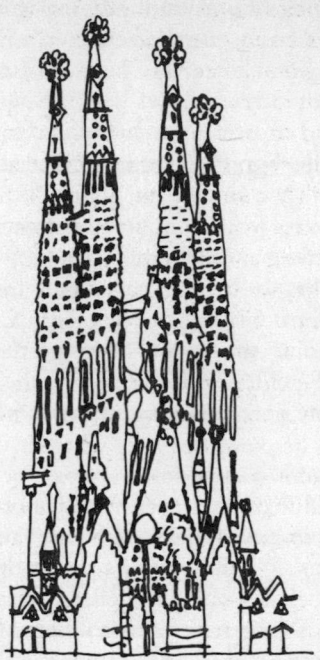

here, no tearing around the aisles with a trolley full of pre-packed rubbish. Food shopping is a serious business and there is no hope of literally keeping a customer's nose out of it. Hygiene falls by the wayside.

Wandering around Barcelona, it is impossible not to keep stumbling across flamboyant buildings, fountains and street-lamps designed by the city's most famous architect, Antoni Gaudí. He was to modern architecture what Salvador Dalí (another Catalan) was to surrealism. Gaudí is best remembered for his bizarre, nonconformist approach to design: he did not so much design buildings as sculpt them. His creations, with weird and wonderful curves, sparkling and twisted roofs and melting metal balconies, were the most daring of all art nouveau.

All the tendencies of his outlandish style (which echoes the shapes of natural phenomena) seem to clash at random in the unfinished symphony in stone of his most famous building, the church of La Sagrada Familia, which he began in 1884. In 1926, Gaudí had too close an encounter with a tram and his death two days later was treated as a Catalan national disaster. The church is still incomplete but is one of the most prominent structures in the city, with its eight perforated spires (there were supposed to be four more, symbolic of the Twelve Apostles) and three exterior walls, parts of which are framed by enormous stone bones. Inside, this roofless 'ruin' resembles an abandoned building site: a tall, rusting crane stands in what might one day be the nave and tufts of grass sprout from the altar steps. Many people believe that this neo-Gothic masterpiece will never be complete but, whether it is or not, it will undoubtedly remain magnificent.

With feet tired from unaccustomed walking, we remounted and headed out of the city. We rode past the centre's spacious cafés where, after a hard morning's shopping, fashionable folk refreshed themselves with Fundador (Spanish brandy) in glasses the size of fishbowls. We pedalled past small, crowded harbour-front restaurants where convivial customers pulled and scooped and sucked an assortment of squid, lobster, crab and prawns, mopping up the juices with *pan con tomate* (bread smeared with tomato and soaked in olive oil) and on past the enormous monument of Christopher Columbus, which stands proudly looking out over the harbour towards a reproduction of his ship, the *Santa María*, which seemed far too small to have sailed across the Atlantic with forty men aboard.

The 'plan' was to cycle south down the Costa Dorada and so be within easy dipping distance of sea and sand. After a morning's ride along the traffic-laden highway, we gave up that idea and decided to venture inland into the mountains. It was the right decision and it was beautiful. The narrow, rocky roads wound their way among flower-spangled villages and groves of oranges, almonds and gnarled old olive trees.

By chance, we came across the mediaeval fortress town of

Morella, rising from the plain around a small hill crowned by an almost impregnable castle which dominates the Castellón countryside for miles around. Here, away from the outrageously priced coast, we treated ourselves to a £5 double room (with bathroom en suite) at the El Cid Hotel. The lager louts who invade Torremolinos and Benidorm and the culture vultures who throng Granada, Seville and Madrid felt miles away.

Weaving our way south among terraced fields, we passed through small, white-washed villages with narrow, winding streets festooned with window boxes ablaze with colour, and filled with the songs of caged canaries. Cycling slowly past windows and doorways, we peered into dark, cool, cavernous interiors which exuded pungent aromas of cooking, garlic and herbs. Towards evening, as the incandescent heat dissipated, wizened old women with leathery, wrinkled faces brought their wooden chairs out on to the streets and sat in black lace shawls, preparing vegetables, sewing, chatting and watching their quiet world go by. Grubby-kneed children with big, dark eyes played late into the warm night, kicking footballs and running barefooted down the streets. In the bars, where huge hams hung from the ceiling, men in dark clothes and black berets picked at *tapas* and scratched their heads as they confabulated in earnest discussion.

Mid-flight down a mountain, I noticed a bee hitching a free ride on my knee. It was no ordinary bee: it was a buzzing beast as big as a bat. Cautiously, removing my left hand from my rear brake lever, I attempted to flick the creature into oblivion but it had dug in its haunches and was obviously determined to get a run for its money. The big, black patches around its eyes gave it the droll look of wearing goggles and, with its tight-jawed expression, it reminded me of a grizzled pilot in an early flying machine.

With growing concern, I tried to brush it aside and managed to dislodge it. It taxied along my thigh before buzzing into take-off — but not before leaving me with a painful reminder of its visit in the form of a dagger-like sting, which I carefully removed and stuck in my diary.

My knee swelled to the size of a tennis ball and for three days I lolled around, out of operational order. But I did not mind. We happened to be camping in Elche, famed throughout Spain for its exotic palm forest (originally planted by the Moors), and the delay gave us the unexpected chance of being in the city during its remarkable fiesta. The celebrations culminate in a centuries-old mystery play, the *Misterio de Elche*, and are one of the best examples of the mock battles between Christians and Moors which characterize many of the festivals in the region. The elaborately costumed warriors, clad in cloaks and Jesus sandals, fight it out over several days before the Moors are eventually driven from the city and the Christian king enters in triumph.

That night there was a fireworks display of fantastic proportions. We merged with the convivial crowds and jockeyed for an advantageous position on the bridge, eating a bagful of deliciously sticky local dates as we stood squashed and waiting. At 11.15 the action started, with a show of colourful explosions bursting into the blue-black sky. At first it was a fairly tame and controlled display, greeted with roaring cheers of approval as fireworks fountained in a multitude of multi-hued splendour. Little did we know that the Battle of Elche was about to begin.

Suddenly the air was alive with the sound of artillery fire. Fastened to the opposite side of our bridge was an armoury of rockets — but they were only fireworks, being set off with gay abandon. Had it been Guy Fawkes Night back in safety-conscious Britain, the bridge would have been cordoned off and spectators made to stand well back, but this was Spain and the Spaniards like to dice with death. A lot of the rockets shot off vertically into the sky, as intended, but a lot did not and spun off at speed into the crowd. Pandemonium ensued as people screamed and tried to run away in panic. A hysterical woman pushed past me, her hands clasping her bloodied face. Some people fell and were trampled underfoot. And still the rockets were firing off, scudding in every direction. The noise was deafening; explosions and screams and sirens filled the air and, in a state of bewilderment, I reminded myself that this was supposed to be a fiesta, not a fiasco.

Ward and I escaped by jumping from the bridge to the bank and sliding down to the river. We ran along the edge to calmer crowds who were quite unaware of the air-raid attack taking place on the bridge: they were gazing wide-eyed and open-mouthed into the night sky as it flared in a burst of continuous colour. On the dot of midnight, in true war-time fashion, the whole city was plunged into a complete black-out.

A silent suspense fell upon the spectators and then, in a succession of laser-like lights, a sequence of fireworks streamed up into the darkness before exploding into a mushroom-cloud finale of cascading brilliance. A massive and dazzling phosphorescent palm tree appeared against the black sky, momentarily turning the night into the shimmering luminescence of day.

The show had literally ended with a bang. For us, however, the main excitement was yet to come. Returning to the campsite was a terrifying but hilarious ordeal. It was impossible to walk back sedately along the city streets marvelling at the sights we had seen — we would never have made it alive. Gangs of wild-eyed youths, armed with burning and flaring fireworks, lurked behind parked cars or hung off balconies hurling their lethal homemade missiles at helpless unarmed passers-by like us. It was as if the city was under siege. We darted from dark doorway to hidden alley in sporadic bursts. Our ears were screaming from the high-pitched wail of treacherous creations which scudded aflame across the ground like remote-controlled warheads to burst at our feet with a blinding explosion.

With pounding hearts and sweaty skins, we finally arrived back at base in one piece. We were filled with pumping adrenalin and felt as exhilarated as if we had made it across a battlefield alive. We congratulated ourselves on our survival techniques, took a cold shower and fell into exhausted slumber.

*

Granada is one of Spain's most celebrated towns but it has always had sorrow at its heart. Being the last Moorish stronghold in Spain, it was the arena for many a battle over the centuries.

Before the Christian crusaders slowly expelled them from the land, the Muslim kings built their last fortress there and today it must be one of the seven great tourist wonders of the world. High on a hill, with the permanently snowcapped Sierra Nevada as a backdrop, stands the Alhambra — an awesome and romantic palace that towers over Granada in sublime and commanding style.

Lorca loved Granada but said that he thought of it 'as one should remember a sweetheart who has died'. Shortly afterwards, at the outset of the Spanish Civil War, Lorca was shot and became the most famous victim of the city's terrible atrocities during that time.

Just outside Granada, on a road that heads into the mountains, stands a sign: *La carretera mas alta de Europa* — the highest road in Europe. We followed its direction eagerly and embarked upon a thirty-two mile ascent that seemed to rise into the sky itself. Up, up, up we toiled and sweated; up, up, up, into wild and rugged scenery marred only by Solynieve, a truly hideous ski resort which at that time of year resembled a concrete ghost town. Up, up, up — emitting creaks and groans from both bikes and bones, until finally, after six slow hours, we arrived at the 3392-metre Pic Veleta.

Panting like a salivating bloodhound, I collapsed in a crumpled heap. When my breath returned, I was able to appreciate the view — and what a view! To quote what all mountain climbers say, I felt on top of the world. The day was so clear that we could see Castile in the north and the Rif mountains of Morocco shimmering to the south. Feeling like a couple of conquistadors, we perched on a rocky overhang restfully munching our well-earned sandwiches and savouring the scenery as we congratulated ourselves on having pedalled the equivalent of over a third of the way up Mount Everest.

Then came the moment we had been waiting for, the moment that makes slogging masochistically up a mountain all worthwhile: the descent. We launched upon it with exhilaration and our only complaint was that it was over too soon. It had taken six hours to get up but only forty-five minutes to come down.

We hit the Costa del Sol and headed for Rincón de la Victoria, where Brian and Feli Baybut (friends of Dad's) had a holiday home. Leaving Malaga along the N340, Ward stopped to photograph what he saw as the epitome of this part of Spain: a litter-strewn beach packed with sun-worshipping bodies and the complementary backdrop of high-rise blocks and factories.

We found the Baybuts' flat and stayed the night. The next morning there was a surprise phone call from my brother Dave and his girlfriend Melanie, who were in Malaga, having just motorbiked in two days the distance that had taken us two months. We arranged to meet at four o'clock that afternoon outside Malaga's tourist office.

Not long after three we were waving goodbye to the Baybut family and pedalling down the fast traffic-laden road to Malaga. Ward, as usual, was ahead by a good hundred metres. I glanced down momentarily to check the distance on my cycle computer.

When I looked up, I saw Ward flying through the air in slow motion. I thought I was dreaming but, no, he really was airborne and was veering off the righthand side of the road, his bike to the left. In the couple of seconds while I had glanced down, a van travelling in the same direction had careered into him. It did not stop.

Although in reality it took no time at all to cycle the short distance to the point of impact, it seemed to take forever. I became oblivious to everything around me. I was shut into my own muffled, slow-motion world, my eyes focused only on

In the Sahara Desert, which puts the likes of Bournemouth beach in the shade

After Algeria - relaxing on Marseilles beach - Ward had lost weight and I'd gained!

The Ardèche Gorge in France, which we were all too soon to canoe down.

Iceland's main traffic-laden highway!

Bubbling mud pools and burnt feet in Iceland

High up and warmer in Iceland

A dive-bombing great skua and Red'ed (he's the one on the ground) in Iceland

Cooking up another trip abroad - meals on wheels - caught in action with multi-course lunch on board

Practice road marking in the Faroe Islands

Posing, like so many have posed before me, beside the Arctic Circle sign in Norway

Trying not to look too out of breath atop the Atlas Mountains (Tizi-n-Tichka Pass) in Morocco

Pristine teeth in Drâa Valley, Morocco

Demonstrating the versatile port-a-loo cape method

The uncanny sight of tree-climbing goats. As there is nothing to eat on the ground, they have adapted themselves to skip along the branches, squirrel-fashion

Mel looking concerned about some mobile haystacks in the Atlas mountains, Morocco

Holy cow and stupa in Nepal

Ward's flying form. And I thought: what's he doing in the air? He doesn't look right up there. And then, when he landed in a splayed heap, I thought: this can't really be happening.

I would like to be able to say that I threw down my bike when I reached Ward and ran to his rescue. Instead, within my dream world, I remember dismounting and carefully laying my bike down on its non-gear side, as I had been taught. At that moment I was inexplicably more concerned about bending my derailleur than possibly saving Ward's life.

But then, in a sudden burst, the real world returned: the noise, the speed, the fright. I was sure Ward was dead. He lay flat on his back, motionless, his eyes wide open, unmoving, glazed and staring. From his head trickled a steady stream of rich, dark, sticky blood.

I could quite easily have become hysterical but managed to hold back. By this time a huge crowd from the beach had gathered and everybody was shouting and flapping their arms around in an over-excited and unhelpful manner. Many were intent on trying to get hold of Ward's legs and drag him across the sharp, dusty gravel to the shade. I managed to prevent them by clumsily indicating that he might have broken bones.

We needed an ambulance but it had not occurred to anyone to summon one, despite my repeated requests. It struck me that, this being Spain, it would no doubt take all day for one to materialize anyway — a thought that later proved to be correct.

I realized that we were outside the entrance to a factory and I sent some workers into the place to fetch their van and a first-aid box. Meanwhile I removed Ward's bandanna from around his neck and fashioned a makeshift bandage, which I dipped in antiseptic and held tight against his badly bleeding head wound. With my other hand I carefully mopped his brow, using the remnants from my water-bottle. All the time I babbled away to him in as comforting a manner as I could muster in the circumstances. Although he seemed dead to the world, I kept repeating that I would soon have him out of this mess and he would be as right as rain.

With a back-up team of several Señores, I helped to transfer him gingerly into the waiting van. I was much relieved by his apparent return to consciousness — there was life in the old dog yet.

All set to leave in the ramshackle van for a hasty dash to hospital, it suddenly occurred to me that the bikes were still lying on the ground with our money, passports and possessions. Scuttling back to them, I rounded up Ward's panniers (which had flown off on impact), removed the handlebar bags containing our valuables and locked the bikes in an old shed. I scampered back to the van and, after an inauspicious splutter from the engine, we were off.

Glancing back at the crowds and the scene of this nightmare, it dawned on me that the sight was familiar. It was the exact spot where, on the previous day, Ward had stopped to take his photographs of the beach.

Ward was in a state of delirium in the van and had no idea what was going on.

'What happened? Where are we going? My head hurts. Who had an accident? Where are we going? Don't leave me — don't leave me, will you? Who had an accident? I had an accident? Where are we going? Where's my head? Did the driver stop? Bloody hell, the driver didn't stop? Don't leave me. Why are you covered in blood? Did the driver stop? My head hurts. What's that trickling down my neck?'

I kept holding him, propping him up and truthfully answering his continuous babble of slurred questions — apart from the last one. I told him it was water (not blood) that was running down his neck.

After a horrendously bumpy ride of erratic swerves and near misses, we reached Malaga's local casualty hospital. There was no one around to receive new arrivals and the van driver and I had to stagger in with Ward, who collapsed on to a bench in the reception area. I felt a faint sense of relief now that we had made it to hospital — medical help was at hand. But this was Spain. No one wanted to know. A group of staff carried on chatting happily together, right next to us, as though we did not exist. When I forcefully intervened, looking fraught and desperate, I was brushed aside and curtly told to wait. Wait! I could not wait. I had a friend who, for all I knew, was close to death. I ran frantically down the corridors looking for someone to help. There was no one. The whole place seemed to be in a state of siesta. Then I bumped into a sleepy-eyed assistant who told me they were not admitting emergency cases. I had to go to Carlos Haya, Malaga's main hospital.

I asked for Ward to be transferred by ambulance immediately. '*No! No hay ambulancia!*' came the reply. I demanded an ambulance. Finally one appeared with a disconsolate driver — I think I had woken him up.

Then I remembered Dave and Mel. It was way past our rendezvous time and they would be worried. I had to get word to them, quickly. I saw a police car parked by the gates, its doors open and the driver languishing inside. I ran up to him and tried in Spanish to explain my predicament, asking if he could possibly pass a message to the tourist office.

'*Imposible*,' he simpered. And I knew he meant it.

As we headed towards Carlos Haya in the ambulance, I thought: at least Ward will get proper treatment now. It was wishful thinking. Despite showing staff that we were insured, we were made to wait in the crowded chaos of reception for an hour and a half. In the meantime I had to do everything myself: I put Ward in a wheelchair; I found a bandage and some antiseptic and tied up his head. It did not stop the bleeding but it was better than nothing. Ward sat slumped in the wheelchair in a semi-conscious state. I kept reassuring him that all would be fine, though by now I was far from sure myself.

The road that follows the Costa del Sol is said to be the most dangerous in Europe and there are scores of accidents, with at least two fatalities a day. As we waited in the painful confusion of the reception area, victims from these road accidents arrived through the doors in a steady stream of blood and bruises. Some were just badly shocked, others were seriously injured. A man lying beside me on a stretcher had stumps of bloody bandages where his feet should have been.

Chatting doctors occasionally sauntered past, clutching clip boards and oblivious to the mayhem around them. Countless times I intercepted a doctor or nurse, urgently requesting them to see to Ward, but they waved me away and told me to wait.

Eventually a Dr Rengel took Ward aside and heavy-handedly stitched up his head without cleaning or dressing the wound. He carted the patient off, supposedly for an X-ray. On being questioned later, Dr Rengel stated that he had carried out a thorough investigation of Ward's head wound by placing his fingers in the hole to ensure that the skull was not fractured. He did not bother to remove Ward's bloodstained clothes to check for further injuries and altogether missed the deep cuts and gashes that covered his back.

Dr Rengel then tried to eject us from the hospital, saying that the patient was in a fit state to return home: he had asked Ward (who was only semi-conscious) if he was feeling all right and had received the answer, 'Yes.' When I explained that we were camping, this medical practitioner merely said that there were no spare beds in the hospital and that we must leave immediately. With rough impatience, he took hold of the wheelchair and pushed Ward out through the exit door, although he was in the midst of vomiting. I pushed him back in again, scarcely believing what was happening.

Fighting back exasperated tears, I tore around the hospital in one final effort to find someone — anyone — to help. I found no one. The only doctor I came across who spoke a little English laughed at my predicament and asked irrelevantly how old I was. When I said I was twenty, he simply looked heavenwards and told me I was too young to be running around his country.

I was at a loss and did the only thing I could in the circumstances: I found a taxi and took Ward back to the Baybuts' flat for help. Feli ran down the stairs to the taxi, where Ward sat slumped in the passenger seat, verging on unconsciousness. Three hours after the accident, blood still ran from his head and he was in a filthy condition in torn and bloodstained clothes and wrapped clumsily in a bloodstained sheet provided by the hospital. Even the taxi driver was shocked and told Feli that he could not believe a hospital could release a person in such a serious condition.

We took Ward upstairs and laid him on a double bed, where he passed out. From that moment, Feli took command. It helped that she was Spanish herself but without her determination and encouragement I would not have known what to do. In hurried detail, I told her exactly what had happened. The hospital was telephoned to find out more about the treatment given to Ward and Dr Rengel himself stated that he had already administered all the treatment that was necessary and that Ward only needed to rest.

Ward was still lying unconscious and bleeding profusely from his head wound — the pillow was saturated with blood. Brian came home, took one look at him and insisted that he must immediately be readmitted to hospital for proper treatment and observation. Knowing something about the workings of the Spanish medical services, he took my insurance policy and phoned their local office in Malaga. He explained the circumstances and said that an ambulance was required to take Ward back to hospital but was told that this would not be possible until they had full details of the insurance policy. It was only after the Baybuts had given personal undertakings to pay for any charges that the manager grudgingly agreed to send an ambulance, saying that it should arrive in roughly twenty minutes, but that nothing further in the way of treatment could be arranged until the insurance policy had been checked.

The ambulance finally arrived over an hour late. Thankfully Dave and Mel arrived simultaneously on their motorbike; Feli and I accompanied Ward in the ambulance back to the Carlos Haya with Dave and Mel in pursuit.

Feli collared Dr Rengel and expressed her disgust at the way he had handled the patient. He advised her that Ward's alarming symptoms of vomiting and continuing to bleed were perfectly normal and not serious, and that there was nothing further he could have done. The argument continued until the doctor at last capitulated by sending Ward for a head scan.

It was midnight before Ward was brought back from the scanning department and transferred into intensive care. At last he had been thoroughly cleaned up and his bloodstained clothes removed — some eight hours after his accident. The results of the scan took another hour and a half to come through. Fortunately he had no fractures or internal haemorrhaging but was to be kept in intensive care.

At 2.30 in the morning Brian and Feli went off to report details of the accident at Malaga's central police station. Dave, Mel and I spent the night sitting outside a bar across the road, reliving the day's events. Every now and then I scampered over to the hospital to check on Ward's condition.

The next morning the British consulate arrived, represented by an amenable middle-aged woman. She had liaised with our insurance company and been told that Ward should be kept in for a few days but that there were no spare hospital beds. He would have to be transferred to a private clinic. Feli took responsibility for all charges, knowing that Ward was covered by valid insurance, and later that day Ward and I were taken by ambulance to El Angel clinic. There we were given a private room with our own bathroom. The doctors and nurses were friendly and efficient and it was like moving into a five-star hotel. Dave and Mel gallantly insisted on staying with us, camping on the waiting-room floor next door. Some holiday!

It transpired that Ward had lost at least two days of his life and could not remember a thing about them. Having a hole in his head also accounted for some curious behaviour towards me. For example, when he discovered that I had transferred the valuables from his handlebar bag to my own for safe keeping he promptly accused me of stealing them. Naturally I assumed he was joking but he was serious.

The real bombshell dropped when we discussed the accident itself. We had had a slight altercation a few days earlier and Ward, who could remember nothing about the moment of impact, accused me of pushing him. This struck me as such an outrageous supposition that I assumed he really was having me on this time and I made light of the affair, playing along with him and jokingly admitting that perhaps I had slightly overstepped the mark and been a little too enthusiastic with my imaginary push.

Unfortunately my facetiousness went undetected. Ward was adamant that I was admitting the terrible truth. It was, he said, a joke that had nearly cost him his life. In his eyes, I was no longer a happy-go-lucky girlfriend but a thief and his potential murderer.

Despite such wild and vehement accusations, I stayed at his bedside and administered to his needs like a true Florence Nightingale for over a week. The only time I ventured out was to buy him big, sickly edible treats in the hope of rekindling his rationality. Then he began to accuse me of doing nothing to help and never being around when needed and I thought: to hell with him. I escaped for a morning with Dave and Mel at the gigantic Aqua Park in Torremolinos. Shooting down a near-vertical 100-foot water-slide towards potential death is highly recommended for releasing pent-up frustration.

Back at El Angel, I became suddenly and violently ill. Emerging from the bathroom feeling none too good, I blacked out and collapsed in a heap at the foot of Ward's bed. Dave and Mel lifted me on to the neighbouring bed and urgently called the nurse. She came careening round the corner, automatically heading for Ward who, propped up in bed, was haughtily reading *The Times*, quite unmoved by my plight. Wrong patient. The nurse was redirected to the next bed, where I had turned as white as the sheets. For some reason the nurse found my sudden misfortune of great amusement and she emitted short bursts of stifled giggles as she took my temperature, took my blood pressure and took the piss.

'You're always ill,' said Ward, before resuming his perusal of the paper.

Had Dave and Mel not been at the hospital I think I, too, would have turned loopy. Until then Mel had always been just

Dave's stand-offish girlfriend as far as I was concerned. Although she had been on the scene for over four years, she was someone I knew of but never really knew and she was certainly not someone with whom I would have chosen to spend much time. We passed formal niceties but we preferred to keep our distance. Basically, we did not see eye to eye.

Suddenly, and literally overnight — in a hospital ward — all that changed. For the first time in four years we really talked, opening up completely and hiding nothing. She was a new person and we became the best of friends.

Although Ward and I were only a day's ride from Morocco, we had once again failed to reach that mystical country. The doctors steadfastly agreed that to continue our ride was out of the question. Anyway, if we did so, Ward would require a new head and a new bike — and I would need a new boyfriend. We were put on a flight for home.

Looking back on it now, I have perhaps drawn Ward as an unsavoury and argumentative travelling companion. Frankly, he was, but for some inexplicable reason I still adored him. And even today, though he still insists he was pushed, we remain the greatest of friends.

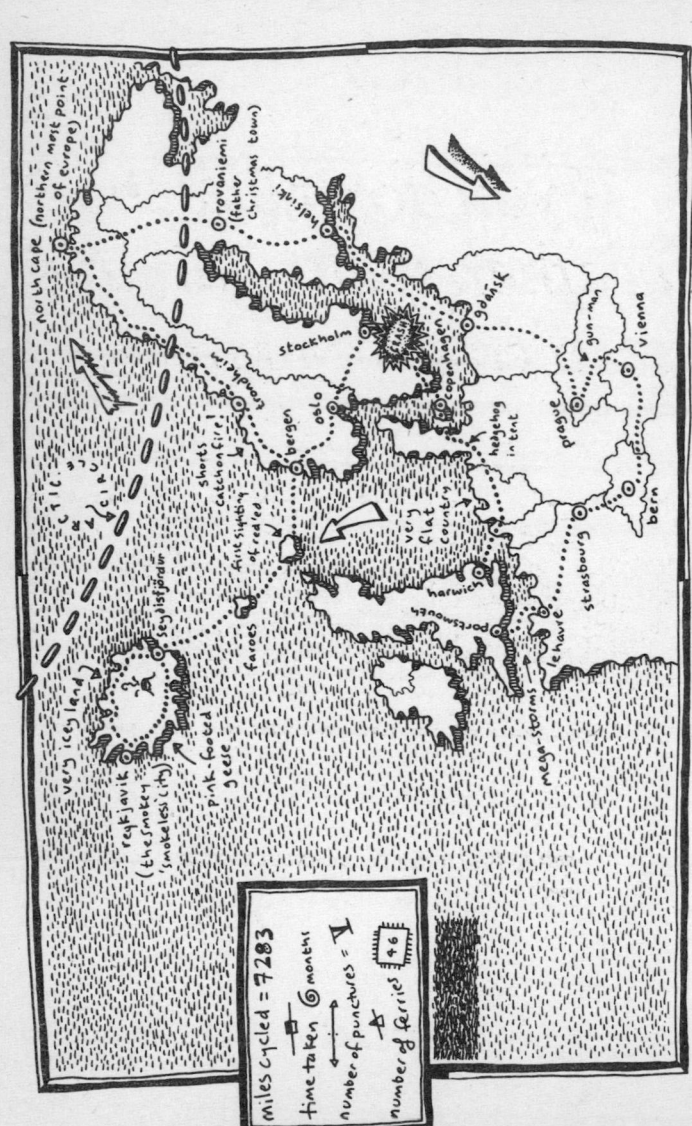

3

'If you don't like the weather, wait a minute'

TO ICELAND AND BEYOND

'It is easier to find a travelling companion than to get rid of one.'

ART BUCHWALD

Seven months after Malaga, I found myself with itchy feet and no cycling companion. For the third summer running I set out for foreign parts, only this time I was alone.

For each of my previous expeditions I had headed south into sun, heat and trouble. It was time for a change. Instead of turning right as I stepped out of my front door, I turned left. I was heading north to the Arctic and my destination was North Cape, the northernmost point of mainland Europe.

Almost immediately I met the first in a long series of curious characters. The guard on the London-to-Harwich train was unlike any British Rail guard I had ever encountered. He smiled. He also treated my bicycle as if it was a living and lovable creature.

'Your super, shinin' steed 'as be'aved bew-tifully, me darlin',' he said. 'Ya know, not once did it answer me back, unlike that bleedin' awful ferret I 'ad to escort yesterday to Saff'end. Bleedin' nightmare it was — give me a bike any day.'

Into pancake-flat Holland I rolled, past fields littered with windmills and scarecrows. The scarecrows were actually dead magpies, hapless black and white birds suspended by their feet from stakes driven into the ground. I wondered what winged creature deserved such an ignoble end, even if magpies were the thieves of the feathered world.

Crossing the river Waal, I met a wild-eyed Dutch woman swaddled in multi-coloured hippie garb and festooned with beads. She smelt of joss-sticks and garlic and told me she was on her way to visit a favourite castle for the fifteenth time in as many days. She went there for meditation and a bit of a chant.

'I lived in Chiswick for a year, working as a dog-walker,' she told me. 'I loved London and dreaded returning to Holland. But sadly I've never been back there.'

'Why not, if you loved the place so much?' I asked.

'Oh, I couldn't!' she lamented. I thought she was going to burst into tears. 'I would find it all too emotional.'

As the ferry came into dock, she reminisced about London's Underground. 'Just the most fascinating place. No one speaks to each other, but everyone stares. I found the tension thrilling.'

After that first day, the sun went down and I did not see it again for two weeks. I had chosen to cross Holland and Germany during their wettest May on record. Every day was the same: heavy-laden skies, torrential rain and fierce, cold, blustery headwinds. I had never been so wet for so long. My fingertips remained moist and as shrivelled as old prunes while my numb feet began to look disconcertingly toad-like.

I squelched steadily onwards, although thoughts of Arctic conditions did little to warm my enthusiasm. But I was determined not to give up (not yet, anyway) even when I nearly died of fright one night when waking to find a bedraggled hedgehog at the bottom of my sleeping-bag.

Denmark was memorable for its five hours of sunshine and Sweden was memorable for a bright yellow van that shot through a set of red traffic lights, quite oblivious to the fact that it was on a collision course with me until it was too late. Lying sprawled in the path of a juggernaut, I sensed that all hopes for my Nordic adventure were about to be squashed but a quick-thinking lorry driver plucked me to safety.

After ascertaining damage to body (bruises) and bike (buckled wheel), he kindly took me for a recovery breakfast. Over a smoked herring and rye-bread sandwich, with coffee so thick and strong it resembled tar, he told me his name was Christer and that he would prefer not to be a witness to my accident (although he had taken the hit'n'run driver's number) as far as reporting it to the police was concerned. This, he admitted in lowered tones and with shifty looks, was because he himself was something of a shady character and his best friend was currently mixed up with a murder. This was heart-stopping news. Ward would have been proud of me. There he had been in Italy spicing up his diary with imaginary meddlings of the Mafia, while here I was in real life mingling with Stockholm's seedily suspect underworld in squeaky-clean Sweden.

I had the address of a friend of a friend of my mother's who lived on the other side of the city and I arrived just as the family was going away for the weekend. Despite the fact that they did not even know me, they handed me their front-door key and told me to make myself at home.

It is an odd feeling to find yourself suddenly in charge of someone else's house when you have not even stepped into it yet. Then, when you have, it is hard not to be nosey. Other people's decorations, possessions and furnishings fill me with fascination — especially when I don't even know them. By being inquisitive, it is possible to gain a clear insight into the character and idiosyncrasies of those who live in a place. Telltale signs such as choice of books, pictures, records, ornaments and furniture (whether tacky or tasteful) or the degree of tidiness (pigsty or pristine) and the contents of the fridge all help to piece together an accurate impression of the inhabitants. And I am glad to report that the information gleaned about Celia and Stein Sylten from their abode proved highly favourable.

Cycling through hundreds of miles of dense pine forest can become rather monotonous and can affect your head. I speak from experience. I would sing a dirge to the trees in trying tones:

> Oh trees, trees and more trees, tra-la-la,
> And yet more trees, tall trees, the same trees, tra-la-la.

Then, to amuse myself further, I would practise riding 'no hands', then 'hands, one-foot pedal', then 'one-foot pedal, no hands'. Then I would select a tree (one of the green trees, the tall trees, the same trees, tra-la-la) way up the empty road and sprint towards it, legs pumping, heart pounding, as if there were no tomorrow. Then I would savour the sudden surge of momentum this provided and practise free-wheeling while tottering on my cross-bar in a dangerously unwieldy acrobatic fashion. Then I rigged up a bookstand on my handlebar bag and became so absorbed in Somerset Maugham's short stories that I narrowly missed ending up as pulp beneath the massive bulk of an eighteen-wheeler logging truck. Every now and then my monotony would be relieved by the appearance of a moose or a hurriedly lolloping hare.

People ask me if I get bored cycling alone. Well, as you can see, there just isn't time.

At one stage I came to Öland bridge which, at nearly four miles, is the longest bridge in Europe. After such arboreal tedium, the excitement of this discovery was almost too much for me and I so enjoyed being battered and blown by the tumultuous, salty-sprayed crosswind that I turned round and rode over it again. As I said, an overdose of spruce can affect the mind.

One lunchtime, perched on a pine stump and eating a banana sandwich, I was puzzling over my map of Scandinavia wondering how many more miles it was to North Cape when suddenly something caught my eye in the top left-hand corner of the map. It was an island. To be more precise, it was Iceland. Being a great disbeliever in route planning, it was only now that I had got around to opening my map to its full extent, thus revealing this distant land of *Is ok Eld* (Ice and Fire). I noticed a thin red line leading from Norway to Iceland via the Faroe Islands. My map-reading skills went as far as recognizing this as a ferry route.

The more I brooded on this remarkable discovery, the more I wanted to visit it. As I swallowed my last mouthful, I brushed the crumbs from my map-covered lap and rose resolutely to my feet. That's it, I thought; I'll make a quick detour to North Cape via Iceland.

Umpteen punctures later, I arrived in Oslo and headed straight for the bike shop to buy a new inner tube.

'Ah — so where are you going on that?' the Norwegian shop owner enquired, pointing to my jaded mount.

'Iceland,' I said, and promptly wished I had not.

'How old are you?' he asked.

'Twenty-one,' I replied, not quite sure what that had to do with cycling to Iceland and wondering why someone always asked my age whenever I hit dubious times.

'Ha, ha!' he crowed. 'And do you know what you head for?' No, I had to admit, I did not.

'Hell!' he announced with vigorous glee. 'Absolutely hell! Five years ago I take my bicycle there and never again. Beautiful country? Yes. But not for bicycles and ...' (casting a derogatory glance towards my visibly trembling steed) '... especially not yours. You need a mountain bike. No, I think you must need a jeep.'

This encouraging Norseman then proceeded to take great delight in relaying the grim details of how, after only two days, his bicycle had literally disintegrated beneath him. He drew intricate diagrams to explain the atrocious road conditions which resembled more a cross-section of some savage mountain range than a cycling surface. As if that was not enough, he then enthusiastically described the morbid details of how a French family was washed away and drowned in a 2CV when attempting to cross a flooded glacial river. I thought such folly served them right but decided not to air my opinion. I did not want to excite him further.

'So now I think you stay safe in Norway?' he said.

Clearing my throat to dispel any shaky tones of doubtfulness, I said: 'No, no. Of course not. You've only whetted my appetite. But I will have *two* new tyres and every puncture repair kit you have — just as a precaution, you understand.'

Crossing Hardangervidda, a rocky mountainous plateau (the largest in Europe), I was taken completely unawares by a snow storm. The morning was blue, and hot by Norwegian standards, and I thought I was in for a good day's ride to cross the pass. After only a few miles the weather had changed completely from sunny to surly, the skies obliterated by ominous dark clouds which soon engulfed me in stinging, torrential rain. As I climbed progressively higher, the rain turned to sleet which turned to snow and I was in a full-scale blizzard.

My biggest mistake when embarking upon my excursion to Iceland was not taking a jacket. This is not to say that I left for an Arctic adventure totally ill-prepared. I possessed a cycling cape but, as I was now discovering the hard, wet way, what good is a cape? It flaps voluminously like a billowing spinnaker and blows up around your neck, simultaneously half-strangling and blinding you, which is not helpful when negotiating anything from rush-hour traffic to a vertical mountain descent.

As wet on the inside as I was on the outside and with icy rivulets of slush trickling down my neck, I climbed higher still. The blizzard was blowing from the north, hitting me broadside and covering half my body with hard-packed ice — I was half human, half snowman. I kept thinking: I must try to cycle faster — try to warm up. But it was impossible. My mind was no longer connected to my body and I had lost all contact with feet and fingers. I sensed that I was in a bad way.

Very few cars passed but an Austrian camper-van pulled over up the road when I was within striking distance of the summit. The bearded driver jumped out of his fugged-up cockpit and aimed a camera in my direction. I presumed he wanted to photograph the white-covered wastelands, which were indeed spectacular, though in my refrigerated state I was in no mood for appreciating the scenery. I thought: bloody hell, what a time to take a photo. However, I was considerate enough to stop, as one does so as not to ruin someone else's picture by getting in the way.

Much to my amazement, this furry-faced fellow actually wanted to take a photograph of *me*, battling against the elements.

'No, no!' he cried. 'Please keep cycling. I cannot believe what I see. You must be the Crazy British.'

As I drew level, his smiling wife handed me a steaming cup of tea, which I was incapable of holding because my hands had moulded themselves into the frozen shape of their grip on my handlebars. I was also incapable of speech: my mouth and brain were no longer co-operating with each other.

Slowly the hot tea thawed my vocal muscles but when the Austrians offered me a lift the sounds I emitted were not those welcomed by the rest of my body. I heard my voice say, 'No thanks, I'll be fine,' while my mind and limbs and ligaments explosively shouted in contradiction, 'Wonderful! You saviours — I'd love one!' Somewhere among the internal mechanisms of my body there was a massive breakdown in communications.

Cold arms waved as the Austrians disappeared into the distance. Then I was all alone. The downhill was almost as horrendous as the uphill. The driving blizzard blinded me, stinging my scarlet cheeks. With teeth chattering like castanets, I withdrew my head into my ice-encrusted cape like a tortoise but still the knives of that perishing wind stabbed through every layer of my saturated clothing. My only thought was to get down the mountain as fast as possible but I could not see and everything hurt too much. Although unaware of it at the time, I was on the brink of hypothermia. I felt light-headed and giddy; I was panting in short, hurried gasps and my arms and hands became seized in a tingling paralysis. I thought: I mustn't stop, I must keep going.

When I finally reached the small town of Eidfjord, I stumbled through the door of a small supermarket and collapsed dramatically in the trolley park, gasping and shivering uncontrollably, much to the consternation of onlooking shoppers. In my head, all I could hear were the echoing cries of the laughing Austrian: 'Crazy British.'

Early the next morning my spirits rose with the sun and I pedalled towards Bergen along the glorious Hardangerfjord, lined with blossoming apple trees. It was easy to see where the composer Grieg had sought his musical inspiration. In Bergen I treated myself to a bed at the youth hostel, which was full of assorted Interrailists complaining and comparing notes about the ludicrous expense of the country. Only twenty-four hours after my worst day's cycle, when I thought I was almost certain to die, I did my bit for the bicycling trade by proclaiming the virtues of two-wheeled travel and saying they did not know what they were missing.

I am not sure if the message got through but whatever I said had a profound effect on one Swiss boy. He approached me and said, 'Shall I have it off?' He was referring to his shaggy beard, which bore the unappetising remnants of a spaghetti supper.

'Yes,' I said, 'that's a good start.'

Half an hour later he returned with battle-scarred but baby-faced features, looking confidently chuffed with himself. I did not have the heart to tell him he had looked better before.

The Dutch girl in the lower bunk had arrived at four in the afternoon, like me, and had immediately gone to bed. I think she was suffering from sleeping sickness, as she did not surface again until 5.30 the following afternoon. In fact, had she not sporadically lapsed into a reverberating snore, I would have taken her for dead.

'Crikey!' I said when she finally stirred from hibernation, 'You must have had an energetic time to be able to sleep for so long. What have you done — hiked from the Arctic?'

'No,' she said listlessly, 'I came on the train from Oslo and slept all the way. There was nothing else to do.'

She then gave me two of her unused colour-slide films as she did not think there was anything worth photographing. I gave her half a pot of honey in return.

The next day I went to the docks and bought my return ticket to Iceland. There was no going back now. Oiling my chain made me feel slightly less apprehensive about the uncertain days that lay ahead.

I boarded the MS *Norrona* for the forty-one-hour voyage across the choppy North Atlantic and was much relieved to find myself in the company of a handful of fellow cyclists. However, it was short-lived: they all disembarked at Lerwick in the Shetland Islands, leaving me once again in a state of anxiety with the only two-wheeled transport on board.

I took my mind off this worrying fact by trying out my bunk, deep down in the bowels of the ship. It was the first time I had seen multi-storeyed bunk beds. As my fellow cabin occupants all suffered from vertigo, I gallantly elected to sleep on the precarious uppermost berth, which had only a tiny and ineffective bar to prevent you from rolling out and crashing unceremoniously to the ground. Such sleeping quarters were all the more perilous when we hit a furious storm that pitched and plunged and bumped the ship from side to side: clambering up the inadequate footholds as the bunk swayed and oscillated like an out-of-control see-saw was a major expeditionary feat. When I finally heaved myself to the top, breathless but triumphant, I discovered (by way of my stomach) that it was no place to weather a storm. Outside was the place to be so, teaming up with Kev, a Geordie and fellow disillusioned upper-bunker who was 'hitchin' round Scannie', we secured ourselves firmly on deck in a leeward and strategically-situated nook beside a lifeboat. Next stop: Faroe Islands.

Hopes rose as a small cluster of cyclists embarked at Torshavn. Close inspection revealed that they all possessed mountain bikes, except a skinhead school teacher from Switzerland who had a rare but sturdy recumbent. Wielding these mean machines with tyres the size of tractors, their faces grim with determination, they looked as though they meant business. With my spindly and wheel-buckled roadster I felt I was truly stepping out of my league and I quickly removed my Mickey Mouse mascot from the top of my handlebar bag, replacing him with my spare tyre and Swiss Army knife.

The passengers on board this ferry were of an entirely different breed to those who plied the cross-Channel routes. There were no parties of screaming schoolchildren or fuddleheaded football fans causing havoc here. Nor was there a car deck of geriatrics in caravans. People did not loll around below decks watching *Rocky IX* or cling to the hypnotic Space Invaders machines. No, these were weatherbeaten, outdoorologist types: biologists, geologists, seismologists, ornithologists. They strutted purposefully around deck clutching reading material like *Geological Formations of Iceland* and *An Ornithologist's Guide to the Arctic* and were draped with an impressive array of telescopic cameras and equipment. Whereas on a cross-Channel ferry a bag of chips or can of beer is never far from hand, here on the MS *Norrona* it was a pair of binoculars. True fanatics never seemed to remove these magnification devices from their eyes — they were constantly scanning the skies or some distant rocky outcrop for signs of rare feathered prey.

I fell into conversation with a robust and ruddy-cheeked Scottish professor who was travelling to Iceland to study pink-footed geese. He had visited Iceland many times before and gave me the encouraging information that the roads were the worst he had ever experienced. On previous visits his re-inforced Land-Rover had suffered from innumerable punctures and engine trouble; even the chassis had been fractured.

I first saw Makl leaning casually against the deck rails, nose directed skywards, scrutinizing the weather conditions. I sidled up to him and said, with a meteorological air, 'Looks like rain,' as if I knew what I was talking about.

'Not at all,' he replied in authoritative tones. 'The strato-cumulus are far on the horizon and with the wind blowing a fresh south-easterly force five I think precipitation very unlikely.'

I had chosen the wrong person to impress with my Michael Fish act. Makl (whom I instantly dubbed Red'ed for his vibrant shock of fiery-coloured hair) was a trained Canadian pilot — which explained his superior knowledge on the vagaries of the weather. He knew everything and anything and was also an expert bicycle mechanic. In comparison, my mechanical capabilities were nil, my motto being: if it contains a nut or bolt, leave well alone. The only thing I could administer without too much trouble was a liberal dose of lubrication. I realized I was well out of my depth with Red'ed and endeavoured to change the subject.

'Where are you headed, then?' I asked. Even as I spoke, I recognized what a senseless question this was and my face turned as red as his hair. There was only one place he could be going — the only place the boat was going: Iceland.

My first impression of Iceland was a good one. I usually rate a country by the cleanliness of its public conveniences and I was immediately impressed by the one at the ferry terminal at Seydisfjordur.

My second impression was a misty one: the cloud was so low it was almost hurting my head. This turned out later to have been an advantage because it hid the fact that the dirt road out of Seydisfjördur climbed over an almost vertical mountain. I only felt the gradient, without seeing it.

Amongst the motley collection of travellers at the quayside was a continually grinning Japanese boy called something like Wakazakitakamoto. He told us to call him Ken. Ken was one of those cycle tourists who like to play safe by carrying two of everything: two tents, two sleeping-bags, two stoves, two front lights, two helmets. He probably had a duplicate bicycle tucked up his sleeve somewhere. Ken was highly proficient at 'Ahhhh' and 'Zorrring' but not too hot with his English. Yet it was possible to gather that he planned to cycle up an apparently active volcano. The more he was told that this could be a potentially cataclysmic exercise, the more he broke into radiant beams of ecstatic delight. There was no dissuading him.

For an apprentice map-reader such as myself, Iceland proved to be a paradise due to its lack of roads. Basically the choice lay between cycling clockwise or anticlockwise round the island on Route 1 — the national ring road. I left Seydisfjördur at the same time as Red'ed along the only road to Egilsstadir and we found ourselves teaming up together.

We opted for the clockwise direction, heading first along the south of the island for no other reason than we thought it would be warmer. That was our first mistake: it is the north that offers the finest weather, often basking in hot, crystal-clear days, whilst the south is prone to low clinging mists, perpetual drizzle and thrashing winds that blow off the Atlantic. For the first few days the mist was so thick that we literally had to feel our way. It was no good turning to a compass for guidance either as the magnetized volcanic rock made compass swings misleadingly erratic.

I have to admit that I had always imagined Iceland to be somewhere near the North Pole and alive with Eskimos and polar bears. Even when Gorbachev and Reagan carried out their abortive disarmament talks there, my impression had remained unaltered. In fact the only Eskimos to touch its shores were sailing radically off course for Greenland and the only polar bears to touch down had hitched a casual lift on a passing iceberg.

'Iceland' is something of a misnomer: it should swop names with neighbouring Greenland. Although Iceland sits just south of the Arctic Circle, it benefits from the warmth of the Gulf Stream and the average temperature in January (the coldest month) is higher than that of New York or Vienna, while in summer the only ice is on the glaciers.

In geological terms, Iceland is a mere stripling at sixteen million years old. If the aeons of time in which the Earth was formed were compressed into one day, Iceland would have been born at five minutes to midnight — and it is still developing. Being the largest landmass on the mid-Atlantic fault, it is a tremendously volcanic place, adding bits and changing bits in violent convulsions. It is as though it cannot decide what it wants to be when it grows up. You never know what shape it is going to be from one millennium to another. It gained a whole new island in 1963 when Surtsey rose steaming and roaring from the ocean one November day, giving everyone a bit of a fright.

Even though I had been warned, the state of the roads still came as a shock and by the end of the first day my nerves and my bicycle had been rattled to pieces. Red'ed, however, was irksomely smug and confident. Hailing from deepest, darkest Nova Scotia where there is an abundance of dirt roads, he was well conditioned to a spot of rough-ridin'. He also had a machine to match the terrain — a self-designed model with intricate expeditionary detail which appeared to bump and bounce and crash its way over every obstacle with no trouble at all.

On the second day we nearly met with disaster. Leafing through the small guide provided by the tourist office, I saw under 'Hours of Business' that shops were only open from 9 AM to noon on Saturdays. Synchronizing watches, we were alarmed to discover that today was Saturday and it was 10.45 AM. We had precisely one and a quarter hours to pack up the tents and ride fifteen miles over rough and rutted roads on which we had been averaging a mere 6 mph. But now was no time for concern about the fate of our machines or plunging down roadside ravines or into the hungry maws of the ubiquitous pot-holes. No, food was at stake and so we crashed and pounded our way full-throttle towards the alluring supplies of a store, goaded into action by the urgent demands of our stomachs. With pulsating pectorals and sweat-sticky skin we arrived wheezing, red-faced and desperate as if our lives depended on this store (which was the only one for many a mile). But it was 12.04 — four minutes too late. I felt like crying. But wait, there was hope yet: there was movement within. Oh joy of joys! We had struck lucky. The store was open. It was the only one we ever found in the whole of Iceland that opened its door at twelve noon on Saturdays instead of closing them. The Nordic gods were on our side.

Shopping or stopping for food has to be one of the highlights of any cycle touring. Usually the only thing that spurs me on across harsh and desolate landscapes or through days of continuous rain and headwinds, when energy has ebbed and the mind is opaque and heavy, is the ultimate sighting and satisfaction of sustenance. Visions of food override all thought.

Eager anticipation of this much needed fuel subconsciously lifts the mind, fills the stomach and ekes out that last gram of energy that you felt certain had long since gone. It gives hope and the only reason for going on. Nothing sends the spirits plummeting more readily than the shocking discovery of no food or a shut shop when all sights have been focused on this one target.

I rarely eat out if I am touring alone, preferring to be self-sufficient, visiting local markets and stores and carrying supplies. Such is the importance of food that I use two whole panniers as my larders. These are the most important ones — the front ones, always within sight.

The daily pounding of pedals produces the most prodigious appetite. Consumption capacities are phenomenal and can send any non-cyclist into a speechless gawp of wonder. I often amaze myself and at the end of a sizeable intake, I think: surely I can't have eaten *that* much? But I have and I do and will no doubt continue to do so.

For two reasons, Icelandic cuisine does not do a lot to satisfy the raving appetite of a cyclist. One is the expense (omelette and chips can cost £10) and the other is the delicacies the country offers — fish dishes like fisky fangs and reyktum lax, ram's testicles, svid (singed sheep's heads), 'filly' (young horse) or the delightful hakarl, made from strips of half-rotten shark-meat buried for weeks in gravel beds to cure. However, one of my greatest finds and fondest memories of Iceland was skyr — an affordable national dish which was a mixture of cottage cheese and yoghurt. I gorged on it daily, by the tubful and with any combination of food: bananas and honey, treacle and tuna, dried fig and cheese sandwiches. Icelanders say that it is not advisable to take coffee and skyr together just before riding horses as the combination gives you diarrhoea. Can it be comparable to the effects that rotting shark must have on the innards?

As Red'ed and I deviated from Route 1 and twisted our way

along such tongue-tying places as Reydarfjördur, Fáskrúds-fjördur and Stödvarfjördur, a rare vehicle loomed out of the damp, low-lying mist. Drawing level with us, it stopped. The steamed-up window was wound down to reveal a native Icelander with ice-blue eyes. It was our first meeting with a local on the open road.

'Where are you two from?' he enquired in perfect English.

Red'ed said, 'Nova Scotia,' which met with a blank look.

I said, 'London.'

'London. I was there once,' he stated and then drove away.

We rejoined Route 1, which was gradually being tarmaced although apparently at random. For most of the time we would bump and clunk and rattle along mile upon mile of rough dirt roads where in many places the ferocious Arctic winds had torn the surface into rutted formations like corrugated iron. Then, suddenly and inexplicably, we would hit a short section of velvety smooth, fast-rolling tarmac. Just as suddenly, it would end and we would brake-plunge down on to dirt for another long, dusty, bone-rattling experience. I was baffled why such brief bursts should be chosen for surfacing. Red'ed suspected that there was a dartboard covered with a map of Iceland in the Road Metallers' Manager's office and that decisions on the next stretch to be tarmaced were based on where a dart happened to land.

Cyclists in Iceland, while not subjected to the usual dangers of traffic that pervade most other European countries, face perils of another kind. Because there are no trees, birds have little choice other than to build their nests on the cliffs. Those who do not find seaside space, or who perhaps have no head for heights, choose to set up home on the ground. This is fine until they are rudely disturbed by some alien but unsuspecting cyclist coming upon them unawares. Their natural reaction is to protect their eggs, their livelihood and their territory by launching a vicious dive-bombing sortie on any two-wheeled intruder. I did not enjoy being repeatedly swooped upon by a bomber squadron of determined Arctic terns and great skuas, nor did I appreciate it when they misjudged their target and hit me on the head like a full-force rocket. What with dodging these airborne attacks, the cavernous pot-holes and the multitudes of dim-witted, shaggy-haired sheep, cycling in Iceland can be quite hazardous.

Approaching Höfn, the road fell away and plunged down an almost vertical mountain of mud. On one side there was a good 100-foot drop straight into the windlashed, icy ocean and I was in danger of testing its temperature as I perilously slip-slided my way towards the edge with my mud-clung brakes failing.

We made it safely down to Höfn and were escorted by a gang of fresh-faced BMX boys who led us over their acrobatic route of jumps and obstacles to the youth hostel. And just in time, too, before a beefy-tyred bus pulled up and disgorged a gaggle of tourists. We had the pick of the beds and were into the showers before they had even found the front door. We dried out and warmed up for the first time since landing in Iceland.

By morning the mist had finally lifted and at last we could see the awesome landscape. Leaving Höfn, we were greeted by the sight of Vatnajökull, the biggest glacier anywhere outside Antarctica and Greenland. Although only a tiny portion was visible, it still looked massive as its giant tongues spilled over the rugged purple mountains.

That evening we came to a glacial lagoon in the river Jökulsá á Breidamerkursandi and sat watching the black and grey-blue icebergs. As the glowing sun sank over the sea, they changed into red-pink ice and cracked, creaked and groaned as they slowly drifted their way out to sea along the world's shortest river — it was barely half a mile long.

It had occurred to me that it might be a nice idea to tackle the vast, empty bits in the middle of Iceland rather than keep to the coast road. This was a particularly unusual year, however, as even in July the 'roads' of the interior were still closed by snow and glacial floods, but I continued to peruse *The Visitor's Guide to Iceland*, which provided such useful tips as: 'Check unbridged rivers by wading across them before attempting to drive over,' and: 'Don't let the current hit you behind the knees.' That sort of thing.

Five days after leaving Seydisfjördur, Red'ed and I were still together. It was nice to have his company as we cycled across desolate lava landscapes and the black, empty deserts of volcanic ash — and one of the most alluring things I found about him was not his thicket of red hair but his camping stove. I had steered clear of such contraptions since that fateful day when Ward's had died a premature death and, although I was quite happy on a diet of sandwiches, I have to admit I was pining for my porridge. It did not take long to win Red'ed round to the early morning ritual of a good dose of thick, steaming stodge and it made me realize just what I had been missing.

Down and around the south coast we ventured, camping wherever the fancy took us. This was a country where there was no need to worry about hiding from rowdy gangs, potential thieves or murderers. With a population of only a quarter of a million people living on an island the size of Belgium, Denmark and Luxembourg put together, Iceland does not seem to accommodate undesirable types.

In Vik, a shopkeeper with turnip-yellow hair told me that there had only been one reported bank robbery in the whole of Iceland's history and even that one was not pulled off with any success. It is not really surprising. Attempting to make a speedy getaway would be pointless — a puncture would undoubtedly stop you before the police did.

Iceland is like the 'good old days' that my grandfather Frankie used to talk about, when you did not bother to lock homes and cars and could leave something valuable in the public eye and return to find it still there. After living in London, it took me a while to condition myself to this sort of trust and I amused Red'ed by adamantly locking my bike at night even though there wasn't a soul for miles. 'You can never be too safe,' I told him. After the first week, however, I would leave my bike and valuables willy-nilly, unlocked and un-attended, with the satisfaction of knowing that I would return to find everything intact.

After riding through a lichen-covered lava field with contorted mounds of rock like Henry Moore sculptures, we were greeted by our first Icelandic dog. Cyclists know all too well what it feels like to be chased at high speed by evil-fanged, salivating canine beasts and Iceland is no exception, although the animals are thinner on the ground. Our dog doggedly raced along beside us for nearly seven miles, growling and barking excitedly but fortunately content just to accompany us rather than maul us.

In contrast to much of England, Iceland's farm dogs still find cars a novelty and come rushing out to bark at them and snap at their tyres. Most English dogs abandoned that sort of behaviour in the thirties, recognizing it as exhausting, dang-erous and pointless. The fact that Iceland's dogs are half a century behind the times indicates two things: the relative scarcity of cars and the slow speed at which they are obliged to travel. Cyclists, too, are rare and comparatively slow ...

I preferred the roaming Icelandic ponies and we saw many, shaking their shaggy manes and galloping gloriously free. For centuries these stocky beasts were the farmers' only form of transport over the rough terrain but now, sadly, they have been exchanged for four-wheel-drive vehicles — British Landrovers, Japanese Toyotas, German Hefflingers, American Fords. Luckily there are still many herds of these stumpy, hippie-fringed ponies roaming the land and they possess the unusual ability to break into a *skeid*, moving both legs on the same side in unison like American pacers. They are descended from Viking stock and some say that they are amphibious — they can even swim a river with someone in the saddle, as long as it is the right someone. There is a legend of an Icelander who, in the early days, used to swim his horse two miles out to sea to meet the tobacco boat.

'If you don't like the weather, wait a minute,' is the standard Icelandic advice about their unpredictable climate and one that your hear many disconcerted tourists mumbling. Never had I known weather to change so radically so quickly. One moment I was dressed as if for a bask on the beach, and the next as Scott of the Antarctic. It really did change that quickly and I spent much of my time clambering into and out of my clothes trying to regulate temperature control.

One morning, I decided that I really did not like the weather and so 'waited a minute'. One minute went by and the torrential rain and ferocious winds showed no signs of easing. Something had definitely gone wrong. Feeling rather cheated, we cycled to the nearest petrol station and sat drip-drying at the tea bar. It seemed that everyone else had the same idea. The pink-footed geese man was there and said that he had been plagued by mechanical problems, punctures and broken fan belts since leaving Seydisfjördur — so far he had travelled only the same distance as we had on two wheels. The German mountain bikers from the boat were there too; they sidled up to me and said sneeringly, 'And zor, 'ow manee veels 'ave you broken?'

'None, *dankeschön*,' I said, feeling smug. 'And I haven't had any punctures either.'

Apparently that was more than they could claim for themselves.

There are nineteen youth hostels in Iceland and we stayed in four of them. The most memorable was the one at Fljótsalur, an enchantingly traditional turf-roofed cottage lying at the end of an almost unridable track which wound its way deep into a desolate valley encased by a glistening glacier. It was owned by Dick Philips, who is the most respected British expert on Icelandic travel and renowned for his courage, humour and eccentricity. Sadly we just missed him as he had left for a trekking tour but his wife told us how, in 1958, Dick had set out with three companions to make what he believed to be the first bicycle crossing of the Sprengisandur (a huge, icy desert in the heart of the island) in the days when the most ferocious rivers had not been bridged. With a rubber dinghy and a third of a mile of rope strapped to his rack, he completed the journey on a fixed-wheel Viking. He still toured on this ancient bike, with panniers improvised from a battered cardboard box and a worn leather briefcase with a toe-strap for a handle.

Feeling in need of a shower, I was a bit surprised to be directed outside to stand in my birthday suit beneath a tree from which a bucketful of water was suspended. This would have been a welcome respite from the suffocating heat of the Sahara but shivering in a chilly tunnel of wind blowing straight off the glacier was not the sort of relaxation I had envisaged after a hard day's bumping around in the saddle. When my circulation had returned, Mrs Philips casually told us that we had only just missed an earthquake; she made it sound as if she was referring to the local bus. 'One of our guests was on the toilet at the time,' she said, 'and he was a bit confused as to whether the shuddering movements erupted from him or the ground.'

The next morning's ride was far from swift. The winds were so strong that it took a demoralizing three-and-a-half hours to cover twelve miles — on flat ground, too. I came a cropper more times than I would care to mention, partly because of the savage batterings of the wind and also because of the unnavigable boulder-strewn road and a storm of dive-bombing birds.

It was the latter that led me to be the cause of a minor pile-up. Stuck in one rut on the wrong side of the road, I was too busy shrieking at and fending off the unwelcome antics of the swooping skuas to notice a vehicle bearing down. Rather than plough into me, the driver took evasive action and jeopardized his vehicle and life by swerving and plummeting off the road into a five-foot ditch. At this stage I became aware of the terrestrial events around me and paused from my aerial battle to take note of the scene. As I did so another vehicle appeared (one vehicle was rare enough, but two in succession was unprecedented). It attempted to haul the first vehicle out of trouble but skidded and ended up joining it in the ditch. I waited to see if a third vehicle should arrive, either to help or to follow the tyre tracks of its predecessors. When it did not, I cast a sheepish grin towards the hapless victims and bumped off down the road to Gullfoss.

The man in the tourist office explained that 'foss' meant 'bicycle' as well as 'waterfall' because when bicycles were first introduced to their island Icelanders could not think of any other sufficiently swift comparison. Gullfoss looked nothing like a bicycle to me, but it did look like a very wet, very big and very impressive waterfall. The furiously flowing Hvita (White) river has created a clean-cut fault gorge to tumble in a thunder of water, crashing and cascading its way down the narrow ravine. As I approached the falls, the spray was so thick that I walked through archways of rainbows and it was easy to see why they called it the Golden Waterfall.

In 1910 an English company had come up with a scheme to turn it into a hydro-electric plant. All the local farmers had agreed to sell except one, whose daughter threatened to throw herself into the falls sooner than allow her beloved Gullfoss to be destroyed. Instead of ruining a spectacular phenomenon and making a beefy profit, the farmers shelled out to build a memorial to her and it remains as glorious a waterfall as ever. Greenpeace would have made her an honorary member.

Changing direction, the wind bowled us along the road to Geysir, the King of Geysers, which gave its name to all the hotsprings around the world. Known as the Great Gusher for continually sending up a spurting tower of water, it now holds a very badly kept secret: it just cannot get it up these days — not without some therapy, that is. When Elizabeth II paid a visit, the Icelanders stimulated it into action by their old trick of dropping hundreds of bars of soap down its hole. Enraged, Geysir threw a great plume of boiling water sixty feet into the air, right on cue.

With the King dead, Strokkur (Geysir Junior) has taken the limelight some 200 paces from the deceased. I took up position on the front line with my camera dutifully poised, waiting for the heir to blow his top. My first impressions were of a docile pool of water, green and clear. Then it became a little agitated and began to steam and hiss as the water fluctuated into a crystal-clear dome that heaved and sighed with increasing speed. Then, as I dropped my camera in shock, a gigantic, surging shaft of steam and boiling water burst forth and shot skyward into a 100-foot high scalding column which hung in the air for several momentous moments before dispersing into a spectral cloud and blowing off down the valley like a lost ghost.

Before leaving Geysir we bumped into two French brothers who recognized us from the *MS Norrona*. Didier and Dominique were motorbiking around Iceland on BMW 1000's and seemed suitably impressed that we had ridden as far as they had in as many days. Didier handed me his address and said, '*Visitez-moi.*' I stuck it in my diary and wondered if I ever would.

That night, we set up base amongst the mossy crusts of a lava field. As I stood on a lump of volcanic rock under scarlet skies, marvelling at the fiercely beautiful and bleak landscape, I could understand why early churchmen who visited the country described it as a 'desert of the ocean'. Romantically, I thought: I'm in the midst of a desolate sea with not a soul for miles. (I tried to forget about Red'ed.) Then, from over a distant rocky outcrop, a vision materialized in the unwelcome form of a loud, obstreperous German backpacker. Having shattered my illusion of peace and solitude, it became evident

that Heinz had just stridden across a few hundred miles of an
empty lava-crinkled land, which perhaps explained his excitable air on his reacquaintance with human life. Any lingering
serenity was hastily dispersed as, without hesitation, he erected
his tent (the size of an average town hall) and gabbled away
about his exploits. That night a rampant wind roared and his
tent collapsed.

Iceland is a fishy place. Lining the sides of the roads were what
I first took to be acres of socks hanging out to dry. They were
actually cods' heads festooned over row upon row of neatly
arranged trellis tunnels. Although heads predominated, there
were also whole sides of fish drying in the summer sun. Most
would be sold to the Third World — the heads for fishmeal,
the rest as dried fish to be reconstituted and eaten. Ironically,
the only aggression this peaceful country has seen recently was
over fish in the 'Cod War' when Iceland extended its maritime
boundaries, much to the chagrin of British fishermen.

For once, the wind was in our favour as we tore towards
Reykjavik. We sped past the broad lava plain of Thingvellir
where Icelanders used to have their *Thing*, or parliament. In
930AD the settlers established the world's first free parliament,
the Althing, on the shores of Thingvallavatn (the biggest lake
in Iceland), where no king presided over free men. Today it is
the world's oldest surviving parliament still in session.

Approaching Reykjavik, we returned to signs of the modern
world: metalled roads signified the unwelcome presence of
traffic and fast cars. The majority of the population live in and
around the capital in low, earthquake-proof and brightly
painted Lego-like houses. It can be an expensive place — £2
for an ice-cream, £4.50 for a lager, £10 for a gin and tonic —
but in two respects it is a cyclist's paradise, as cities go. For a
start, there are no dogs at all. It is illegal to own one and the
police wield the ultimate dog deterrent: they may quite
legitimately shoot dogs on sight. It must be the only city
in the world where you do not run the risk of breaking

your neck from skidding in the stinking sludge of a doggie deposit.

The other advantage is that, apart from the car fumes, Reykjavik is free from atmospheric pollution. The inhabitants do not need coal-fuelled power stations to heat their homes. Instead, the abundant geothermal energy is harnessed and carried from the nearby volcanic springs along two heavily insulated pipelines ten miles long. The heat lost while the water runs from the subterranean streams to the kitchen tap is less than two degrees Fahrenheit. The only disadvantage is that a sulphurous odour like that of bad eggs can pervade the house. The steam rising from the springs gave the city its name: Reykjavik means Smokey Bay, although paradoxically it is a smokeless city.

Not only is its air clean but so are its streets — and not just from dog dirt. No rubbish can be seen. For a start, Iceland's drinks come mainly in bottles rather than cans and each bottle has a greater value than its contents, so it is treated as negotiable currency. This not only saves resources but also brings a welcome respite from wading through Europe's seas of empty cans blowing in the wind.

Of course, Reykjavik is not completely free from problems. It suffers from high rates of alcoholism and suicide, possibly because of the interminably long, dark winters. Some say boredom plays a big part, too, and it is claimed that Saturday night in downtown Reykjavik is about as lively as Sunday morning in Surbiton. Although I witnessed no suicides, I saw plenty of drunks tottering around in various stages of inebriation. One of them who refused to leave us alone as we sat in the park eating our picnic was also a chainsmoker, so that we were sitting in this smokeless city enveloped in a wafty haze of cigarette smoke.

We cycled on into the constant wind and passed a tumbling river where two fishermen, their faces glowing, staggered under the weight of salmon the size of a small submarine. The lack of pollution in Iceland extends to its waterways and the life within them: everywhere the flowing, crystal-clear and naturally pure glacial torrents were so cold that the water stung the gums as you drank.

We raced to the busy little fishing port of Stykkishólmur (whence the outlawed Eric the Red had set sail and discovered Greenland) just in time to board the ferry across Breidifjördur. The *MS Baldur* was a car ferry but not in the familiar style — there were no unwieldy snub-nosed roll-on roll-offs here. For the four-hour crossing to Kikafell we were transported on a fishing-boat which could accommodate twelve cars, transferred from the quay into the hull by a crude winch. The boom improvised as a small crane to which thick bands of webbing were attached. These were passed under the chassis and the vehicle was hoisted into the air, hanging and swaying as it was precariously lowered over the other cars until, with infinite skill, it was deposited precisely into the tightest of spaces. With slightly less dexterity, the same loading method was used for the bicycles which disappeared into the hold with an ominous crunch.

The boat paused for a while at Flatey, a pinprick of an island. I jumped out to stretch my legs and tripped over a parade of dead seals lying flat out on the quay. It was not a pleasant sight and I looked out to sea instead: I could just make out the snow-capped, cone-shaped Snaefellsjökull glacier on a distant peninsula, where the Vikings once thought they had discovered the entrance to the Underworld. Centuries later, Jules Verne made this awesome mountain famous in his *Journey to the Centre of the Earth*.

With food supplies perilously low, we joyously came across a small store where we were momentarily distracted from the ill-stocked shelves by a basketful of kittens, among which romped a tiny fox cub. The store owner told us that its mother had bitten off its foot but it was now living quite happily among the kittens and was suckling from their mother.

We pressed onwards over conical mountains and craggy fells until we could go no further. We had arrived at Latrabjarg, Europe's most westerly point. Magnificent cliffs, 450 metres high, were lined with thousands of brightly beaked puffins, periodically plunging vertically into the seal-infested ocean below. Just down the road, near an empty white-sand beach, we stayed at youth hostel number three where I tinkled the ivories and with gloating satisfaction played my party piece, Mozart's *Adagio in D minor*, on Europe's most westerly piano.

The experience of almost twenty-four hours of perpetual daylight was sending my bodyclock haywire but clock time seemed to be of little importance to the locals. Sitting in the sun and eating my lunch at two in the morning, I was never surprised to see people hay-making, fishing or mowing their lawns. Even golf tournaments started at midnight. After hibernating through their dark winters, it appeared the locals made the most of their summers and apparently never slept. Insomniacs who did want to sleep could always count sheep — there were well over 1.3 million of the beasts in Iceland, which meant about five sheep per person.

Tending to the call of nature alfresco soon becomes second nature for cycling campers (and a lot more preferable to using public conveniences) and Iceland must provide some of the world's most impressive panoramic vistas for such private moments. Often, hunched on my haunches, I would admire the spectacular view stretched out before me and think: no five-star hotel could better this. It was free, too. Tending to nature in nature — what could be better?

There were times, however, when the convenience of a five-star hotel's bathroom next to my tent would have been appreciated. One morning, camping outside Patneksfjördur, I was desperate and leapt from my tent with a pained expression. Usually it would not have been a problem in Iceland; rarely was anyone else around and I had the freedom to perform at a safe distance from camp. However, this morning it was different. I was camped on the outskirts of town and found a small clan of school children waiting for the bus on my right and a farmer out on the moorland to my left who insisted on waving to me. Had I been in almost any other country I could have dived into the foraging toileter's best friend — nearby shrubbery — and been concealed from sight. But Iceland has no shrubbery. My only potential screen was a small outcrop of rock on the other side of a small glacial river.

Barefoot and bursting, I entered the icy waters and they shot through my soles like daggers, freezing me to the spot. Thus immobilized, I became even more aware of my urgent bodily needs and my pained expression grew. Then the confounded farmer, who was surveying my every move, realized I was marooned in the river and started approaching, calling to me. That was all I needed. Please! Please! No! No! I'm fine, I signalled. Suddenly I wished I was in somewhere like India, where privacy was thrown to the wind and you went where and when the urgency took you, with none of this time-consuming modesty. There they do the job and that's that.

I did eventually manage to reach the safe haven of the rock but it was not half as big as I had imagined. The pointing, guffawing children and the slightly sheepish, smirking farmer knew exactly what I was doing. Oh well, from each bad experience stems a learning. From this one it was: always size up a convenient convenience the night before.

Up and into the mountainous, claw-shaped peninsula of the western fjords we wandered. Here signs of life were even more rare, although we did see one surprisingly audacious Arctic fox.

High up a mountain we came across a bright orange rescue hut. We did not need rescuing but there was no one in when we called and so we decided to spend the night there. It did not take long to wish that I *could* be rescued. The temperature dropped so low that I dreamt I was sleeping in a deep-freeze during the brief moments when I was lucky enough to be asleep at all. Most of the time I lay awake, quaking in a spasm of uncontrollable shivers which made me comfortably aware of the inadequacy of my almost bald down-filled sleeping-bag.

Red'ed, lying on the opposite bench, claimed to be 'as warm as toast' in his twenty-five-season, internally heated sleeping-bag.

Suffering together is not as bad as suffering alone and to be able to commiserate with a companion in equal chilliness takes the edge off being cold. Suffering body-numbing pain while your comrade revels in radiating warmth is, frankly, not nice at all.

I was surprised that a mountain rescue hut provided no blankets. It seemed illogical. I searched high and low but to no avail. Desperately I asked Red'ed if he could see any but I think he had sunk into a complacent heat-haze of comatose contentment. There was no reply. On rising the next morning as stiff as a frozen fish fillet, I discovered that he had been sleeping on top of the blanket supply all along. I was not amused.

Soured feelings were not harboured for too long, though. Being Iceland, there was always a surprise in store and I chanced upon a thermal pool that had me thawed out in seconds and tingling with ecstatic glee.

Well away from Route 1, the road surfaces became even worse and careering down boulder-strewn, mountainous descents while shunning the skuas and weaving among a platoon of pea-brained sheep required endless concentration. Red'ed, momentarily distracted, found himself nursing a badly grazed limb and a severely buckled wheel that was more a square than a circle. The thought that the nearest decent bike shop was in either Canada or Norway would have put me in a state of utter despair in a similar situation but Red'ed seemed more concerned about his upturned jar of peanut butter. Being a bicycle mechanic of truly impressive skills, he sat on a lump of lava and whistled nonchalantly as he rebuilt his wheel, spoke by spoke, until it miraculously became a functional circle again.

In Isafjördur an American girl with buck teeth and bunches scuttled over to me and immediately shattered the tranquillity of the small fjordside town with a bombardment of querulous questions.

'Hey, hi there! Ma name's Macey. How d'ya find the biking? Have you had many flats? How d'ya find the highways? Gee, you folk sure are carrying one helluva load!'

When she paused for breath, I grabbed my chance and asked, 'So, Macey, how are you travelling round Iceland?'

'Well, I had planned to cycle on my racer, but when folks warned me my tubular tyres would never make it I gave up the idea. So I'm touring with an airplane pass instead. Gee, it sure is great. Beats biking any day. You folks should try it!'

We boarded the fishing-boat ferry *MS Fagranes* to cross the fjord to Baeii. When I climbed down into the hull to get a jumper from my bike, I saw huge bundles of netted sacks containing feathers. They were in fact dead puffins. The puffin may be Iceland's national bird but it is also Iceland's national dinner. A crew member told me: 'We catch 100,000 puffins every year and we roast them, fry them, grill them, smoke them and salt them.'

Up on deck I met Thelma, an American from 'Noo York', who told me I was 'out of my mind' to be cycling around Iceland on all those dirt roads. 'In the States, if you wanna bike in Iceland you're advised to keep only in and around the urban areas. That way you can be almost guaranteed paved roads.'

I said I had not come to Iceland to cycle on tarmac. Thelma looked a little piqued and walked away.

The highlight on reaching Akureyri (the capital of the north) was replenishing our larders, which had run stomach-rumblingly low. At Hagup supermarket we cleared the shelves of Solgryn (the Icelandic version of Quaker Oats) and restocked with dried fruit, honey, crispbreads, tinned kipper fillets, bananas (grown in greenhouses heated by natural springs in the south of the island), carrots, fruit juice and my essential skyr. We bought enough to last a good week and see us back to Seydisfjördur but somehow (and with surprising ease) we managed to consume most of it during a four-hour lunchbreak in the park.

With lunch over by 9 PM, we remounted and tottered off down the road feeling like a couple of pregnant hippopotami. We did not go very far: after a few revolutions we camped in a cove. The small beach was littered with wood, a rare sight on the island, but it was not home-grown. Any wood you see in Iceland is imported and this was Russian wood — flotsam which had drifted north and become frozen into icecaps that had floated into the Gulf Stream and melted, so that the driftwood was washed ashore, imported for free by courtesy of the sea.

We crossed the magnificent volcanic plateaux to Godafoss (another of Iceland's splendid waterfalls) where we met Markus, a tall, fine-featured Swiss biologist on a mountain bike. We cycled together into the gusty winds towards Myvatn where he was meeting his friends — or what was left of them. After only two days one had decided she did not like cycling and had deserted the party; they had come to blows with another and were no longer on speaking terms; and the third had left and got lost.

Myvatn means Midge Lake and the clouds of these insects are often so thick that they block out the sun when it shines which, as Myvatn is the sunniest and driest place in Iceland, is quite often. The lake is also one of the most important bird habitats in the world and more varieties of duck can be found there than anywhere. I watched the eider ducks (after which I viewed my eiderdown in a new light) but their numbers had been catastrophically reduced since mink first escaped into the wild in the 1960s. Ducks make a tasty dinner and mink can down an eider in no time.

Near the lake we climbed up a big, black, voluminous volcano which gave the most uncanny views of subarctic deserts, glassy waters, sulphur-smoking hills, labyrinthine cones of volcanic ash and lava-strewn moraines.

We travelled eastwards past mountains like vast slag heaps, emerald-green valleys and monochrome moonscapes. We came across some extraordinary pink-and-ochre hills where the land was alive with bubbling blue, grey or red mud-pools, steaming and hissing like a witch's cauldron. The air was acrid with sulphur and notices warned you to watch where you walked. It was a dangerous place. Under our feet burned a subterranean furnace, its surface like a hot-plate capable of frying your soles.

Iceland is indeed a wonderfully varied and weird land — so weird that the Apollo astronauts trained here: it offered the Earth's nearest imitation of a lunar landscape. It is also an unspoilt country. There is a marked absence of high-rise buildings and (except in Reykjavik and Akureyri) hamburgers. There is a merciful scarcity of crowds, crime and traffic and no frogs, snakes, trains, trees, tipping or curiously, as a local told me, television on Thursdays. Certainly it is a land of vivid contrasts of which I could never tire. But for those who prefer the proximity of a chip shop to a bubbling mud-pool, or the animations of an amusement arcade to a conversation with a puffin, a holiday in Blackpool would be a much safer bet.

Back in Seydisfjördur, it was still misty. Once again we boarded the MS *Norrona* and headed for Norway, stopping off at the Faroes to spend a few wet and windy days cycling round those wild islands of twisted rock formations where, they claim, it rains for 363 days of the year. I believe them.

We hit a dilemma in Bergen. My original idea had been to cycle to North Cape and I was still intent on doing so — alone. Red'ed had decided that he, too, wanted to ride to North Cape, not alone but with me. I liked Red'ed and hated the feeling of awkwardness arising, but I preferred my original idea of going it alone and I told him so.

Parting was not easy. We were both going to North Cape, we were both on bicycles, we both travelled at the same speed and both took the same road — the only road. Unless we staggered our starts like a handicap race, it was hard not to keep bumping into each other. Jestingly I said I would cover my eyes and count to a hundred but my flippancy was not appreciated.

The problem finally resolved itself at a fork in the road. I knew that this was Separation Junction. The whole scene then turned comically tragic.

'Okay, Red'ed,' I said, 'choose ya road.'

He selected the right-hand fork, leaving me little choice but to take the left. We parted, giving each other a big hug and a peck on the cheek before pedalling forlornly down our respective routes, waving and calling until we could no longer see each other. It was a real tearjerker, straight out of the movies.

At first I felt a little anxious and guilty about going solo but I also felt tremendously free. I could go wherever I wanted, whenever I wanted, with no need for pensive consultations, earnest discussions or bitter altercations. And I knew then that I had made the right decision.

During the first night, the weather turned so nasty that it was really rather enjoyable. Rain fell in stair-rods (as it would continuously for a week) and the world around me disappeared into a thick, blanketing mist. After miles of soggy and boggy ground, I counted myself lucky to come across a nice patch of grass beside the road. There I squelched and pitched my tent. As morning dawned, I emerged from my damp and dripping home. The mist had lifted sufficiently for me to see that I had in fact camped on someone's lawn. I thought: better scarper before I get caught. But the owners had already spotted me. They were bearing down fast and I sensed that I faced some awkward explaining. However, their reaction was not what I had anticipated. A smiling family threesome stepped forward bearing gifts of hot coffee, bread and cheese.

Since leaving Red'ed I had been aware of a sudden sharpening of my senses as I realized how vulnerable I was on my own. Yet vulnerability had its advantages and provided the best opportunity for meeting people. In their eyes I presented no threat. I was just a little girl meandering on a bicycle far from home.

People seemed to feel sorry for me; they wanted to protect me and could not believe or understand that I was actually enjoying myself. I may have looked small and defenceless but (secretly flexing my biceps) I knew otherwise and that I could put up a fight should trouble come my way. After all, I had two years of karate training under my belt.

Although my male counterparts may not be threatened with harassment, molestation or rape, they have the disadvantage of the very fact that they are men. People are much more wary about approaching a lone male than a female and I found that, compared to being a man or even when I was travelling with a man, I could open more doors and see and learn much more about the country and its inhabitants when I travelled as a lone woman. For me, one of the main excitements of visiting foreign lands is meeting the people and experiencing the way they live.

At the end of each day I would calculate my distance on the map and was always a little disillusioned to see what slow progress I was making. Despite a daily average of about seventy miles, it looked as though I was hardly moving. Norway, with a coastline of more than 12,000 miles, is an incredibly long country and I thought back to my school geography lessons: if you flipped Norway upside down, it would stretch from Oslo to Rome. North Cape was still a long way ahead.

The closer I rode towards the Arctic, the longer the days became. Indeed, the only time I encountered darkness over the next few weeks was when I was repeatedly plunged into the blackness of the numerous unlit tunnels which weave and carve their way through the spectacular mountainsides, sometimes for miles on end. They are a cyclist's nightmare. Careering into their yawning, cavernous mouths from the brilliance of daylight left me practically blind to blunder on against the dripping rock walls and it was the only time that I ever felt frightened in Scandinavia.

A straight tunnel was manageable: even if it was a few

kilometres long, I could get my bearings and head for that tiny, life-saving chink of light at the end. The most harrowing were those that twisted and curved so that my eyes strained into an inky blackness, my bicycle lights having no effect against the enveloping darkness. Slowly and cautiously I would *feel* my way out.

Being caught in one at the same time as a thundering truck made the ordeal twice as bad. The crashing roar of its engines filled the whole tunnel with deafening reverberations and I often found myself stuck half way, pinned up against the rough, slimy walls and paralysed with fear, unable to move either forwards or backwards, with the unpleasant prospect of being well and truly squashed.

Sometimes, as an alternative, I used the old abandoned roads that snaked their way round the mountainside, but these were often strewn with boulders and landslides and in such a state of disrepair that it was impossible to pass. I met one stocky, tough-looking Mancunian cyclist who was so terrified of the tunnels that he would retrace his tracks, even if it meant a lengthy detour, rather than be engulfed by a horror chamber of dripping blackness. Eventually I found that the best solution was to wait at the entrance, flag down the first vehicle and ask the driver to drive slowly while I raced ahead in the light of the headlamps.

Norway was awash with German tourists and I was constantly mistaken for one of them. To put an end to misunderstandings, I suspended a Union Jack from the back of my bike — and this immediately worked wonders. Apparently the British are a popular lot. People would toot and hoot and wave and cheer as if I was a member of the royal family. The greatest advantage of flying the flag was that British vehicles would invariably stop and shower me with edible gifts.

One day, as I laboured my way towards the top of a mountain pass, a picnicking family greeted me with a lusty rendition of 'She'll be coming round the mountain when she comes, tra-la-la ...' As I breathlessly approached, a hefty but appealing woman who resembled a doughnut welcomed me with: 'Tea or coffee, luv?' The family was from Blackburn and had passed me on and off for four days.

Tea, coffee and light refreshments were not all that they offered. Beryl, the buxom daughter, appeared from the camper with a cauldron of steaming stew and whisked off the lid to a round of applause.

'Lancashire hot pot,' she announced proudly. 'We thought you mahte lak soom.'

It had been made specially for me. No one else ate — they just watched. They had passed me at the bottom of the mountain three hours ago, driven to the top, started culinary preparations and, knowing that I would eventually pass their way, sat and waited for me. It was a strange experience to be sitting on top of a remote Norwegian mountain eating a plate-load of Lancashire hot pot. I was so dazed and amazed by this heart-warming, stomach-filling display of British comradeship that I completely forgot to get their address. I never saw them again.

Norway has a lot of water which, together with modern television, joins the different pockets of civilization cut off from each other by mountains and vast distances. I was constantly crossing deep, dark, motionless lakes and fjords that mirrored green landscapes under fresh, brilliant skies. I passed countless rivers and streams foaming white through the hills and cycled beneath waterfalls that hung like silver threads.

I became adept at arriving just as the ferry had left, which often meant a wait of a good few hours before its return, but I did not mind. I was in no hurry and would spend my time doing useful things like eating or having a snooze.

The captain of one ferry invited me up on to the bridge, gave me lunch and asked if I would like to take a hold of his controls, as it were. I took up his offer and held the helm for over an hour as we plied the glassy waters from island to island, after which the captain offered me the job. It was a nice idea but North Cape was calling and I went on my way.

The unsightly elephantine bulk of a motor-home squeezed alongside and a triple-chinned, baseball-capped head protruded from the window.

'Hey, kid! Where ya headed?'

'North Cape,' I called.

'Catch ya there, then, but sure as hell don't miss Briksdal.'

With that he lumbered off up the road in a dark cloud of noxious fumes and I decided to follow the American's recommendation.

I clambered through a scrub forest in order to reach Briksdal, which turned out to be an offshoot of the Jostedal Glacier, the largest ice field in Europe, rearing its milky-blue, eerily creaking mass above the scrub. I had stayed with a family in Oslo who said it was possible to go on special hiking expeditions across this vast, dangerous ice-cap.

'But don't try it alone,' Pierce had warned. 'Many fools do and are never seen again.'

With a twinkle in his eye he told me the story of how, in the 1940s, an Englishman had climbed up the glacier dressed as if for the office in suit, cap and brogues, his briefcase and umbrella in hand. He had slipped and fallen hundreds of feet through a crevass and was never seen again — until a few years ago when he was discovered drifting in an iceberg from the glacier. He looked exactly as he had on the day of his fall except that, of course, he was dead.

I was grinding up Trollstigen (the Troll's Path), a twisting and turning road over the mountains near Andalnes, when the weather turned unpleasant. Rain and sleet threw themselves at me and the ice-blast wind blew so strong that I could only travel just fast enough not to fall off. I knew the descent would be even nastier and so I was determined to cycle in just my shorts and T-shirt right to the top, where I could at least look forward to donning a few extra layers.

When I reached the summit, it was entombed in whiteness. I stopped in the panoramic-viewing park where there was a solitary orange VW Beetle. A couple sat behind the steamy windows, staring at me. I think they were a little surprised to see me loom out of the freezing, swirling mist dressed more for a tropical tramp than for an Arctic snowstorm. I felt a bit self-conscious as I removed my ice-encrusted shorts with numb fingers before climbing into two pairs of longjohns, two thermal vests, three T-shirts, a sweatshirt, a tracksuit top, a cycling cape, a scarf improvised from a pair of longjohns, a pair of gloves, a pair of mittens, an Icelandic woolly hat over which I attached a plastic bag, and two plastic bags serving as over-shoes. Looking like a multi-coloured Michelin man, I felt ready to do battle with the elements. I gave a jolly wave to the dumb-founded couple who, on realizing that I was human after all, beeped back enthusiastically. Later I met them at the hostel and they told me my one mad-woman show on the mountain had been better than any view and had made their day.

Staying at a campsite the next day, I washed my two pairs of cycling shorts and laid them over a tepid heater in the games-room to dry. I was doing some darning back at my tent when some Dutch friends came tearing towards me, shouting, 'Quick! Quick! Your shorts are on fire!' Panic-stricken, I rushed inside to find my indispensable and trustworthy shorts a mere smouldering shadow of their former selves. It was a truly tragic sight.

As any cyclist knows, when it comes to saddles, bottoms are a sore subject. It was in the days before 'smuggled goods' short liners so my shorts were reinforced with an unsightly padding of chamois leather — horrible stuff, but a bottom-saver. What would I do without them? The implications were almost too painful to imagine. There was only one solution. I got on the hotline to Mum who, on learning of my terrible tragedy, broke into infectiously unstoppable giggles which wasted a good five minutes of trans-North Sea telephone money. Finally, stifling my own sniggers, I managed to convey the seriousness of the situation and sent her to rummage through my drawers (so to speak) for a spare pair of my DIY custom-made cycling shorts. She came up trumps and sent them on post-haste to Narvik, where my grateful hindquarters were joyously reseated in comfort.

I kept to the jagged and dramatic coastline as I cycled up Norway, jumping from ferry to ferry across the many fjords and waterways that divide the land. The Norwegians use ships like sea-going buses to visit family and friends, for shopping expeditions and to get to school and work. The only time I ventured inland on the tourist-infested E6 was for a snapshot and suitable pose beside the graffiti-covered 'Arctic Circle' sign that straddles a road at the crest of a windswept, barren mountain. From then on, as I embarked upon the last 600 miles of my assault on North Cape, I began to shiver more and more each night. That Arctic sign had certainly marked a temperature frontier.

Most of Norway's four million people live in the south and at these latitudes they had become thin on the ground. Those I did meet, however, remained as hospitable as ever. I was camping down a leafy track not far from a small cluster of houses when a farmer stumbled upon me as I sat cross-legged eating my sandwiches. He presumed I must be so uncomfortable that he raced all the way home and brought me a chair.

I was eating again when I met a Norseman with a weathered face out for a hike near Å (one of only three places in the world called A). He stopped to chat and as he rose to leave he handed me the equivalent of £3 'for beeger sandwiches'. When I protested and refused his generous offer, assuring him I had money of my own, he simply ran away up the mountain.

The Lofoten Islands are an extraordinary sight. A sheer wall of granite mountains bursts out of the Atlantic like the sculptured tail of a giant dragon, lifting their snow-covered peaks high up into the unpredictable skies and dwarfing the tiny wooden buildings of the fishing communities that nestle into their ragged cliffsides. Boats were the main form of transport and I had the spray-lashed, undulating coastline roads to myself. Europe's populated mass seemed far, far away. There were no billboards to insult my vision, no factories belching fumes — just rocky shores covered with wooden racks for drying cod, colourful fishing-boats bobbing on the waves and, high above me, the glorious forms of soaring eagles forever on patrol.

Sometimes I would shiver, not just from the cold but also because I felt so ridiculously happy from the excitement and exhilaration of cycling among such scenery. Everything would be right: the wind behind me, the skies clear, the mountains dramatic, my bike functioning, my stomach replete, my energy endless. Feeling fit to explode, I would race along without a care in the world and break into lusty song, warbling with fervour to the sun, the sky, the sea.

This was not always such a good idea. Blackflies, bugs and mosquitoes flourished at these latitudes and my trap would hastily shut in mid-song on a mouthful of assorted winged insects.

The temperature at night, as I neared North Cape, reminded me that the North Pole was not so very far away. The cold often became so intense that I would have to pack up my tent and start cycling to rekindle my circulation. When I removed its poles, the tent remained standing — frozen to the ground. But living outside for four months had made me quite hardy. When a family invited me to sleep in their centrally-heated house, I found I could not and tossed and turned between the sweat-soaked sheets. I felt trapped in a claustrophobic furnace and sneaked back outside in sub-zero temperatures to put up my tent in the garden, whereupon I immediately fell into unbroken slumber. In the morning the family seemed a little shocked at my nocturnal ramblings and thought I had gone loopy.

Sightings of reindeer multiplied as I entered Lapland, while signs of habitation diminished even further and opportunities for conversation became extremely limited in such desolate wilderness. It came as a welcome relief to be overtaken by a Lapp in traditional costume on a snow scooter one day. He was delighted to discover my nationality and broke into torrents of fluent English. Dismounting from our vehicles, we sat on a couple of cairns overlooking a herd of grazing Rudolphs and chatted excitedly like long-lost friends, he exercising his English and I my vocal chords. He told me how he had paid an astronomical amount of money to travel to London's Oxford Street for a hair transplant, which was not quite what I suspected from a Lapp.

The only hostility I experienced on my Arctic excursion was at Skaidi when I went in search of some hot water to thaw my water-bottles. I knocked on the door of a small cottage and the wild-eyed woman who answered threw my bottles back in my face, flying into a rage of Nordic abuse. I sensed I was unwelcome and was not going to succeed in replenishing my water supply, so I thanked her politely for her time and looked elsewhere.

After fifteen weeks and 4,572 cycling miles from Harwich, I found myself waiting with the locals for the ferry to Honningsvag on the final burst to North Cape. Not for the first time, a tourist coach screeched to a halt and shattered the peace with its passengers. I was shocked to find myself engulfed by these rumbustious and animated Americans who obviously classified me as something of a rare species along with the Arctic fox and white-tailed eagle: with their clicking, whirring cine-cameras they filmed me eating my banana as if I was some curious primate in the zoo.

'Hey, Mavis!' exclaimed a very fat man. 'C'me on over here. I swear to Gahd you'll never b'lieve this but ...'

On the final stretch, and with only a mile to go, I had my first puncture since Sweden — in spectacular style. I was swooping down a lush green hill past a jeep full of Germans when, without warning, my back tube exploded with such ferocity that it sent me skidding to the bottom like a slalom skier.

After a speedy repair job, I at last reached the isolated promontory of my destination: North Cape. I succeeded in elbowing my way through a thicket of coach tourists and into front position on top of the towering 1,000-foot granite cliff that plunged down into the icy waters of the Arctic Ocean. Ignoring the clamour and gasps of trans-Atlantic delight around me, I stood gazing out towards an infinity of frozen polar horizon, feeling as triumphant as if I had just conquered the Pole. With an overwhelming surge of satisfaction I knew that, no matter how hard I tried, I could cycle no further north. Fighting my way back through the throngs, I found a secluded spot and ate my last banana to celebrate.

Later I phoned home to announce my arrival at North Cape. Whenever I spoke to Dad from wherever I was in the world, he would without fail take my precise bearings to pinpoint me on the map kept beside his telephone, ask when I was coming home, and inform me that I could catch such-and-such a ferry from such-and-such a place and be home in so many days. The formula was the same this time and, as usual, I told him I was still enjoying myself and wanted to go a bit further.

Finland was flat and freezing and full of trees — and reindeer which kept tripping over my tent in the night. After the extravaganza of Norway and Iceland it seemed an unspectacular place and I missed the sea and the mountains. It rained a lot, too.

I had planned to take the boat back to Sweden when I arrived in Helsinki and work my way home from there. Then I realized I had only made this decision because my map of Scandinavia ended at Finland and, as my knowledge of geography left a lot to be desired, I was not quite sure what happened underneath. I knew Russia lurked down there somewhere. It would be fun to ... but I gave up that idea when I was refused a visa.

At the youth hostel I met Albert le Blanc, a French-Canadian from Quebec who was cycling around the world from one Olympic Game to the next. Attached to his handlebars was a large globe (his navigational aid) and it was from this that I discovered what really happened south of Finland. Across the Baltic Sea lay Poland — a mere ferry-ride away. I decided that Gdańsk would be my next port of call.

Plunging into poverty-stricken Poland after the affluence of Scandinavia came as a shock. Huge, unsightly sculptures of hammers and sickles stood incongruously in the middle of the beautiful rolling countryside; food was worryingly hard to find and its inhabitants appeared cold and dour-faced. But that was just my immediate impression, merely skimming the surface. After the first few hours I dug down underneath and began to experience the real Poland, the tragic history, the unpretentiousness and above all the warm stoicism of the people.

It was no wonder I was feeling a little unsettled. After living for four months in the pathological cleanliness of Scandinavia and amongst Sweden's fast, gleaming Saabs and Volvos, I was suddenly faced with the decay of poverty, the noxious fumes of Polski Fiats struggling to reach 30mph and an abundance of horse-drawn carts. One moment I was paying £1 for one tomato, the next 10p for ten. Like the people, the fruit and vegetables looked tired and disillusioned.

For four months I had been free to come and go as I chose in Scandinavia. Now I had a visa that allowed me only a set number of days to cross the country and a wodge of irrelevant documents that I was supposed to get checked and stamped for each night's accommodation. This was a Communist country where life was made as frustratingly complicated as possible.

That the Poles appeared aloof and grim was not surprising in view of the hardships they suffered — but it was deceptive. The first time I stopped to ask for some water in a small, dusty village outside Gdańsk, the woman I approached stared at me stonily and then slunk back indoors. I stood for a moment, puzzling over my next move, when the door opened cautiously and the woman, in her scarf and layers of print-patterned aprons, re-emerged. My knowledge of the native tongue went as far as a few mispronounced grunts so I resorted to smiles and drawing little pictures of who I was, where I was from and where I had been. The transformation was remarkable. Shaking off her shackles, the woman broke from a worn look of suspicion to an expression of twinkle-eyed merriment. She sketched some pictures — one person — alone? Aren't you scared? And then she invited me into her simple home and gave me a delicious meal of rough bread, tomatoes and some strange, potent cheese. All I had asked for was water! When I rose to leave, she took my hands tightly in hers and beckoned me to stay. I could not; my visa did not allow it and I was still a long way from Czechoslovakia.

Not far from Chojnice a car stopped and a woman jumped out, calling excitedly — she had spotted my Union Jack. In broken English she told me that her brother was manager of Selfridge's book department in London and said I must come back to her home. Her name was Irena; her husband, Eugeniusz, worked as a television technician and they had once been to England to visit her brother. The only English words Eugeniusz uttered were: 'Hen-lee. Goote bee-air.'

They brought out the best crockery for supper and a spread of bread, sardines, salami, green peppers and cheese was carefully laid out with pride. They took only bird-sized portions for themselves while serving me a huge plate-load. 'No, no,' I said, embarrassed, knowing that most of this food was their monthly rations, 'you must take more.' But they refused and offered me more and more, so that I had to pretend I was full rather than eat through all their supplies.

Irena told me that, during the war, the Germans had knocked on her door and asked to see her father and oldest brother. Her worried mother asked what they wanted with them and the Germans replied that there was nothing to worry about, they just wanted to speak to them. The two men were led away and Irena never saw them again.

After supper, Eugeniusz ignored my protest and opened a bottle of advocaat. It was a strong, sickly drink made from vodka, egg yolks, vanilla and sugar, and it had cost the equivalent of his monthly wages. All the time they enthusiastically plied me with questions about England, about London, about the life of the British. Irena said that their television and newspapers never gave news or pictures from the West. 'They tell us we're free,' she said, 'but we're not.'

When I left, they insisted on packing me a food parcel which included the whole of their cheese ration. They hugged me and waved to me and, as I cycled off down the road, Eugeniusz shouted, 'Goote-bye — touriste sportife!'

Then I met Stanislaw, a truck driver who took me sailing on a choppy lake with his family and friends. All fourteen of us crammed into a twelve-foot boat, the water rising to the gunwales. It was like a *Carry On* movie: Stanislaw's potbellied brother tripped over somebody else, who then got hit by the boom and they both ended up overboard.

I was camping in some woods near Poznań when I heard footsteps prowling around outside my tent. Sensing trouble, I was surprised to hear exclamations of: 'Ahh! Marg-a-rite Taatcher. Hello Houseeze off Parly-ment. Yaah — Bigge Benne.'

Three slightly befuddled students who had seen me earlier had managed to track me down and they invited me to a lakeside party. Anna and Katarzyna both studied and spoke excellent English but their friend had already exhausted his vocabulary with 'Houseeze off Parly-ment'. His name, so Anna said, translated into 'On the Corner'. Later, On the Corner fell out of a tree and into the lake. He was very drunk.

I passed into and through but very nearly not out of Czechoslovakia. Three miles from the Austrian border, I stopped on a quiet road to attend to nature in some nearby shrubbery. Duty done, I went to remount when suddenly a man sprang from the foliage and grabbed hold of my bike. Naturally this gave me a nasty turn but, illogically, I felt less concern for what he might be about to do than for what he might already have done or seen — after all, we had both been in the same bushes.

Shouting roughly, he demanded my passport. I thought: who the dickens does he think he is? Dressed as a peasant in worn, baggy trousers and a faded blue jacket, and leaping at me like a lion from a lair, he certainly was no border guard. I was darned if I was going to give him my passport and I tried to cycle away. It was only when he produced a pistol from his pocket that I knew he meant business, although it took a while to register this. I was a bit shocked. I thought: good grief — that's a gun. In the meantime he could have shot me and I would be thinking nothing at all. I had never had a real gun pointed at me before and I could only think how shabby it looked and that surely this was not really happening to me.

Again he shouted frantically for my passport and then it dawned on me that maybe he was a fugitive and wanted it to forge one of his own before escaping his country. Anyway, whatever he wanted, I would rather let him have it than me end up dead. With hands shaking wildly, I discovered how impossible it is to undo a series of fiddly zips and buckles on a handlebar bag. But such jelly-shaking trembles had their advantages: I was still struggling with the fastenings, certain that my moments were numbered, when an army truck rumbled into sight in the distance. My aggressor bolted back into the shelter of the woods while I, waiting for nobody, flung myself on to my mount and high-tailed it into Austria.

Up and over the Alps I went and stopped at the home of Didier and Dominique near Strasbourg. The brothers were amazed; they had thought they would never see me again after Iceland. I parked my bike in the garage, where I was surprised to see a couple of gleaming Campagnolo-equipped bikes suspended from the roof. Didier, I discovered, had once been a junior road-racing champion.

I stayed for a few days, brushing up on my abominable

French, going for long walks into the Vosges mountains with Didier and Raphael (his three-year-old son), participating in the consumption of gastronomic delights and helping Didier's wife Christine to change nappies for her newly born son Colin, who I became godmother to on my next visit to them.

One final spurt brought me to Le Havre where I found myself feeling a little weary after six months and 7,283 miles of pedalling. I was looking forward to some home comforts, notably a hot bath and a bowl of porridge. (Since Separation Junction, I admit that I had missed Red'ed's stove.) All I had to do was board my forty-sixth ferry of the holiday and it would be plain sailing to Portsmouth.

It was not that simple. The Great October Hurricane of 1987 struck with all its force mid-Channel and then rampaged over the whole of southeast England. I finally arrived in Portsmouth feeling decidedly green and made it home to find the place in turmoil: no trees left standing, no electricity, no hot baths and, worst of all, sandwiches for lunch.

4

Saddle Bound and Fancy Free

TO MOROCCO WITH MELANIE

'If you look like your passport photo, then in all probability you need the journey.'

EARL WILSON

I was up to my elbows in rough-puff pastry when the telephone rang. With the receiver in my floury hand I heard Melanie's voice, phoning me from work for the third time that morning.

'*Now* what do you want?' I said.

'I'm bored,' she replied.

'Well, let's cycle to Morocco.'

'Okay,' she said.

So we did.

It was not quite that simple. Mel did not possess a bicycle and when I recommended some 'serious' training she borrowed Dave's mount but could not make it even half a mile down the road to the local supermarket without major heart palpitations. She would not be deterred, however. We paid a visit to our friendly local bike shop and selected a dashing frame from a catalogue, a method not to be recommended. Unfortunately there was a ferry strike and the machine never materialized.

Two days before our departure date, we picked up her replacement frame and discovered that none of the components (each from a different source) was compatible. We knew what the desired effect should have been but had no idea how to achieve it. F.W. Evans had kindly but foolishly told us that they would be happy to check our bikes over before we left — 'check', note, not 'build', and I was amazed that they did not slam the door in our faces when we appeared in the shop the day before a bank holiday weekend with Mel's bike in bits in the back of my bicycle trailer. Gary Smith calmly took matters in hand and solicited the expertise of chief mechanic and HPV enthusiast Glen Thompson. (HPV? Human-powered vehicle, of course.)

April Fool's Day had seemed appropriate for our departure. It sounded slightly warmer than March and, as people told us, we were fools. With only minutes to spare, we found ourselves ensconced on a Brittany Ferries boat sailing from Plymouth to northern Spain.

I had deliberately chosen this crossing rather than the usual cross-Channel route to France, just in case Mel should come to

her senses on landing in Europe and wish to return home. My
ploy was to whisk her as far away from base as possible in one
move, making the chance of a quick dash home that much
more difficult for her. I had also tried my utmost to hide the
map from her until we were firmly on our way.

'There won't be any mountains where we're going in Spain,
will there?' she had enquired when we were preparing for the
trip back in London.

'No, of course not,' I had replied casually as visions of Picos
de Europa peaks loomed in my mind, 'just a few ups and
downs.'

Although we had been warned at length that the Arabs would
stare at, pester and pursue us, we were taken completely
unawares by the amount of attention we received on the ferry
itself. We were sitting quietly enough on the sunny but chilly
deck, swaddled in our sleeping-bags and doing some last-
minute sewing on our stripy shorts which, we had decided,
might benefit from reinforcement. We were industriously
stitching in the latest furry polartex inserts, which in due
course would make us feel as if we were sitting on dead cats.
The gathering onlookers were intrigued and one man
commented on our novel method of smuggling a domestic
moggie abroad.

Before setting out, we had decided to use our expedition to
raise money for the Wishing Well fund for the children in
Great Ormond Street Hospital, largely by way of sponsorship,
and we now attempted to make the most of our captive ferry
audience by requesting their contributions towards the appeal.
The majority of them thought we looked such an unlikely pair
to be cycling to Morocco that we raised very little money on
this occasion.

Reclining in a deckchair behind us was a rotund Geordie
with a knotted hankie on his head. As his wife tottered off to
the duty-free shop he called after her, 'Buy us some cigars—say
King Eddies—as a treat, would yer, Hilda?' Hilda turned quiz-

zically in the doorway. 'Eeeya, Harold man,' she said, 'what the devil d'yer want with pa-tay-tas?'

The sunshine we had soaked up during the crossing would be the last for the following few weeks. We crossed northern Spain during one of their worst springs on record and were greeted by an icy wind and sheets of freezing rain. Mel did not look too enthusiastic about her first expedition. As we dived into a steamed-up café that first morning in an abortive attempt to warm up, it did nothing for our morale when a television weather report depicted not only umbrellas but also snowmen covering our area of Spain. The slick-haired weatherman was smiling and I felt like hitting him—no, I wanted to shoot him, though I think it was the boys across the road who put that idea into my head. They were dangling out of a window and firing down into the river below with an air rifle, which struck me as an unusual method of fishing.

As the weather showed no signs of easing, we settled ourselves for a lengthy sojourn in the café. I took the opportunity of acquainting Mel with the contents of my sophisticated Blue Peter handy pack. Basically this small assortment included Prittstick, miniature collapsible scissors and Sellotape. Armed thus, it was possible to turn what might otherwise be a sensible and informative expedition diary into a childish mess. I revelled in it and thoroughly enjoyed attacking tourist office leaflets, newspapers, posters, food containers, mementoes, memorabilia and paraphernalia with my handy little scissors, to snip and stick and tape them into a confused collage in my diary. Mel, I was encouraged to note, appeared sufficiently impressed although I grudgingly admit that, as time wore on, she became even more proficient than I was at cutting and taping and creating an aspiring artistic mess.

The first night was a disaster. We were camping in monsoon conditions and I was hit by a severe bout of sardine poisoning which meant that I had to crawl over Mel on numerous occasions in a desperate urgency to leave the tent. Every time I unzipped its door a deluge of water cascaded on to her; and as I clambered over her on my return I would deposit a morass of mud as well. She did not see the funny side and said she wanted to go home.

It was even bleaker in the morning. Relentless winds and rain battered both the tent and our fast-fading enthusiasm. Nor was Mel altogether encouraged when, bravely venturing out to relieve herself, she discovered with dismay that the few hills to which I had previously alluded were in fact almighty snow-capped mountains which loomed into the glowering skies like a tall and menacing wall. (They had been named Peaks of Europe by sailors nearing the end of their passage from Africa or America because they were usually the crews' first sight of Europe.) Mel said that if any mountain got in her way she would cycle round it. I said that was a very defeatist attitude and that it was fun to half-kill yourself by cycling over them.

By the end of the second day we had cycled all of eleven miles. That night it rained so relentlessly that we awoke to find our inflatable sleeping mats had doubled up as lilos, making the prospect of floating right back home not such a ridiculous one.

Then Mel started having trouble with her nuts—the nuts on her headset. They kept coming loose. Headsets are a delicate area, as all cyclists are aware, and I am sure my concern will be appreciated when a brutish Rambo of a garage mechanic set about forcefully tightening Mel's nuts with an enormous monkey wrench. It was hardly 'precision adjustment' and they came loose again, so much so that her handlebars visibly moved a couple of inches. I took a look and quite confidently declared it contained a superfluous washer. 'If in doubt,' I said, 'leave it out,' and did just that. We received no further trouble.

The rain continued to fall—not for hours but for days. We could only keep our heads down and spirits up as we hastily made our way past the grey-slate villages, through the lush rolling valleys of Galicia and down into the hazardous cobbled descents of Portugal. To help weather the storms, we attached an impressive array of plastic carrier-bags on to our heads and feet in an attempt to divert the channels of water from cascading down our necks and feet. It was far too much trouble to disentangle the medley of Spar bags every time we stopped at a café and we would sit there in a sea of polythene, impassively drinking *café con leche* and busily Blue Petering our diaries while old men with sombre faces and sombre clothes stared at us in speechless disbelief.

The weather, the roads and Mel's fitness at last began to improve. I was at the top of a mountain pass awaiting Mel's imminent arrival, delayed not by her ascent speed but because she had begun to take considerable interest in identifying wild flora that lined the roadside. Finally she appeared from her botanical foray with a fine collection of flowering shrubbery sprouting from her handlebar bag. We embarked upon our hair-raising hairpinned descent down a peaceful mountain road. It was a beautiful, balmy evening; the air was sweet, the birds were singing and the sinking sun was a golden glow betwixt the mountains.

I was up front with Mel slipstreaming close behind. The gradient was steep and the speed fast—and rapidly increasing. As we rounded a bend, I was suddenly distracted by the glorious sight of incandescent peaks and verdant pastures that spread along the valleys below. To my detriment, I was much more intent on this riveting view than the road, while Mel, oblivious to such scenes, was attempting to beat her all-time speed record and had her attention fixed upon her on-board bicycle computer. A major absence of communication on my part and a momentary lapse of concentration on hers caused us to collide in an ugly confusion of metal and muscle. Bodies and bags and bits of bike flew in all directions.

For a few brief seconds we lay sprawled in a state of shocked silence, wondering whether we were dead or alive. Having established that we were both still breathing, our first reaction was to laugh and our second to survey the damage: a badly buckled wheel for me and a badly buckled body for Mel.

A car arrived and stopped, narrowly avoiding a splattering of escaped panniers. Help was at hand. But, oh no — the occupants nonchalantly stepped out of their Fiat Uno, gathered for a scenic snap of the view and them oblivious to the bloodied and dazed souls beside them, calmly drove away.

A second vehicle, crammed full with windsurfers and suntanned flesh, stopped and provided gestures of comfort. Then by chance a friend of theirs passed in a pick-up. We limped and bundled ourselves into the back and were driven down to the nearest village.

Unfortunately it was a Sunday and also a public holiday, so that the local doctor was unavailable. Instead the fire station (a hut and a truck) had to suffice and an oil-engrimed mechanic slapped on a few consolatory plasters at random. This skilled medical procedure was interrupted by a phone call from a hysterical woman desperately announcing a fire in her house some fifteen kilometres away. The mechanic replaced the antediluvian receiver as calmly as if he had just taken a weekly meat order. He shuffled listlessly to the grimy basin and, like Lady Macbeth, scrubbed his hands in a futile attempt to rid them of the marks. With visions of a screaming Signora dithering on the brink of an upper floor window as hungry flames licked ever closer, I felt there should be slightly more sense of urgency. But this was Portugal, where a somnolent air prevailed — even, it seemed, in an emergency.

Adjusting his oil-soiled trousers, the mechanic yawned and stretched and sauntered over to the manually operated fire alarm. It reacted with equal inertia, sounding like a drunken air-raid siren. Slowly, and in various stages of undress, a motley bunch of lethargic firemen appeared from the village — either on foot or on bicycle, but all taking their time. On arrival at the station, they clattered around, laughing and joking and looking for things that apparently were not where they thought they should be. At last, with an unhealthy splutter, the 'fire engine' coughed into life and chugged off down the road at the speed of a milk float, over half an hour after the initial panic-stricken summons.

*

After a week's convalescence in Lisbon, we and our bikes were back in operational order and we sallied forth to Spain. Kestrels wheeled in limpid skies as we rolled from the clifftop town of Arcos de la Frontera down to the plain below. It was a relief to return to peace. Arcos is typical of villages and towns all over Spain and Portugal — beautiful, but bedevilled by the infernal and ubiquitous scooters which buzz and whine like electric hairdryers through the narrow streets, causing an ear-splitting din which rebounds off the steep whitewashed walls. And then there are the television sets, their loud, distorted sounds emanating from every open window and doorway, rattling the eardrums and numbing the mind. We might call it intolerable noise pollution but to the Iberians, whose normal tone of conversation is a shout, such a label would mean nothing.

We spent that night in a farmer's field of rustling wheat. It was dark and hot and late; Mel was lulling off to sleep while I, transistor pinned to my ear, was tuning in to Radio Gibraltar, atrocious as it was. Suddenly and violently Mel elbowed me in the ribs.

'Ow!' I said. 'I thought you were asleep.'

'Ssshhh,' hushed Mel, 'something just brushed past the tent.'

I gulped and momentarily stopped breathing. Rigid as corpses we lay waiting, ears straining into the silence. Nothing happened. I was beginning to think Mel had imagined it but then we heard prowling footsteps and low, sinister voices. A beam of torchlight flashed erratically across the tent.

Again I gulped, only louder. I looked at Mel who, from what I could make out, had apparently died of fright. Sincerely hoping she had not (I did not want to face whatever was outside alone), I nudged her.

'Mel,' I whispered urgently, 'are you alive?'

Her answer was barely discernible but at least it was a response and indicated that we were in this together.

'Quick,' I said, 'we've got to do something.' We pulled on our shorts.

The sounds of men's voices approached and they started shouting at us in Spanish. We did not want to shout back and disclose our sex—for all they knew, we could be male. Tension mounted in the tent. Mel was once again playing dead. I had adopted the dog pose, squatting on my haunches ready to spring to the attack. Time was running out. I detected the voices of at least three men at close proximity. I thought: we must take preventative measures. I stirred Mel into action.

In the dark, we frantically gathered together a supply of weapons: a Swiss Army knife, bicycle pump, Perry whistle and a cup of fresh pee. (My self-defence course had taught me that, if thrown in the face, urine's acidity stings the eyes. Pepper would have been more convenient but we were out of stock.) It was a meagre collection of arms and did little to boost our confidence.

It is on occasions like this that you realize how vulnerable you are in a tent. There is no window for sighting the enemy, there are no sturdy walls for protection and there is no emergency exit. Zipped up in a mesh of rip-stop nylon, you are all ears but no eyes. You are trapped—an invitation to be attacked. What is needed is a periscope and an underground bunker. An armed guard or two would not go amiss; failing that, a Rottweiler would go down a treat. We had none of these and suddenly wished that we were safely tucked up in our own beds instead of lying in a wheatfield miles from home surrounded by a bunch of potential pants-droppers.

One of them crept up stealthily and unzipped—not his trousers (yet) but part of the outer tent. Within the inner shell, we were ready. All was deathly quiet. As he proceeded to undo the next zip, inches from my face, I suddenly switched on my bike lamp and blinded him not only with its beam but also with my cup of pee. I then issued a war-cry and leapt from the tent, wailing my head off and wielding my bicycle pump.

As suspected, we had a bunch of flashers on our hands. Mel flicked open the knife and blew so enthusiastically on the Perry whistle that my hearing was impaired for days to come. Such a howling fracas was obviously not what those Señores had bargained for: never have I seen three pairs of boxer shorts being pulled up so fast. Fumbling with fright and holding up their trousers, they stumbled over each other in their haste to retreat.

The rest of the night passed uneventfully.

Leaden English skies heralded an appropriate approach to Gibraltar, where we were faced with the aftermath of an IRA shooting incident and the infamous apes of the Rock. One ape mistook me for a banana and, leaping from great heights, landed on top of me in an ungainly heap.

To enter or leave Gibraltar by road, you have to cross the phenomenally wide airstrip. (Having a runway that doubles as a public highway seems like a recipe for disaster but it is a necessary compromise: Gibraltar is so cramped that there is scarcely room for a Portaloo, never mind a separate runway.) We had almost made it across when an alarm sounded, signalling the approach of a landing aircraft and warning you not to cross. An old woman, laden with shopping baskets, was a quarter of the way across when a megaphoned voice urgently instructed her to return to the side she had just left. Ignoring all warnings, she continued shuffling on her way. By now the approaching plane could be seen glinting silver in the sky as it prepared for its landing. Still the hunched crone continued on her deliberate way, quite oblivious to the fact that she was on a collision course with the aircraft. She had set her sights on reaching her destination and nothing, not even the prospect of being flattened into the tarmac by tons of metal, would deter her. With only moments to spare, a police car accelerated over the strip and whisked her to safety.

Gibraltar exuded British tackiness and came as a harsh and unappetizing shock after the romance of Spain. We had become accustomed to the lilting phonetics of the Spanish language and it did not feel quite right to be greeted suddenly with 'Mornin', luv,' from a swarthy, suntanned British bobby. The whole place had an air of parody. Main Street was full of contrived fish 'n' chip shops, pretentious tea-houses and British-style pubs and hotels. Lager-swilling skinheads hung around wearing Union Jack shorts or cut-off jeans and Doc Martens — and very little else. Underneath all this lay a thriving smuggling industry, mainly in Moroccan cannabis.

Since the border opened in 1985, the Rock had turned into a duty-free paradise but a traffic-congested nightmare. Motorists flooded into this already crowded community, queueing for hours in serpentine lines, jamming and polluting the narrow streets to fill their boots with booze.

The Gibraltarians are an ethnic blend of Spanish, British, Moorish, Maltese, Asian and Genoese descent who speak bad English and perfect Andalusian Spanish. To find yourself buying a packet of Kellogg's Cornflakes or Tate & Lyle Golden Syrup in Lipton's among such a mix of people feels somehow unreal. The place tries too hard to be British and, despite its impressive claims to law and order, how can Gibraltar be a 'model society' when most of its dirty work is done by impoverished Moroccans on one-year contracts who are accommodated in decaying army barracks without their families?

Many people think that it is high time Gibraltar was handed over to the Spanish and believe that the opening of the border was a first step in this gradual process. Perhaps, but legend relates that the British will remain in Gib as long as there is a colony of apes on the Rock. For that reason, 'ape security' is big business.

Down at the docks we met a couple of beefy American boys, Larry and Wayne, who had just returned from what should have been a two-month tour of Morocco. It had lasted no more than two days and they were lucky to have survived even that. While they were waiting for a bus, a group of Arab

youths had set upon them with fists and knives, robbing them
and threatening to kill them. The Americans had taken to their
heels and now spoke venomously about the whole Arab race,
writing them off as thugs and thieves. They said that we, as
two fair-headed females, would be mad to go to Morocco but
we said we wanted to judge the country for ourselves. Then
they gave us their *Let's Go* guidebook to the country.

'Here,' said Wayne, 'you have it. We don't intend to return
to that shit-pit again. We're off to take it easy in Torremolinos
— to lie on a beach for two weeks.'

'You're just as likely to get mugged there as in Morocco,' I
told him.

Rather than brood about the possible hazards, Mel and I
ventured straight into a travel agency to make enquiries about
a return boat ticket to Tangier. The staff fell about laughing
when they learned of our bicycling intentions. They said that a
one-way ticket would be far more appropriate because the like-
lihood of our surviving was very slim indeed.

Two such unpromising encounters within half an hour did
not fill us with confidence but our minds were made up.
Unfortunately the only boat service from Gibraltar was a
hydrofoil which refused to take our bikes, despite happily
transporting all sorts of black rubbish sacks, cardboard boxes
and crates containing the household goods of itinerant Moroccans.

'You'll have to go to Algeciras,' they said, 'and take the
boat.'

A few smarmy smiles and ingratiating words won the
officials round (females do sometimes have the advantage) and
we strapped our steeds to the deck.

The Strait of Gibraltar is one of the world's busiest waterways, with a ship passing every six minutes, and was no plain
hydrofoiling. We hit a violent storm: the wind tore under the
hull, thrashing at the sides as the vessel repeatedly pitched and
plunged and hit the great wall of waves at such an angle that I
was sure we would capsize. The captain said later that it was
one of the worst storms he had weathered.

We arrived in Tangier feeling decidedly fragile and were greeted by torrential rain, with the wind howling through the palm trees. This usually sun-saturated African clime felt as dishearteningly cold and wet as a mist-dripping Scottish moor. Local men shuffled past in their thick, brown camel-hair cloaks, their spacious pointed hoods firmly tied on like a ship's tarpaulins before a gale.

Stepping outside the ferry terminal, we were immediately set upon from every direction by suave hustlers clad in Levi jeans and black leather jackets who greeted us with offers, innuendos, hard sell, hotels and hash all in the same breath. One youth with rotting yellow teeth and a pencil-thin moustache, wearing a 'Be cool man' T-shirt, sidled up to me and said, 'Hello, my friend, how are you?'

'Very well, thank you,' I replied politely.

'Welcome back,' he said.

'Welcome back? I've never been here before.'

'Ah yes you have. I remember last May. You come with big red suitcase.'

'Sorry to disappoint you,' I told him. 'Wrong person. Anyway, I don't have a suitcase, only bicycle panniers.'

'No wrong person!' he insisted aggressively. 'You think I forget. You shit. You forget yourself.'

Tangier is no longer the stylish place of old. Since Morocco's independence, the famous writers, spies and jazzmen of the thirties have all long gone but the elegant architecture remains as a sad reminder of more prestigious times. The cafés and bars that line the once-stately promenade are no longer fashionable; they present a scene of gloomy decadence and are filled with hawking Moroccan men in pale, tired djellabas, staring out at passers-by.

Seeing no reason to linger in Tangier, we rode off down the Atlantic coast to Asilah where the sun came out at last, glaring off the whitewashed walls of the town with scalding brilliance. It raised our spirits — until we fell prey to the notoriously zealous carpet salesmen.

Being constantly hassled and hustled, it would have been all too easy to judge every Arab with contempt but of course not all of them were bottom-pinching money-grabbers. If we were to shun the services of each man who approached, we would be forever eliminating the chance of meeting a nice one. Travelling without male company in an Islamic nation, where women keep a low profile, we knew that we would be construed as 'loose' Westerners which meant that it was risky to judge a man as having good or bad intentions. But we also knew that there was little point in visiting such a mystical country if we coldly pushed aside every invitation of hospitality. If you trust no one and take no risks, why travel? You might manage to see a country as an observer but you will not be able to feel it. The rewarding fun of it all is to get behind those closed doors, to experience the life of the natives and to be able to eat and laugh with them.

However, we played safe when Mohammed approached us in the vegetable market and said, 'I am summer drummer at Club Méditerranée. I show you souk?'

'We're fine, thanks,' we said.

Strangely, he seemed quite content with our answer and left us alone to wander at will among the stalls of white radishes, candles, incense and fresh goats' heads, which is perhaps why, when bumping into him again, we decided to accept his offer. He explained that he wanted no money.

'I am not bad Arab,' he said (gullibly, we believed him), and he seemed genuinely interested to 'show two bicycles round my souk'.

'Why you bicycle and not bus?' he said, obviously perplexed that two rich Westerners who could afford the local transport chose to travel by such arduous and lowly means.

'Because we love bicycles and hate buses,' we said, and we meant it.

When we felt we had exhausted all the possibilities of the souk, we bought Mohammed some *kaab el ghzal* ('gazelle's horns' of crescent-shaped pastry stuffed with marzipan and cinnamon), thanked him for his time and made to leave. Then he invited us to his home to meet his family and we immediately thought, 'No, we must go,' but rather naively said, 'Yes, okay, we'd love to.'

We wandered down the winding alleys of the medina, not to his home as he had led us to believe but to the local carpet warehouse. Mint tea was poured from impressive heights into tulip-shaped glasses — a sign that negotiable business was pending. Mel and I both knew what this meant (after all we had been warned about it often enough) but we found the whole atmosphere enticing. There was something compelling about the fact that we were experiencing the conman at work and we knew that we wanted to stay. The kelims were indeed wonderful and Mel, knowing a lot about textiles, could tell that the goods on offer were genuine. She quickly persuaded me that I needed a new rug in my room to replace the hideous one my brother had given me years ago.

Not content to show us just one rug, the salesmen pulled out most of their shops' contents from the huge, colourful piles that towered around us. The purchase of these rugs was a time-consuming process but we revelled in the whole operation, which was carried out with good humour throughout. As we got the hang of the negotiating process, we bargained hard — scribbling our price on a tattered piece of paper, crossing out a salesman's offer with exaggerated disdain, more mint tea, more numerical scribbles, more crossing out, expressions of spurious discontent, rising to leave in feigned disgust, beckoned back, lower offer, more crossing out, more tea, more scribbles and, finally, the agreement: the exchanging of dirhams for *kelims*, the handshakes, the farewells. Despite claiming to the contrary, the salesmen had of course made their profit. They were happy but so were we and we knew that our carpets were far cheaper than anything of equal quality that we could have bought at home. And above all it had been much more fun than walking into a Western shop, looking at the price tag and paying wordlessly at the cash till.

Mohammed was still around and now repeated, 'Please, come and meet my family.'

'That's what you said last time and led us to the carpet men instead,' I said, knowing that he would have received a commission from the deal.

'Ah, but they are my friends.'

'Yes,' I said, 'I can see why.'

He had taken us for a ride this far and so we thought we might as well go the whole way. He lived in a cool, dark basement of two bare and basic rooms: no furnishings, just rough walls, stone floors, an indoor well, an outdoor communal hole-in-the-floor toilet and, of course, the ubiquitous television blaring forth its wailing Moroccan music.

His wife could speak no English and sat in a corner smiling shyly, every now and then leaving the room as she obeyed her husband's imperious commands. After a delicious supper of spicy chick-pea and coriander soup (which they noisily slurped and sucked from the bowl) Mohammed insisted on dressing us up in a couple of traditional kaftan costumes made by his missus. There was much merriment all round but the evening began to turn sour when it became obvious he expected payment for his hospitality. When we reminded him that he had specifically said, 'My friends — I ask for no money,' he then demanded we give him a selection of our possessions, including some of the clothes we were wearing. All the while his shrew-like little wife sat timidly in the corner, looking embarrassed about the whole affair. It was only because of her mute work-dog role, her poverty, the meal she had prepared for us and her genuine expressions of apology about her husband's aggressive imploring that we handed her some dirhams. Then we left.

We had arrived in Morocco in the midst of Ramadan — the most important of all Islamic celebrations, when Muslims rigorously observe a total fast from sunrise to sunset, abstaining from food, drink, smoking and sexual behaviour during daylight hours. Disregarding these rites results in imprisonment and punishment. Therefore the night-time, in the towns at least, is when everyone gets down to hours of feasting and fun.

Because most people were relaxed and replete after the

night's activities, or simply dozed the foodless hours away, the morning was the best time to look around the markets and medinas: everyone was in good spirits and rarely harassed us. By afternoon the hunger pangs set in, tempers frayed fast and it was best to be in the saddle.

A sense of urgency prevailed as sunset closed in. The air was full of the pungent smells of *harira* — a thick bean soup (our daily diet) — rising from every window and doorway, and children scuttled towards the mosques with brimming bowlfuls for the resident beggars. Cafés filled up fast with people sitting at tables shelling hard-boiled eggs, with tall glasses of milk or orange-juice and steaming bowls of soup at the ready as they waited eagerly for the signal from the mosque. Its ear-splitting, tannoy-distorted wails sounded the end of another day's fast.

The eating was far from over after the *harira* had been wolfed down. Mounds of couscous, chicken *tajine* and strange sticky sweets were consumed at regular intervals until the crowded street stalls and cafés closed just before dawn. It was no wonder (though rather ironic) that many Moroccans actually put on weight during their fast.

Not every Muslim abides by the Ramadan law. In Larache we met an affable young waiter who told us that he found the strict rituals all rather tedious. At the risk of nine months' imprisonment, he preferred to ignore the ways of Allah and acted and ate as he pleased within his own home.

'Anyway,' he said, 'to eat and sleep properly is very important for my biology, geology, maths, physics and chemistry exams.'

'You're a law-breaking brainbox,' I said.

He laughed. 'Study for me is more important than religion.'

One of the major problems about being a bicycle-bound female in Morocco was not so much the persistent attentions of the men as the question of relieving ourselves out in the open. We all know that it is easy for men — a quick turn of the back and the deed is done — but privacy is essential for women and was extremely hard to find. All was well and good if we discovered a deserted wood or field so that we could get on with our business quickly and quietly; but someone would inevitably appear on the scene just when you thought the coast was clear, even with the advantage of a cycling companion as a lookout (Mel was not always to be trusted in this role).

This relieving business is of some importance to cycling campers but rarely seems to be described in practical detail by travel writers — it is almost as if they never feel the urge. Well, perhaps bouncing about in a bicycle saddle all day increases the frequency of that call and, for the sake of fellow cyclists everywhere, I would like to pass on a few tips based on urgent experience.

While in Europe we always made the most of using toilets in bars, shops, garages and restaurants. In Africa, however, the majority of squat toilets were so soiled that navigating a path through the overflowing filth was no easy task and we were well aware of the danger of disease. Then I had a nasty experience when, poised for action, I heard an ominous noise from below. I was certain it had nothing to do with me and discovered a toad in the hole, ready to leap towards vulnerable areas. In the face of such hazards, we preferred to go in the wilds.

Out in the countryside, though, foliage was a necessity to conceal our actions. That was a problem in a flat expanse of African desert, teeming with nomads and not a single leaf or twig or rock to hide behind. Our solution? Dig a hole and half submerge yourself. We devised several other alfresco methods, one of which involved camouflage. Instead of squatting *behind* a bush (should we be able to find one), we would literally get into it. Although this produced scratches and bits of shrubbery in sensitive areas, the results were remarkably effective. Mel would tell me not to look as she dived into nearby foliage and then give a yoo-hoo or a whistle to see if I could detect her whereabouts. I never could, nor she mine.

In Morocco there was the combined hazard of Ramadan and the native djellaba (the hooded, wide-sleeved cloak worn by most Moroccans) to add to our privacy problems. During Ramadan especially, people tended to flop down anywhere to sleep, often in the most unexpected places, and the colour of their djellabas blended perfectly with the landscape. On one memorable occasion I sprang full-bladdered from my cycle to retire safely behind a rock, which promptly came to life. It turned out to be a large and startled Arab who had been peacefully snoozing in his native camouflage among the genuine rocks in the landscape.

By far the best idea we devised was the 'portaloo' cape method. In fact it is the only good use I have ever found for a cycling cape. By way of a bonus, its setting-up involves no complicated instructions in two dozen languages — it is quick, simple and practical. Don a cape, sit on your haunches and — hey presto! — an instant toilet tent that exposes nowt.

Brilliant as this invention was, in very populated areas I tried to emphasize to Mel the crucial importance of positioning herself so that the workings within the cape were undetectable from the outside. To distract unwanted attention, the method I suggested was to crouch to one side of one's bicycle and pretend to meddle with one's equipment (as it were) — bottom bracket, or rear derailleur, for instance — as if tending to a mechanical fault. But Mel would not listen. Instead, she chose to squat like a stuffed turkey plonked on the roadside. This drew quizzical looks, especially on hot, cloudless days when a cape seemed utterly superfluous.

Riding down the coast, we took in Rabat (the capital) for elevenses and Casablanca ('Play it again, Sam') for lunch. There was nothing in the least romantic or mystical about Casablanca. It was fast, ugly and modern. With a population growth of over 50,000 a year, it was also full of poverty, prostitution and shanty towns where children in rags foraged through mounds of rat-infested rubbish for anything to help their poor families survive.

Travelling south, the roads were surrounded by trees; there

were blossoming almonds, silvery olives, spiky palms, stout eucalyptus and sweet-smelling mimosa. They were also full of chaos — cars, camels, trucks, ducks, scraggy donkeys and sad mules which, when returning from market, often had an assortment of mangy sheep and goats strapped to their backs, baaing and bleating in plaintive cacophony.

There were bicycles too — ridden by men who would frantically give chase whenever we overtook them. The prospect of having their macho self-esteem shattered by a couple of females gliding effortlessly past was more than they could take. Rather than lose face, they would splutter and wheeze alongside on their rusty old boneshakers, a practice which could become irritating, even dangerous, as they attempted to initiate conversations while we slalomed through groups of dithering goats or convoys of supercilious camels.

These boys would demand to know our nationality and we soon discovered that it was inadvisable to admit we were English — the majority of them knew enough words to drive us insane: '*Bonjour! Française? Allemande?* American? *Non? Non?* Where you from? Ah, English! Good morning, bread and butter! Hello! Fish and ships — hello! Ha! Ha!'

Our usual ploy was to tell them we were either Icelandic or Martian and then communicate with each other in our own gobbledegook. Generally this worked wonders and would baffle them for long enough to make a speedy get-away.

Travelling in such a male-dominated world, deciding whom to trust could be a problem and the local gendarmes did not make it any easier. Every police jeep that passed would invariably stop and wave us down, oblivious to the fact that we might be enjoying a swooping descent. First they would bumptiously demand our passports and then invite us back to their post for 'mint tea, couscous and a relationship' — always in that order.

By the lovely old Portuguese ramparts in El Jadida, the only eyesore was a greasy-haired, gangling German who thought he was the bee's knees. He spoke English with an American twang. I asked him where he had been and where he was going.

'Hey man,' he said, 'I ain't headed no-vair. I'm just cruisin' around from one hash hangout to zee next. Maybe cruise over to Marrakesh for zee veekend and zen cruise on up to Casa.'

Hey, yeah! Groove it! And cruisin' he was, in a money-oozing Mercedes estate slob-mobile.

South of the town we passed the fortified monastery ruins of Tit (you may snigger, but it means 'eyes' or 'spring' in the local Berber dialect) and entered a scene of salt marshes and acres of long, industrial greenhouses. The fields were full of people digging and picking and crating and stacking. Dilapidated lorries groaned and swayed unsteadily beneath loads of tottering crates full of tomatoes, cucumbers, melons and onions as they slowly lumbered past us on the road.

Finding a lunch spot was impossible. We could not stop anywhere for a moment without attracting a crowd of curious onlookers who fired a barrage of ear-battering, senseless questions at us. Finally we dived into the thicket of a maize field and, lying low, managed ten minutes of peace to make and wolf down a cheese sandwich before being discovered.

The small fishing port of Oualidia gave us our first (and last) chance to sprawl on a beach out of view and out of range of the Moroccan male. It was a beautiful crescent of white sand, empty and clean. There were no ice-creams or cold fizzy-drink stalls here, just a vendor bearing a big reed basket full of smelly fish—not exactly thirst-quenching refreshments.

The empty campsite was appalling. The floor of the toilet block was awash with soiled, stagnant water and alive with croaking frogs. As a result, the camping area was covered with faeces and reeked of urine. Perhaps that is why Mel was suddenly and violently ill. In the darkness, I transported her to a nearby hotel and deposited her on a bed. She was terribly sick all night.

The next day I played the role of nurse and the day after that she was better and we left. Five miles down the road a man buzzed alongside on a moped, waving a British passport. We wondered what he was doing with such a thing and then it dawned on us it was Mel's. He was the hotel manager. After all we had been told, it was nice to find an honest Moroccan.

It seemed to be a day for integrity. At Cap Beddouza we sat on a stone bench outside a small bar eating raw carrots and playing with a little boy's kitten. The barman saw us, walked over to a scraggy vegetable patch and plucked out some of his own fresh carrots for us. Later, we had paid for our drinks and were about to leave when the young owner of the bar ran out, apologizing that he had made a mistake with his addition — he had charged us too much and handed us back a small sum. We gave him back twice as much as a reward for his honesty and left him looking puzzled.

In the pottery-producing town of Safi we met Omar, a rich Moroccan living in Paris. Dressed in expensive and immaculate clothes — checked trousers, polished shoes, pressed shirt — he had set upon us in the street telling us that back home he, too, was a cyclist and raced at weekends round the Bois de Boulogne. After that he would not let us alone; he followed us everywhere — through the market, into cafés, down alleyways. We once managed to give him the slip but he soon reappeared, in our hotel: he had moved out of his own and booked into ours. He seemed to be monitoring our every move. I told Mel that the only way for us to leave the hotel undetected was to disguise ourselves in native costume. I demonstrated by entwining myself in the curtains and sheets, my head topped with a towel. Mel was not impressed and said I looked ten times more conspicuous than before. We decided to simply make a run for it instead.

We escaped successfully and sat in a first-floor café overlooking the bustling square. Mel ordered a cup of tea with milk and was given a tea-bag floating forlornly in a glassful of lukewarm milk. Then a drama unfolded before our eyes as we peered down over the chaotic scene in the square below: a bus ran over a man on his moped. The crowds were drawn irresistibly to the scene, everyone shouting and arguing about what to do but no one doing anything. There was no sign of the man — he was pinned beneath the bus. After a good ten minutes a policeman arrived and started viciously attacking the crowd with his baton, a fruitless activity which only resulted in his injuring a number of people rather than dispersing them. Finally he reached the bus but it seemed like an age before the moped man was extricated, looking in a very poorly state. With assistance, the policeman dragged him away.

Forty-five minutes after the accident an ambulance (a wreck of an army jeep) rattled round the corner at walking pace. When the driver was told he was too late, he smoked a cigarette and then drove away again with the same degree of urgency. After witnessing the emergency services in action, Mel and I decided Morocco was no place to have an accident.

Entering Essaouira, I narrowly missed entangling a snake in my spokes as it slithered its way across the road close by my wheel. Squashed snakes were as frequent a sight on the Moroccan roadside as flattened hedgehogs in Britain or dead dogs in Spain.

In the scorching light of the brilliantly whitewashed and blue-shuttered town of Essaouira, the clamouring hawkers greeted us with, 'Hello — Jimi Hendrix.' Hendrix had rolled up during the sixties and established a legendary hippie hangout full of spaced-out junkies at the village of Diabat, an hour's walk along the beach. The place had closed down ten years later when a mob of local druggies murdered a handful of hippies. Berbers live there now, but the Hendrix name lives on.

High up on the top floor of the Hotel Majestic we found a tiny room for £1.40. There was a small window, a wobbly wooden table, a rickety chair and a double bed so perfectly concave that we had to tether ourselves to the sides to avoid tumbling into the cavernous dip in a sticky amalgamation of sweaty flesh. Yet it was one of our favourite rooms. We won over the hotel owner who gave us a key for the roof, whence we could look down to the narrow street far below. It was full of donkeys, carts, cyclists (one hand on the handlebar, upturned fowl in the other) and women like giant snowballs wrapped from head to foot in voluminous, pristine white robes. Off to the side were the dark, cool workshops of thuya-wood craftsmen who produced exquisitely intricate marquetry work, which they justifiably claimed to be the best in the country (we bought a beautiful miniature chess-set from them, its tiny wooden pieces painstakingly carved to perfection, for the same price as our hotel room). Flat, white, sun-scorched rooftops, splattered with colourful washing that dried in seconds, stretched out all around us, while not far away, over the old Portuguese ramparts, was the deep, dark blue of the Atlantic.

We spent many gloriously peaceful hours on that rooftop, out of sight of any pestering onlookers, reading, diary-writing, eating or sleeping. Unfortunately I underestimated the powers of the sun and hoicked my swimming costume up a little too far so that a portion of rump was sunburnt so red that it blistered. Later, a programme on the World Service reiterated the well-known facts of sun and skin cancer and gave a few tips for lessening the painful effects of a bad burn. That night I went to sleep with slices of cucumber strapped to my buttocks.

Down at the harbour corpulent fishermen lined the quayside, sweating over burning grills to cook freshly-caught sardines. Hungry crowds packed around the rough trestle tables and sandwiched the hot, pungent fish between great hunks of bread. It was a lively scene of chatter and clatter and crumbs.

We walked for miles along the sandy, windswept beach until we both got caught short. A gang of Arab boys lurked ominously close by but we managed to make a dart for the dunes and dug a hole undetected, planning to build sand-castles should anyone walk past. The relief operation was relatively successful until Mel, failing to take the blustery wind factor into account, sprayed her foot and leapt into the air, dropping her rationed piece of toilet paper which blew off down the beach. To some, this might not sound particularly serious. To us, however, the situation was indeed grave: we had failed to find any toilet paper to replenish our dwindling supplies since arriving in Morocco.

I knew how much that piece of 'rare and rationed' meant to Mel and I gallantly tore off down the beach in hot pursuit. Whenever I caught up with the escaped sheet, a strong gust would infuriatingly blow it out of reach again. I zigzagged over the sands in a game of cat and mouse until I managed to fling myself prostrate in an impressive rugby tackle and came up trumps with the dog-eared Andrex in hand. I trotted back to Mel in triumph like an obedient dog and my efforts were generously rewarded with a donation of half the catch.

We headed inland from Essaouira across the dry, dusty desert of Al-Hawuz, riding into an exhausting headwind as hot as the blast of an electric hairdryer. The tourist office in Essaouira had assured us that there were two hotels in Chichaoua and we planned to reach them before dark. However, we were still fifteen miles from the town when the sun slid behind the mountains. We contemplated camping among some haystacks but were put off by a spate of giant, hairy locusts with ferocious forceps and wicked antennae. As darkness encroached, they came out in force and were joined by a particularly unpleasant and sinister crustacean species which scuttled continuously across the road, crunching beneath our tyres.

As we swept down a mountain on the final stretch into

Chichaoua, the spectral vision of a horse-drawn cart driven by a ghostly-white, skeletal man in flapping and flowing robes loomed out of the eerie grey light. It swept past without a sound and vanished into the gloom.

Shaking, scared and breathless, we arrived among the welcome lights of Chichaoua only to discover that the tourist office had misled us — there were no hotels. We spent a long time traipsing wearily around until we found a café owner who said there was a 'residence' about three kilometres away. We set off into the darkness, followed by clattering Arabs on bicycles.

The residence turned out to be a shabby café with a few dark and dingy rooms behind. It was run by an odious youth who said that accommodation was free — as long as we slept in his room. When we declined this unappealing offer, he shouted a stream of abuse. We should have left there and then but the thought of having nowhere else to go stopped us. At last we cajoled him into giving us a room — a windowless hole crawling with cockroaches and covered in dirt. There was no lock on the door and so we pushed both beds up against it. As an extra precaution we contrived an impressive device which would bring my bicycle down on the head of any intruder opening the door.

Barricaded thus, we lay down on our sleeping bags, but we didn't sleep. A gang of youths burst into the courtyard outside our room and for over an hour shouted and banged and hammered on our door. Mel took up her usual crisis posture and lay as stiff as a board.

'Mel, what are you thinking?' I said, mainly to reassure myself she was still alive.

'I'm thinking,' she said, 'that if they get in here just make sure you cut off their balls.'

Fingering my Swiss Army knife, I said, 'Don't worry, I will.'

Fortunately our safety barricade stood the test, the vociferations finally abated and we were left to a night of fitful, knife-clutching sleep. We escaped at dawn and hit the road for Marrakesh.

*

Giant eucalyptus trees shaded the streets leading into this mystical red city of the desert. Together with a sea of hooting scooters, trucks, cars, the clamour of bicycle bells, wooden-wheeled ox-carts and donkeys, we were washed into the city's beating heart — the Djemaa el Fna (Assembly of the Dead), so named for the executions that took place in the square until well into the last century, when heads of rebels and criminals were put on public display.

As we cycled in by the rosy glow of evening it was a thriving scene where east and west, ancient and modern, rich and poor all met in a big melting-pot of sound, vision and colourful splendour like a mediaeval extravaganza. Lanterns were lit around white table-tops; the open-air stalls were preparing for one of the world's greatest fast-food spectacles (an everyday event) and there was not a hamburger in sight. Fat-bellied chefs with meaty arms sweated over their primitive grills. There were kebabs and *kefta* (spicy balls of minced lamb), pigeons, saffron fish and giant *tajines* — Morocco's classic stew cooked in pyramidal-shaped pots. The air was filled with the alluring smell of eastern spices. There were bowls of snails picked from the land and steamed in an earthy, spicy broth. With meat an expensive luxury for many, there was an abundance of offal disguised in soups and stews of turnips, pumpkins, cardoons, artichokes, cumin, cinnamon, garlic and chillis.

Mel and I took our seats and wedged ourselves among a jigsaw of tightly packed bodies that surrounded a huge, simmering cauldron of boiled goats' heads and spicy chickpea soup. At the time we were unaware of the ingredients and demolished a couple of bowlfuls each with no trouble. Everywhere there were mounds of round, flat Arabic bread, still deliciously warm. As we were sharing a third bowl of soup, a skull-capped man slotted himself in beside me; he was clutching a stalk-eyed iguana whose blood, he claimed, cured asthma, haemorrhoids and impotence.

When we had eaten our fill, there was endless entertainment in a square aswirl with fire-eaters, sword-swallowers, child boxers and sad, trick-trained monkeys. Boys danced lasciviously to the clamorous jarring of cymbals, next to a primitive, plier-wielding dentist whose mat was lined with motley molars for sale. Clowns clowned; charming snakes curled hypnotically out of baskets; red-clad water-sellers with large leather hats, pointed shoes and goatskin flasks, jingled their bells, hungry for custom. There was singing and music of every kind on strange instruments — skin-covered, two-string guitars, iron-clashing gongs, crude violins and the battle-beaten rhythm of tall drums hit with long, curved sticks. And there were story-tellers, too, surrounded by a ring of riveted, starry-eyed listeners pressing close together to catch every word. Young girls carrying beads, bracelets and cheap jewellery threw necklaces over our heads crying '*Cadeau! Cadeau!*' and then vanished in the crowds, reappearing moments later to accuse us of stealing and demand money.

Marrakesh was a magnet, drawing us into its mystical clutches, swirling us round in dizzy intoxication. It would not let us go. For two weeks we stayed in the heart of the medina, among its winding alleyways in a small, simple hotel with a sunnily tiled and airy atrium. The hotel was run by Brahime, an extrovert Berber who called us 'disco-dancing monkeys' and who had a suspect habit of hitching up his djellaba to show off his lurid boxer shorts.

I had always had romantic ideas of Berbers living simple and colourful nomadic lives in mountain villages, but Brahime brought this fantasy crashing to earth when he said he had spent most of his life working as a Sainsbury's supermarket assistant in south London and later as a travelling clown. He was eccentric, for sure, and we became great friends. He spent hours in his little rooftop kitchen (a gas burner, table and tap) preparing delicious spicy food for us and his friends. We would all sit cross-legged around low, circular tables, eating and joking as the sparkling stars pierced coal-black skies overhead and all the time the dull rhythmic beat of drums floated enigmatically in the warm night air. Every morning, before it was light, we were woken by the muezzins calling the faithful from red-stoned minarets, the first of each day's five repetitive calls to prayer. The confused, wailing song of entwined voices wrapped themselves around each other like coils of bewitching snakes.

When we ventured into the cool and shady dealing of the souks we were constantly hassled, hustled, jostled, touched, touted, victimized, monopolized and relentlessly harassed. But it was fun. Everywhere we were greeted with taunts and one-line conversation openers.

'Ah, my friends! Welcome to my country. It is me you are looking for?'

'Well, thank you, but no, I'm afraid it isn't.'

Not to be put off, they would then enquire: 'My friends, hello — how are you? You like my country?' It was more a remark than a question, made with smiles too large to be sincere that revealed crooked yellow teeth against coffee-coloured skin. These men were multilingual hustlers, working the streets in the tourist areas to offer both 'hospitality' and cannabis (kif from the Rif) in the same breath.

'I show you souk; get you good price — hey! you want chocolate?' This was the code for hash.

'No thanks, we're quite happy as we are.'

'I show you leather souk — for you best price — yes?'

'Not today, thanks.'

'Come, my friends. I have much to show you. Trust me.'

'Please leave us alone.'

'You think you are the Queen.'

'No, we just want to explore in peace.'

'I think you are racist.'

'Not at all. We just want to be left alone. So goodbye.'

'My friends,' says this 'guide' ominously, maintaining his pace alongside, 'the souk is a very dangerous place for you. Many bad men.'

'Thanks for the warning, but go away.'

'Fuck you, mother fuckers!' comes the hissed reply.

And into the midst of all this confusion we would venture. Importunate hawkers would hound us through the maze of the medina and market, blocking our path in the narrow passage-ways with arms extended, welcoming us with: 'Hey! You English? You come and look. Special cheap price for you,' and even once the bizarre: 'Hey! My friends. You want very good air-conditioned trousers?'

Emerging through the barricade of questions and giving the guides the slip, we spent hours of endless fun down the alluring alleys, haggling over the most inconsequential things like sandalwood sticks and spices, red leather slippers and harira pots, with surprisingly little money changing hands. There was something new around every corner: aphrodisiac dens doing a roaring trade in dried chameleon; towering piles of glazed Safi pottery; brass that gleamed and leather that reeked; and then, into the mire of the dyers' quarters where vast skeins of wool were stirred like spaghetti in bubbling cauldrons and then hung out to dry like bunting.

Back at the hotel an English boy had moved into the room opposite. We christened him Applebottom. He was a peculiar, pale-faced, wispy-haired character who looked like a ferret and spoke like a don; he was 'in computers'. His plan had been to cycle from Morocco to Cape Town but he gave up the idea when he found Africa 'a darned sight hotter than I thought it would be' and sent his mountain bike back home to Oxford.

'So now what are you up to?' we asked.

'Exporting exquisite kelims to a friend's shop outside Oxford.'

That turned out to be just his idea of the day — the next day he wanted to go home.

'I've had enough,' he said.

Applebottom was one of those people who are interesting to talk to for the first ten minutes and then exceedingly boring. And you could never get rid of him. He spent hours in our room, eating our food, smoking copious amounts of kif and talking out of his bottom about 'discovering' himself. I think it is called 'introspection'. I prefer to remain 'lost within' and throw any self-analysis to the wind.

One day we heard loud groans coming through his open

latticed window. We found him writhing in bed and 'dying', or so he moaned. I suspected he had nothing worse than a cold and an excess of hash. However, it was fun to have a drama on our hands and to be drawn running from our rooms by cries of 'Quick, Josie, Melanie — I need medicine!' Like old mother hens we clucked and fussed over him and scurried to the market to buy magic potions or food or bottles of freshly squeezed orange-juice from the rows of brightly canvas-roofed stalls that lined the Djemaa el Fna.

He survived, which was a little disappointing really. To reward his Nightingale nurses, he took us out to buy us a sixpenny bowlful of harira. We were looking forward to a night on the town to see how much less hassle we would attract by being in male company. Ironically, it was the nearest we came to a dangerous situation.

The trouble with Applebottom was that he had no patience. ('Patience is the best remedy for every trouble,' to quote Plautus.) Nor did he have a sense of humour. He treated every approaching Moroccan in pompous and stuck-up fashion, fending off their earnest requests in a serious, supercilious manner. He also seemed to practise the theory that to be understood by a foreigner you merely shout louder. Quite understandably, the hagglers did not appreciate his attitude and one, at whom Applebottom had sworn unnecessarily loudly, lunged at him with a broken bottle. So much for the reassurance of male escorts. He was turning out to be more an embarrassment than a boon and we were far safer alone.

It was time to leave Marrakesh. We could have stayed longer — we loved the place — and maybe if we had we would even have 'discovered' a little about ourselves, though I doubt it. That said, we *did* make discoveries about ourselves: Mel discovered a fetish for Berber bread and I discovered heat rash on my neck. To alleviate the prickliness, a chemist told me to apply his own creamy concoction based on fish-paste. I am not so sure that it dispelled the discomfort but it certainly dispersed the crowds. I stank like an old fish-processing plant and the stench was so bad that even the hagglers gave up haggling. My tip to the Morrocco-bound female is, therefore: never mind the toothpaste, always pack the fish-paste.

We rode through Marrakesh's suburban palm trees, glancing up through their spiny leaves to the snow-kissed peaks of the almighty Atlas. These rugged mountains of purple and red form the northern bulwark of the Sahara and are the mark of Berber territory where the incessant importuning and harassment of the cities are soon lost. Goliath belonged to this white-skinned, indigenous race of North West Africa whose history is lost in the dawn of time.

One of the things I found most intriguing about the Berbers was their idea that love stems not from the heart but from the liver. A girl will look longingly into her chosen man's eyes and say, 'You have captured my liver.' With visions of school-dinner sinewy gristle looking and tasting as tough as old boots, I cannot think of a less appetizing and less romantic organ. Mind you, I have never been faced with a dish of fried heart . . .

We tackled the Atlas by way of the Tizi n'Tichka where, on every corner, groups of men and boys were selling amethysts and immense arrays of vividly-coloured rocks and stones in all shapes and sizes. I was glad that the boys were not my cycling companions: they cast all consideration of weight to the wind, staggering beneath huge boulders as they jumped out calling, 'Madame! Madame! Stop! You must buy very beautiful rock.'

'Ah, *bonjour, Monsieur*. Well, I appreciate the thought and, yes, you're right, your rocks are indeed *très belles*. But we're planning on getting up this mountain on our bikes and I fear, should we relieve you of one of your fine specimens, we would be rolling back to Marrakesh a trifle faster than we had planned.'

Our stone touts did not accept this reasonable explanation as a resounding 'no!' and they continued to force their burdensome wares upon us.

'Anyway,' I added, 'apart from the weight factor, we have no room to put a lump of rock that size.'

'No problem.' (In any language, those two universal words mean you are sunk.) The boy struggled to raise the rejected boulder above his head, with the strength of a Berber Goliath, and then deliberately let it crash to the ground with crystal-shattering force. He then stooped to pick up a sparkling, splintered fragment and proudly passed me a glinting jewel.

'Please now no problem for bicycle. But you pay for damage to rock — yes?'

Stopping for one of many breathers on the long haul up, I looked across the pink valley to a small mud-and-stone village clinging tenaciously to the mountainside and saw a crocodile of self-propelled haystacks gingerly edging their way along a precipitous and dangerous path. Then I realized that they were not only walking but singing. What did this mean? The answer appeared round the bend where we were confronted by a gathering of yattering and spindly old women in colourful garb, each bent double beneath impossible loads of hay. As we stopped to congratulate these strong, sinewy figures on their remarkable hay-carrying capacities, more appeared over the brow of a shale path. Even on such foot-slipping terrain and buried beneath such monstrous loads, these ancient, weathered women skipped a sprightly step up the steep mountainside as sure-footed as the locally acclaimed tree-climbing goats we were soon to meet.

Down the sinuously-ribboned mountain road we swooped and swerved, past dribbly-nosed children crying, '*Monsieur! Monsieur!*' (I think they were addressing Mel, who was often mistaken for my husband). '*Cigarette? Un dirham? Un stylo?*' Down we went, past a river where women washed their clothes, draping them on the ground to dry so that the land turned into a big colourful patchwork, and down into cowboy country full of huge, weird, craggy rocks. Ait Benhaddou, once an important post on the road to Marrakesh, is now famous as Morocco's Hollywood because of its burgeoning film industry. The villagers do not let you forget for a moment that *Jesus of*

Nazareth and *Lawrence of Arabia* were filmed here.

In Ouarzazate a guide came up to me and said, 'Goodbye. I may not have been to English but I speak England very good.' That is all I remember about the place — oh, and the fact that Mel lost her swimming costume (she was forever losing and searching for things in the chaos of her bags; 'Know your panniers,' I said, but she never did) and a pair of freshly laundered knickers from our makeshift hotel window washing-line. They landed with panache on a turban in the street below and the unsuspecting wearer continued walking down the street with a pair of M&S polka-dotted briefs on his head.

Leaving Ouarzazate, we encountered a podgy, pink-fleshed man in shimmering, slinky yellow shorts. He was riding a small-wheeled folder.

'Hi there!' he said. 'I'm not really cycling anywhere — just pottering.'

As well as a potterer, he was also a pilot sent by the American government on a fact-finding mission to eliminate locusts. There had been an invasion of these giant insects, he said, causing devastation by eating all the crops from here to Algeria.

'Go easy,' he warned as we parted. 'They're coming your way.'

From the fairy-castle mountains of the Anti Atlas, we plunged into the Draa Valley — nearly a hundred miles long with date-palmed oases flanked by turreted pink kasbahs and ksour. Long ago these towered and crenellated fortresses, built by feudal families, had formed a series of city palaces and mansions from which an empire was ruled but today, although still impressive, they are crumbling into the dark red mud-clay pisé from which they were built.

We had left behind all major traffic. Apart from the occasional camel, cart or truck, we were quite alone until we reached the small, dusty town of Agdz. We arrived in the midst of a freak whirlwind that swirled across the square. After much searching, we were offered the roof of a rowdy café to bed down on for the night, but the owner insisted that we must first register with the gendarmerie on the edge of town.

Off we trudged, worn out, despondent and hungry. We managed to purchase a stale loaf of bread on the way and it had to suffice as our supper. At the police station we were directed by an armed minion into the Inspector's office, where we were treated with a mixture of suspicion and disbelief. We swayed wearily in front of him in our dusty cycling clothes, concerned to get this bureaucratic charade over and done with as quickly as possible so that we could eat our bread and go to sleep.

'*Bonsoir, Monsieur,*' I said. 'We've come to register before we go to bed.'

We handed him our passports and Mel, as usual, drew attention to my photograph (I looked as though I had a haystack on my head).

'Mademoiselle Worzel Gummidge,' she announced in well-worn form.

The Inspector was not amused and demanded we give him a chronological account of our every move in Morocco so far. When we had finished, he told us that what we had done and what we were about to do were impossible.

'Why you lie to me?' he growled. 'You are I see much problem.'

'No, no, no,' I said, too tired to be concerned with his outburst, 'we travel on bicycles because we like cycling. And we also like sleep. So if you could just sign our form we'll leave you in peace.'

'No!' he shouted. 'You go nowhere.' Slapping our passports on to his desk, he added, 'And passports I keep.'

Oh dear. Thoughts of slumber were fast sliding away. We had trouble on our hands and for nearly two hours we tried to answer calmly a string of nonsensical questions. 'Yes, I have two brothers,' 'No, I'm not married,' 'Iron Lady? Yes, still Prime Minister,' 'No, I know more about bicycles than politics,' 'Yes, in England very many fish 'n' chips . . .'

Finally, with tried patience, we had had enough. Hunger and fatigue made us jump to our feet and act in an exaggerated and cock-eyed manner. We invited Monsieur to partake in a little breaking of bread before going to introduce ourselves to Gendarme Junior, who stood to attention at the back of the room. We complimented him on his dashing hairstyle and then proceeded to make conversation with a map on the wall.

Playing the fool did the trick. The Inspector was so flabbergasted that he made no attempt to stop us when we casually swept our passports off his desk and ran out into the night, back to the safety of our sleeping-bags.

At dawn we slipped away and headed for Zagora on the edge of the Sahara and the supposedly wondrous land of the Tuaregs — the Blue Men of the desert. These tall, elegant, light-skinned desert warriors wrap themselves from tip to toe in indigo-dyed robes, however hot it might be. It is said that the men's faces remain veiled even in sleep, to guard against evil spirits which might otherwise enter through their mouths. The dye from the robes rubs off and becomes ingrained in their skin, giving them a blue sheen. The Tuaregs are pure-blooded Berbers and a remote and mystical race to Arabs as well as to Europeans; townspeople speak of them in wonder, in fear and usually with much ignorance.

The journey to Zagora was not without incident. We encountered swirling whirlwinds, sandstorms that entombed us in an insipid sickly-grey world of hot stinging sands, and the prophesied clouds of locusts. Slinky Yellow Shorts had been right: they were huge and horrible and they were everywhere. The road disappeared beneath their inert forms; their stick-like bodies cracked and snapped under our wheels. Those which were airborne flapped and crashed and collided with our faces and bodies, causing a pile-up when they blinded us — as did the sandstorm which blew with relentless ferocity all the way to Zagora.

In this desolate and unremarkable town, the wind sent lorry-loads of sand hurtling in great clouds between the buildings with a stinging savageness. Simply trying to cross the street was treacherous and painful as we blundered blindly through the swooshing plumes. The locals, though, were equipped for the elements and ventured out barely recognizable as anything other than bundles of protective fabric.

The sand got everywhere. My teeth continually gritted on grainy mouthfuls and when I blew my nose there was enough sand to make a sandcastle. The only time to go out was at the crack of dawn when, for a brief lull, all was quiet and clear and still. Then a teasing breath of wind would brush gently against your cheek; a slight ruffle through the hair and a light rustle through the rippling leaves of a palm tree would hint a warning. In the distance, from across the desert plains, a sudden great wall of murky grey sand would come bowling across the land, blocking out the sun and darkening your world within seconds as it hit you and hurt you and bent you double like the palm trees until you cursed the powers that be.

The weather imprisoned us in our hotel. In our room, everything was caked in sand — even the water that trickled out of the tap was gritty and grey. Downstairs in the dark café we spent hours working on diaries, writing letters, playing chess or reading. It was here that we met Adu, a teacher, whom we quickly judged to be trustworthy. He told us to be wary of the Arabic guides: they were not all that they claimed to be. We said we had already learnt that from experience.

Adu was impressively intelligent and kept lapsing into fluent and erudite prose from Shakespeare, Hardy and Keats — we were way out of our depths. He was also an 'angry young man', as he put it, and not happy with Moroccan life.

'My people are far too crooked and idle for my liking,' he said. 'I long to visit England so I can work hard like the English people do.' Gallivanting around on bicycles, we hardly matched his English ideal.

'I teach for twenty-four hours a week,' he told us, 'which by Moroccan standards is hard work. Here we do not know the proper meaning of work. Things happen, but slowly and only when the time is found which, in Morocco, is rare. For many people the days just pass in a repetitive haze in which little gets done.'

'How easy is it for you to go to England?' I asked.

'To travel is very difficult. The authorities make it very hard to obtain a passport and you need much money. So instead I lose myself in my English books. *Imshallah!* Now I must go to study. I wish you good luck.'

Before he went, he left us with a mind-teaser.

'English,' he said, with a serious, querying look, 'is it the power of language or the language of power?'

People told us that Zagora had had no rain for seven years. However, we brought a taster of British weather with us: not long after our arrival a splattering of fat, wet drops fell from the sky. Everyone rushed into the streets and fell to their knees, giving thanks to Allah. But Allah was only playing cruel tricks. The rain soon dwindled to nothing.

Zagora was famous for being a starting point for a fifty-two-day camel trek to Timbuktu and therefore had an abundance of these one-humped creatures. I suppose it was inevitable that offers fired from every direction finally persuaded us temporarily to swop our two-wheeled transport for their four-legged kind. None of the blue-clad nomads could seem to understand that weaving among Oxford Street's double-decker buses and taxis on one of these ungainly beasts would be far from practical. The prospect of having my furry friend 'heel-clamped' seemed just a little daft.

We took a couple of these spine-jarring creatures for a quick spin in the desert, and were pitched back and forth in the rocky gait that is peculiar to camels. Along the way we spotted the romantically Arabian sight of a caravan, the camels' heads silhouetted over the rise of the dunes like a row of lurching teapot spouts.

Exchanging our haughty and irascible conveyances for our more familiar and smoother-riding bicycles, we embarked upon the final assault into the desert fringes of the Sahara. Rumour had it that, due to a border dispute with neighbouring Algeria, it was essential for foreigners to acquire authorization from the Garde Militaire in Zagora before setting out. From there we would be issued with a local police-approved guide, which would make travelling any further by bike virtually impossible. As it was a frictional military zone, anyone found wandering where they should not ran a high risk of being shot.

The morning of our departure saw us ready and rearing to go at dawn, before the winds and the police had risen. As there was no one around, we decided to start off and see how we progressed — with a white sock at the ready in case we encountered an undesirable situation and saw fit to surrender. Crossing the barren and arid beauty of the desert, which stretched away for thousands of miles to the savannahs and forests of West Africa, we soon spotted the sculptured sand-dunes that we had long sought. We cross-countried through a cloud of locusts until we reached them. As we had not seen a living soul for hours, we felt it safe to remove our shorts so that we could cool down. Then we romped and rolled gleefully among the dunes like a couple of five-year-olds on a day at the beach.

As we collapsed on the sand in happy exhaustion, the silence was suddenly broken by a strange, unidentifiable squawking call. Peering dubiously over a dune, we came face to face with a haggard old hunchbacked woman who was herding a bunch of moth-eaten goats. I suppose the sight of two half-clad, fair-haired females with bicycles must have alarmed her and she burst into a shrill native war-cry. It seemed to be just her way of introducing herself and she promptly mellowed once she had got that little outburst out of her system. Sitting down beside us, she opened her tattered grey sack and gave us a handful of freshly plucked dates.

Back in Zagora, we let our guard slip and fell easy prey to a stalking Berber. We were programmed for mint tea and couscous and were invited back to his home, where we met all eighteen members of the immediate family. The girls were mesmerized by our fair hair and crowded round us eagerly, asking permission to stroke it. When the boys jumped on the bandwagon, we put our foot down. Then one of them who could speak English told us of a curious Berber belief. We were *Rumi*, they said — a corruption meaning 'foreigner'. If a Berber woman is searching for a husband and sees a monkey or a Christian, she must avoid intercourse that night in case her offspring resemble either.

Another Berber custom was for the women to henna their hands and feet in beautifully intricate patterns of leaves, trees, moons and birds. One of the girls offered to dye our hands. I was reluctant, wondering whether the process involved any needles (like tattooing), but Mel was all for it and so, playing safe, I let her be the guinea-pig.

The girl turned out to be a mere apprentice and was using Mel's hands for practice. I watched bemused as Mel underwent the operation, which was not quite the delicate one we had been led to expect. Swirls and splodges were applied with a recycled toothpick and then the finishing process entailed half-baking her hands in a clay oven (along with the Berber bread). The finished product looked disastrous. I found the whole affair highly amusing until I realized that neither Mel nor the daughter would let me escape similar treatment.

Things only got worse after we had both been dyed and baked. Big Mama took great delight in dressing us up in native costume and we resembled two dowdy dumplings. She then commanded her two eligible sons to lead us up the garden path, both literally and metaphorically. The idea was to show us their exotic fruit garden — which was not just out back, as we had been led to believe, but a good twenty-minute hike across the oasis. In our frumpy outfits we were given a guided tour of their prized date palms and pomegranate plants before coming to rest in the shade of an almond tree. Here Hassan announced that their nuts worked wonders for a man's virility — and the amount they consumed prompted a preposterous proposal of marriage. 'Time to get going,' we said and made a hasty dash for our bicycles.

*

Instead of retracing our tracks back to Ouarzazate, we opted to take an unrecommended piste (dirt track) towards Tazenakht and nearly came unstuck. Due to the abundance of rocks and sinking sand, we travelled very slowly — averaging an alarming two mph — and moved laboriously out into sun-desiccated scrub desert. Villages marked on the map, visualized in my heat-dazed mind as minor metropolises, failed to materialize and our water supply went down to crisis level.

Although apprehensive about our predicament I was, in typically irresponsible fashion, rather enjoying myself and revelled in the excitement of not quite knowing what would happen next. Meanwhile Mel, peeved at my Enid Blyton *Famous Five* attitude, said it was obvious what would happen next: we would dehydrate, drop to our knees and die.

'Don't be so dramatic, you silly cow,' I said, with parched mouth and feeling decidedly giddy. 'We've got a good couple of hours' life in us yet.'

Mel hit me after that. She was always hitting me.

She was right, though. We did almost die but, just as the future looked as if it would be no more, a mirage appeared out of the shimmering heat and took the form of a turbaned Berber carrying a basketful of watermelon. A true life-saver! He very kindly cut us a hefty hunk of revitalizing fruit which safely saw us to the first signs of civilization.

For the second time we tackled the Atlas range, only in a different place. People were constantly warning us about the wild wolves and bandits that lurked in the mountains but, rather disappointingly, we saw no signs of either. Had we been travelling in North Africa before the arrival of the Romans, there would have been more than bandits and wolves to avoid. In those days, lions and elephants had been plentiful in the area and their popularity in Rome's circuses and coliseums played a major factor in their extinction.

However, we did come across the famous tree-climbing goats. Owing to a lack of vegetation on the ground, these capricious creatures have adapted to shimmying up the trees, where they skip daintily from branch to branch as they browse the leaves. No doubt they will in due course sprout wings and take to the skies.

The Tizi n'Test pass was hot and hard work but there were plenty of refreshing streams where we made frequent stops to cool off in ice-cold cascades that came gushing down from the mountainside. At one of these stops a small crowd of shepherds had gathered. A scurrilous youth, whose shifty eyes nested in sallow hollows, demanded a donation of dirhams for drinking 'their' water. We gave him a carrot instead.

At the top the view stretched away for mile upon mile of hazy colour. As we posed for the inevitable snapshots, a biblical character with ancient face and long, straggly beard appeared. He beckoned us to follow him behind a rock, where a cloud of smoke was rising. Dutifully we followed, half expecting to find the Burning Bush. Instead the withered old man had built a traditional oven, sunk into the ground, and from it he presented us with two steaming loaves of flat bread. He spoke no English but we all smiled and made sounds of appreciation as we sat on top of the mountain surrounded by peaks and plummeting views while we ate bread and communicated by drawing squiggles in the red sand. Then we began our descent.

We had been looking forward to staying at Hotel Idni, run by an eccentric Frenchwoman, Madame Gipolou. Apparently there were lamps and bidets in each room but no electricity or water. Instead you were given a copious supply of candles and huge dinners fresh from her cottage farmhouse below. There were also no set prices: you paid what Madame reckoned you could afford—and we thought we would be on to a good thing, turning up on bicycles. Unfortunately we learnt on our arrival at Idni that Madame was now *morte* and her hotel lay in ruins.

We stayed across the road in a bar where we discovered a pile of human excrement under the bed. There was no running water or electricity here either but we were offered the use of the owner's private *hamman*, a Turkish-style steam bath. We crawled through a tiny hole into a dark, cramped little cave heated by burning coals. Once inside we found only a bucket and half a candle and, as there were no instructions, we were unsure what to do next. The café owner intermittently rapped on the door, possibly to see if we were still alive or possibly because he had other ideas. Either way, trapped in the steamy gloom, we found the whole escapade nerve-racking and, as usual whenever danger loomed, we burst into a fit of unproductive titterings. Finally, pulling ourselves together, we aborted the whole mission and went to bed.

That night I dreamt I was a flying carrot and had a collision with a goat in the Hyde Park underpass. I woke myself and Mel by shouting: 'There's a lot of people down there!'

Heading back to Marrakesh, we stopped for lunch at Asni and found ourselves back on the heavy-duty tourist trail again — back to hordes of hustlers. As we sat down to a bowl of *harira* within sight of the snow-capped Mount Toubkal, the highest mountain in North Africa, we were pestered by a group of ogling Arabs who offered us sums of money in return for our 'favours'. We were on the point of giving them a sample of karate when an elder butted in, dispersing our tormentors. He apologized for their behaviour, explaining that

they were under the influence of hash. Throughout our travels, we noticed it was common practice for Moroccans to offer excuses of every kind in order to justify the actions of others.

We did not linger for long in Marrakesh due to an influx of pink coach-tourists. We had a last scout around the dark, fierce but captivating labyrinth of souks before heading north.

Spain again. We headed for Tarifa, mainland Europe's most southerly point, and the place to be seen if windsurfing is your sport. More fun than watching these fluorescent-clad fashion followers was meeting Sid and Ethel, a retired couple from Clacton-on-Sea. Ethel had a gammy leg and Sid had a knotted hanky on his head and they both missed *Coronation Street* terribly. We were invited back to their caravan for a cup of PG Tips, some Rich Tea biscuits and a read of the *Sun*.

'When I was a lad,' said Sid, 'I used to do a bit of cycling myself. Raced on a ten-pound Curly Hetchins. She were a beaut, you know. I was hot stuff, eh Ethel?'

'I didn't know you then, dear,' said Ethel, wiping Rich Tea crumbs from her lips.

Sid did not seem to hear and, slapping legs that resembled knobbly sticks of celery, said, 'Made of muscle — that was me. Me and my mate Charlie, used to dance on them pedals.'

But his life was no longer bicycles. His latest acquisition was a Canon movie camera and he said that he had just finished filming the campsite toilet blocks and a statue of a dead dog.

'Alternative photography — that's us, isn't it, Ethel?'

Ethel did not appear to be listening. 'Like another cup of tea, dear?' she asked.

Sitting on the neatly mown grass outside the Prado Museum in Madrid (we felt we had better have a dose of cultural enlightenment at some stage of our tour), we became a prime target for a couple of thieves. A Spanish youth approached with an opened map of the city and asked us for directions. I thought it odd that a Spanish speaker should approach a foreigner, but naively felt it right to try to help — after all, we had constantly asked strangers for directions during the last four months. As Mel struggled to make herself understood, however, I suddenly saw out of the corner of my eye that my handlebar-bag (containing valuables) was scooting off across the grass behind me. It took a moment to appreciate what was happening. My immediate reaction was to exclaim: 'Oh, look! That boy's got my bag! Oh! And he's got yours too, Mel.'

Then, not before time, it struck me that he was, in a very amateurish way, stealing our bags. Having survived the notoriously high theft rate of Morocco, we were not prepared to let these two whippersnappers vanish with all our valuables at this stage. We gave chase, caught them and succeeded in delivering a stinging blow. In the confusing kerfuffle, the boy dropped our bags and disappeared into the crowds.

Back outside the Prado a fellow countryman approached us. He had sat opposite us and impassively watched the whole affair.

'Oldest trick in the book,' he declared condescendingly, before strutting away.

As a result of that near theft, we took certain precautions against a repeat. One of these was to wrap our bagstraps round our chairlegs in cafés, which often resulted in us forgetfully tripping over them and landing in undignified sprawls on neighbouring tables.

It was impossible to travel in Spain and remain impervious to the country's national sport, bullfighting. In Britain, where it is widely condemned and little understood, it is easy to imagine that bullfighting persists only in one or two big cities where foreign tourists can be lured to join a steadfast minority of Spaniards to watch a bloody ritual that has no place in modern cosmopolitan Spain. In fact, bullfighting is more popular than ever in Spain and is actively supported by the government and by the royal family. King Juan Carlos is an avid fan and he has said that his only regret about being king is that it leaves him with less time to go to the bulls.

Bullfighting is more a spectacle than a sport. '*Matador*' means 'killer' and the bulls are always killed — cruelly and painfully. There is nothing sporting about that. For the Spaniards, bullfighting is a long-standing tradition and is regarded as folk art; it is followed by intellectuals because it is a part of Spanish culture. It is also fashionable, and rich 'yuppies' in Madrid will pay up to £750 on the black market for the most expensive ringside seats.

Typically British, both Mel and I abhorred the idea of the magnificent bulls being slaughtered with such cruel and unjust ridicule. However, as all we knew about it was that the bull always ended up dead, it did not seem fair to condemn it without knowing more about what was really involved. We decided to experience a bullfight for ourselves.

In Spain, bulls and references to bulls are everywhere. We cycled past the purple-and-yellow flowering meadows where bulls — the fighters-to-be — dozed and dreamed and ruminated lazily in the hot sunshine. We passed small mountain villages where small boys — matadors-to-be — played in the street, one with his index fingers poking over the top of his head to mimic a bull's horns and charging head down, bull-fashion, towards his friend who skilfully manoeuvred his mother's tablecloth as a true matador would his flamboyant crimson cape. In smoky bars and restaurants, crowds would gather on stools around the televisions which broadcast *corridas*; posters adorned walls, trees, shops and telegraph poles announcing forthcoming fights. Every now and then we would come across a town with its shop-fronts temporarily boarded up as bulls were released to run wild and tormented through the streets, stampeding after the daring inhabitants who chose to run in a festival of fearsome fun.

In the thick heat of evening, we went one Sunday to Madrid's Plaza de Toros to see and judge a bullfight for ourselves. We had done a little research on the subject, learning something from the locals and reading a book on the theory and Hemingway's excellent *Death in the Afternoon*.

There were two choices of seat: *Sol y Sombra* (sun and shade). The *Sol* seats were cheaper and uncomfortably hotter than the cool, more comfortable *Sombra* ones. We took our places and, like everyone else on the sunny side, sat in hats and fanned ourselves as we waited. A demure woman beside me had made her own hat from a newspaper rolled up like a giant dunce's cap. In front of us, an Australian girl with fingernails like witch's claws was far more intent on painstakingly removing her split-ends than observing the events in the arena.

Then the first bull stormed into the ring — half a ton of Andalusian fighting machine. The matador's *cuadrilla* stepped from behind their hideaways and used their wide magenta capes to tease and 'play' the confused, angry beast. Then the *picadores* entered, riding on thick-padded and blindfolded horses, waiting to be charged so that they could pierce the bull's bulging neck muscles with their lances to weaken it. The first spear ripped gruesomely into the flesh, making me squirm in my seat. Then the *banderilleros* ran across the raging beast's path, avoiding its dagger-like horns by inches, and plunged barbed, beribboned, steel-tipped darts into its massive, heaving shoulders. The bull tried furiously to shake them off but if the *banderilleros* had aimed accurately, these 'weapons' would remain embedded in its shoulders until its death.

And then came the matador — the killer who performed his ballet of death with the bull, taunting it with his red cape, drawing it close to his body as the animal charged while he deftly turned it back and forth, this way and that, to the crescendos of the exultant crowd: '¡Olé! ... ¡Olé! ... ¡Olé!' Blood gushed thick and sticky and dark down the powerful, solid, sweaty, steaming flanks and shoulders of the bull and it was weakening fast. The matador waited for his moment and then, standing rigid straight in front of the bull's bowed head, he raised the sun-dazzling sword and pointed it dramatically at his rival. The crowd edged forwards on their seats and held their breath. The end was near.

Suddenly the bull found a last frenzied surge of energy and

blundered bravely at the matador who, with awesome speed, plunged the sword deep between the creature's shoulders and down towards its heart.

The bull jumped with a shudder, spun around crazily, stagger-charged again, veered away, but did not drop. With the sword still thrust into its neck, it whirled frantically, mad-eyed, frothing at the mouth, the blood gushing, brave and dazed and exhausted. Then it collapsed to its knees, jerking its head back, still brave, still proud and refusing to die. This was no clean kill.

At last an official ran in to finish it off. The fight for life and death was finally over. Cheers and whistles erupted from the crowd. Thousands of handkerchiefs waved, handbags and hats were tossed into the ring in appreciation. The matador proudly paraded around the ring, holding aloft the bull's bloodied, severed ear as a reward for his courage, and flinging back the hats and bags to the ecstatic crowd, who revered possessions that had been touched by the great matador himself. The *pica-dores* returned to the ring on horseback, attached a rope to the bulk of the bull and unceremoniously dragged it away across the blood-spattered sand. Another five magnificent bulls had yet to follow the fate of the first.

As we crowded out of the ring, we passed the abattoir where the fresh carcasses, already skinned, hung from huge hooks in the dark interior. On the slimy, wet floor lay the heads of the six great bulls.

The one chance that the bulls have to get their own back is in the *encierro* — the running of the bulls. In villages and towns all over Basque Spain, fiestas are staged where *vaquillas* (wild young cows) run freely through the streets, chasing the locals who want to prove their bravery. The king of all *encierros* is the annual Fiesta of San Fermín at Pamplona, popularised for non-Spaniards by the novel *The Sun Also Rises*, in which Hemingway recommended the event as 'a damned fine show'.

Pushing hard on the pedals, Mel and I made it in time to join in the festivities. Traditionally the *encierro* starts at seven in the morning of the seventh day of the seventh month. By 6AM the town was alive. Spectators lined the route from the Plaza Santo Domingo to the bullring itself, climbing up trees, lamp-posts, walls, fences and rooftops, or leaning out of windows, well out of harm's way. Audacious folk, dressed mainly in white with red armbands and bandannas and clutching rolled-up newspapers, assembled in the boarded-off route, nervously awaiting the crack of the rocket which signalled the release of the bulls. The tension mounted as the deadline approached; the runners checked their watches and swore allegiance to San Fermín at a candlelit shrine. Then the rocket exploded. For an eerie moment there was a deathly silence which hung like bated breath over the whole of Pamplona.

Scared by the blast, the bulls panicked and came stampeding out of the Rochapea corral by the river towards the wall of terrified runners, many of whom were daring American and Antipodean tourists. For the next two minutes it was total mayhem. Spectators screamed and cheered as the mass of people pounded up the boarded route towards the bullring, stumbling over each other, frantic either to reach the ring or to scramble madly out of the way of potential death. The runners dived into doorways, clambered on to window ledges or jumped on to hoardings to be hauled over by a multitude of eager spectators' hands dangling down to help them. Others were not so lucky: they lost their foothold and fell in tangles among the cauldron of whirling, purling, frightened bulls to be gouged or trampled underhoof. The animals burst into the bullring where they were recaptured, their chance of revenge swiftly over because that afternoon they would die in a bull-fight.

And what was the tally of their revenge? Later we learnt that they had inflicted scores of serious wounds and taken the life of one American tourist.

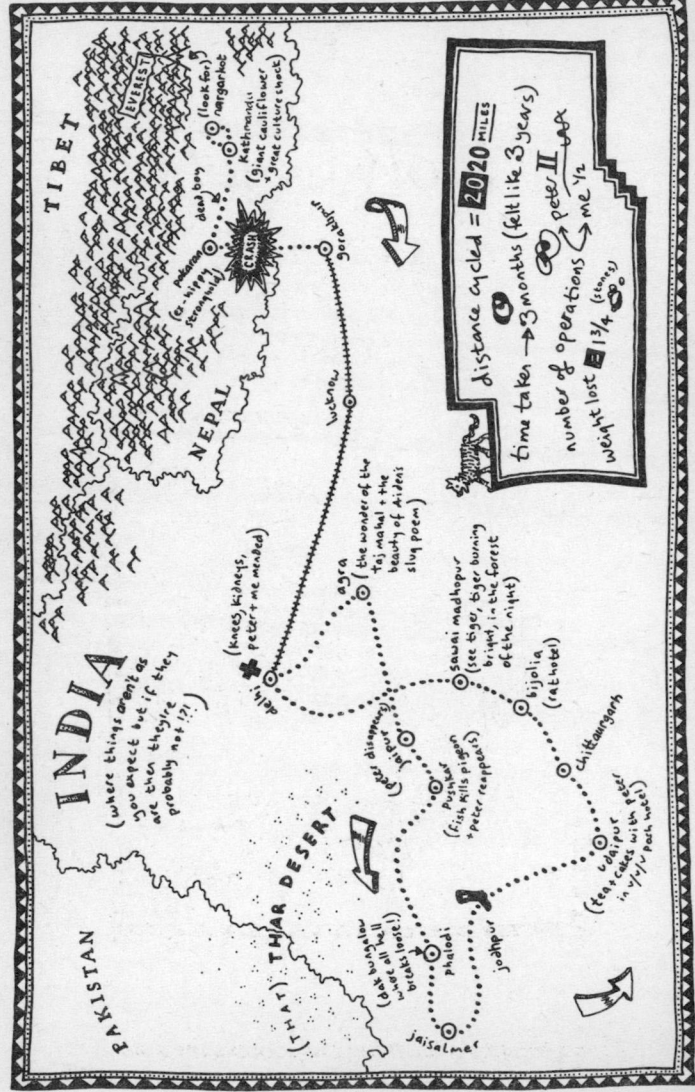

5

Holy Cow!

IN INDIA

'Travel broadens the mind and loosens the bowels.'
ANONYMOUS

The first international flight arrived in Kathmandu only a year before man walked on the moon. At that time a mere handful of tourists a day visited Nepal but, when I landed on the rooftop of the world some quarter of a century later, I was among a daily influx of 700. Today, tourism has grown to surpass the export of Gurkha soldiers as Nepal's largest industry.

At Kathmandu airport, I was expecting to be thrown into an explosion of confused sound and colour. The crowds and the chaos were there but, strangely, not the noise. Everything seemed curiously muffled. I thought: that's funny. Perhaps the air pressure had affected my eardrums or maybe my senses were dulled after a long and gruelling flight on Pakistan Airlines. Perplexed and pondering, I put a finger in my ear and there I found the answer. Lodged firmly within was a broken-off foam earpiece from one of the airline's headsets. I extricated the offending article and the tumultuous sounds of Kathmandu airport burst forth.

My next task was to find my bicycle. The archaic conveyor belt was broken (had it ever worked?), so I hoped that my boxed bike lay somewhere on the tractor-drawn cart that was spluttering towards the terminal with a pile of luggage almost as high as Everest. Several unfortunate packs were lost on the way: one case exploded open on impact with the ground and scattered its contents all over the runway, much to the delight of a couple of scraggy men with dark, leathery bare feet and wearing what seemed to be shabby, grime-stained nightshirts. These two airport officials pounced upon the Western items with worrying glee, making no attempt to replace them.

Finally the tractor shed its load of luggage on to the tarmac with as much panache as a dumper truck. The crash made me cringe as I visualized bent derailleurs and buckled wheels. Tourists swarmed upon the mound to extricate their possessions but I opted to watch and wait, feeling I stood little chance of retrieving my package (twice the size of me) by diving among the elbow-thrusting masses.

The frenzy of aggravated activity diminished, the crowds

dispersed, the luggage dissolved and my suspicions were confirmed. My bike was not there. Feeling a bit sick, I stared forlornly at the emptied patch of tarmac, desperately hoping that my eyes (like my ears) had been playing a nasty trick on me.

I felt a tap on my shoulder and turned to confront a wide-grinning porter with a battered bike box on his head.

'Please Madame bicycle?' he said and deposited it with a rough thud at my feet. Mount and owner were joyously reunited . . . but not yet free.

Customs men with dark, weathered faces aggressively ripped apart the cardboard and peered inquisitively inside. Eager hands with dirty fingernails wrestled with an assortment of camping equipment and bike bits, spilling the contents into a sea of disarray on the floor around me. I watched helplessly as my possessions were laboriously probed and prodded. The hands grappled from every direction, excitedly unwrapping my carefully packaged belongings as if it was Christmas and making it impossible for me to keep an eye on everything. Bits were taken aside, held aloft in front of inquisitive faces, inspected, scrutinized. In the confusion I lost two water-bottles, a T-shirt and a vegetable peeler. Luckily most things were identified and passed off as harmless but one small package had them stumped.

'This explain is what?' they demanded.

'It's a family pack of Cadbury Cream Eggs,' I replied.

'Egg? Why you egg? You think Nepal no egg?'

'I'm sure Nepal has lots of lovely eggs but I'm not sure about chocolate ones. They're for my friend who has a soft spot for them.'

With that I whipped up my belongings and whisked myself away into the crowd. Eventually, outside in the dark, I assembled my bike surrounded by a hundred inquisitive eyes.

So it was that I found myself thrown into the thick of chaotic Kathmandu, a place more renowned these days for its astronomic array of food than for the liberal attitudes towards the smoking of dried vegetable matter which had made it famous as a hippy Mecca in the early seventies. Any culinary taste could now be catered for by places like the Yin & Yang restaurant, Aunt Jane's Wholesome American Fare, The Lunch Box, Pie Alley and Mom's Health Food, serving such tantalizing delights as 'spagetty bollynose', King Birendra Peetza, hash browns with Buffburgers (water buffalo is the usual substitute for beef, which Hindus cannot eat) or 'Apple Pie and Custurd'. So much for exotic and evocative Asian dishes.

For two weeks I stayed at the Cosy Corner Lodge for seventy pence a night. It was anything but cosy with its icy showers and freezing winter winds howling off the Himalayas, whistling under the door and blasting through the broken window. I dubbed it Chilly Corner.

Being on bikes with big ideas appeared to be the current craze. Kathmandu was full of a curious assortment of cyclists, most of whom appeared to be lodging at the Chilly Corner. For a start I was sharing my room with Peter, which was intentional — I had come to Nepal to meet this Geordie from Hartlepool who was on a quick two-and-a-half-year cycling stint from the UK to Oz. Then there was Steve, a Lamborghini salesman from London who, deciding he had sold one car too many, bought a mountain bike and furiously cycled to Nepal in six months, terrorizing inquisitive Indians with his bullwhip along the way. Having reached his goal, he sold the bike and bought a hideously huge lampshade and a ticket for the first flight home.

Next door there were three Frenchmen running from Paris to China with a couple of bicycles between them. Each would run a marathon a day while the other two cycled ahead.

'Often,' they said, 'cars they come alongside when we ride the bicycle and the driver he leans out of the window and is pointing and shouting back down the road and he says, "Hey! Your friend, he lose his bicycle. He is running to catch you!"'

Then there was John Tobbit, a welder from Wolverhampton who had spent three years cycling around the world. He was disillusioned at how easy it had been: in all that time the only mishap to befall him was when he knocked himself out cold in the middle of the Australian desert with a back-firing bicycle pump when pumping up his tyre.

The narrow, twisting streets of Kathmandu were a hive of activity, bustling with a kaleidoscope of colourful fruit sellers, saffron-robed Buddhists, three-wheeled motorized and rasping rickshaws, manic motorbikes, bullock-carts, sacred cows, clanging bicycles, legless beggars scooting around on home-made trolleys, and crazed taxi-drivers who ploughed through this mayhem with hand on horn. When it rained, the dusty, unpaved streets became quagmires. Snuffling pigs and mangy dogs with open sores would nose and pick through heaps of stinking rubbish along with ragged urchins. The place was strewn with fat, bedraggled rats.

I followed a street which suddenly opened into a ramshackle courtyard full of intricate statues of gods and erotic carvings. Vendors on dirty mats spread over the cobbles were selling giant cauliflowers and white radishes two feet long. Beside them a dead dog rotted in the gutter but no one seemed to notice the stomach-churning smell. Across the way were prayer wheels, puppets and papier mâché masks, Gurkha knives, daggers, jewellery and 'yackets' — warm jackets made from yak wool. The wideopen smiles of the hawkers mingled with the smoke and smell of wood fires, incense, jasmine, sandalwood and cow dung.

Wildly painted bicycle rickshaws with colourful awnings and dangling tassles swarmed everywhere like a frenzied army of worker ants.

'Hello rickshaw!' shouted the riders. 'Yes please you take very nice best rickshaw in all world.'

'Thank you,' I would say, 'very nice rickshaw but I've got my own bicycle.'

'No problem take bicycle,' they would say, 'bicycle fit rickshaw easy.'

'But if I put my bicycle on your bicycle it rather defeats the object of me having a bicycle.'

'No problem,' they would say again but I don't think they quite followed. They retreated to more familiar ground. 'You want cheap hotel? Change money — very best rate?' and then, in lowered tones, 'Hash — you want hash? Heroin — brown sugar, I have good brown sugar.'

Sitting in the Two Faces restaurant with Peter over a breakfast of 'banana pooridge, fruit mewsli and big potty jasmine tea', I looked out across the street and saw an American girl having a fit on a second-storey balcony. Hanging from the balcony was a fancily painted sign declaring:

VERY NICE INDEED TRADITIONAL
INDIAN MASSAGE. WE AIM TO
RELAX BODY AND CLEAR MINDS.

The girl, clad in a T-shirt and the briefest of briefs, looked far from relaxed and was screaming her head off in apoplectic abuse at some poor little Nepali man cowering in the doorway. Then she stormed back inside and re-emerged with a contraption that looked like a combination of electric-bar heater, hydraulic foot-pump and rocket launcher. I think she was complaining about it not working. Working or not, it certainly was not going to do much after she had finished with it. Raising it above her head, she let out an exaggerated scream and hurled it over the balcony, heedless of the street-teeming masses below, and narrowly missed decapitating a Holy Cow.

'Holy Cow!' I said. 'What's got into her?'

I suspected 'brown sugar' might be to blame — they say it can do strange things. Deciding the case needed investigation, I quickly downed the rest of my 'potty tea' and then set off across the street and up to the second floor. Topped in a traditional topi stood the little man, still looking a little sheepish.

'Hello — *Namaste*,' I said, 'I've come for your "very nice indeed" massage.'

'No massage,' he said, looking depressed.

Feeling sorry for him, I said reassuringly, 'Don't worry, I promise I won't throw anything of yours over the balcony.'

'That girl,' he blurted out, 'she break my heat.'

I did not know if he meant 'heart' or 'heater'. I trod cautiously.

'Why did she break it?' I asked, beginning to sound like a radio help-line counsellor.

'She say your heat no work was very cold and get much angry.'

'And did it work?'

'No, heat no work.'

'Then she didn't break it, she only damaged it further. But I understand, it was rash behaviour and must have been very upsetting for you to have your heater thrown over the balcony — even if it was broken.'

'Heat no work,' he repeated in mesmerized melancholy, 'now no customer.'

Magnanimously (and perhaps a little foolishly) I said: 'Don't fret. I'm a customer and I'd love a massage — even if it is freezing.'

And freezing it was. As I lay flat on the floor, shivering on a suspiciously stained towel, I thought: what am I doing? But at least I knew that Peter was across the road in the Two Faces, closely monitoring my movements. He had been instructed to get over here quick if I failed to resurface.

A wintry wind whistled through the gaping gaps of the window. Attention diverted from his 'no work heat', the little masseur had snapped out of his doomed gloom and was pummelling me painfully and almost too enthusiastically. Then he took hold of my toes and, with a sort of masochistic delight, seemed intent on yanking them from their sockets. I think he was taking out his frustration on me.

'Hey — easy!' I said, with my nose pressed to the floor. 'I would quite like to be able to walk after this.'

There was no stopping Topi Head. He was engrossed in his work and came seriously close to disjointing me several times. Then things became a little calmer and he covered me in lashings of sweet-smelling oil with bits of herbs floating in it. He had previously warmed the oil over a candlelit burner and I have to admit that it felt, as his sign advertised, 'very nice indeed'. Despite my feet remaining like lumps of ice, the rest of my body started to tingle in oil-sealed warmth.

When it was over he would accept no money.

'Don't be silly, Topi Head,' I said, 'you need to save up for a new heater.'

'No. You feel better, I feel better,' he replied and, placing his palms together, did a touching little bow and bid me good day.

For Western travellers, the favourite mealtime topic seemed to be the state of one's bowels. Diarrhoea, dysentry, Delhi Belly, Kathmandu Quickstep — call it what you will but nothing detracts from the fact that disease and illness run rife in Asia and it sounded as if it was almost impossible to travel in these countries without picking up something.

Referring briefly to the infamous effect that India can have on your insides, a wiry Welshman who had paid only a fleeting visit to the country told me, 'I passed through India almost as quickly as it passed through me.' I had never seen so many people being so sick. Cycling past slow-moving lorries or coaches piled with people proved to be quite hazardous, and on many occasions I narrowly missed being sprayed with vomit by an overhanging passenger. Many of the locals seemed to be constantly ill with hepatitis or something just as serious. With only one doctor for every 100,000 people, it was little wonder that the average Nepali did not live much beyond the age of forty.

Nor was it surprising that people became ill. The water supplies were full of parasitic wiggly things which made themselves at home in your intestines and flourished there; piles of human excrement or decaying dead dogs would lie next to food stalls (where food might be fried in week-old oil); malaria-carrying mosquitoes would whine menacingly, thirsty for blood. Rivers were used as drinking sources and places in which to wash clothes, bodies and elephants, to defecate, to fling dead animals and to cremate humans. When I rode up to the Bagmati river where women were washing or preparing food and children were splashing, no one seemed to notice the vultures tearing into the corpse of a bloated buffalo slowly drifting past.

For some, indulgence in Chang (a Tibetan brew) or the potent Nepalese rum caused them to feel off-colour and there was always a smattering of fuddle-headed people lurching around the streets. There were drunken stupors — and there were Buddhist stupas, the oldest of which was Swayambhu-nath, floating dreamily above Kathmandu in the early morning mists. We cycled up to this 2,000-year-old temple by way of a steep hill which had once been an island when the Kathmandu Valley had been a lake. All the way up, we were under the watchful eye of the Buddha adorning the huge, white dome.

After the human, animal and motorized maelstrom of the city, we were hoping for some peace up here — but it was not to be. Troupes of sour-mooded monkeys were shrieking and hissing and fighting. An amateur film crew was up there, too, filming a video for one of Nepal's pop-music bands, the members of which were prancing and gyrating in ridiculous garb and making the monkeys look positively sensible in comparison.

Beggars abounded. One boy was practically neckless where the horrendously scarred skin had been eaten away into a crevasse of withered wrinkles. I gave him some money, which would only encourage him to follow and pester tourists, but how could I walk past as though he did not exist? What was money to me when someone so stricken and so obviously in need continued to suffer? It felt awful to be one among a rich crowd of camera-carrying tourists, blessed with healthy limbs and good fortune, who had just come to 'see the temple', 'see the view', while beggars lingered with horrific deformities, withered faces, no money, no family, no friends; nothing. I felt wretched, guilty, helpless — and even worse to know that, once I had wandered among them taking my fill of temples and scenes and wonderful mountains to which they were blind, I would turn my back and leave them.

Peter and I took half a day's ride up into the mountains to Nargarkot. No matter how much I had read or heard, or how many pictures I had seen, nothing could have prepared me for the mind-blowing reality of coming face to face with the Himalayas (or, as those in the know say: Him-ah-lee-ers). Big just was not an adequate word; they were bigger and better than big. They were a glorious, sculptured mass of sheer, crisp-white delight tearing high into the tempestuous skies like vast, jagged towers of stone-cloud.

Even though eighty miles away, Everest was supposed to be visible from Nargarkot but, arriving that evening as the fading sun bathed the cone peaks in saffron light, we could not see it. Being an early bird, I awoke at dawn the next morning; leaving Peter slumbering (he liked his slumber) I walked out past 'The Last Restaurant In The Universe' and along the crisp, chill ridge. As the sun rose, the line of snowlit mountains hovered, ethereal, above the horizontal bands of mist. With my *Lonely Planet* guidebook in hand, I referred to the picture of peaks and identified Everest, the king of all mountains, rearing above the rest.

Rattling and rolling our way through the most mountainous country in the world at dizzying speeds down dizzying descents, I had to try to keep a cautious distance from Peter. His well-worn panniers had an alarming tendency to fly off at the most inopportune moments, providing additional obstacles to my high-speed slalom round the deep pot-holes and land-slide remnants. With a life-risking spurt I overtook him — but it seemed no safer to be up front: suddenly a cascade of boulders and rocks thundered down the mountainside just ahead, covering us in a yellow cloud of dusty particles. Rocks crashed across our path; one, the size of a small house, bounced off the road and, with an awesome, reverberating roar, plummeted down into the deep ravine below.

Quivering, I screeched to a halt. All seemed suddenly deathly silent. Jelly-legged, I tittered nervously, 'Crikey! That was a bit close for comfort.'

Peter, blessed with the steely nerves of a serious transglobal cyclist, calmly advised me to keep into the side and we kept going, with one eye scouring high up the rough, rugged rockface and the other on the road.

Dusk set in as we approached Mugling, where we planned to stay the night. In the grey light I made out a small group ahead, gathered around a bundle in the road. It turned out to be a dead youth. He had been catapulted off the back of an overcrowded bus to which he and many others had been clinging as it lurched and swerved and sped its precarious way along the rutted, twisting mountain road.

Road deaths were common and we constantly passed the sobering wreckage of earlier accidents — gruesome remains of collisions, burnt-out trucks and innumerable buses that had plunged over the edge. I was glad I was on my bike. I would not have liked to put my trust in a Buddhist driver who believed in reincarnation. Maybe that was why they seemed to drive like the devil along roads only wide enough for one vehicle. I would not have found it reassuring to travel in a dilapidated bus with such hopeful insignia as 'Good Luck' or 'Trust in God' displayed across the cracked, pitted windscreen. Human life was held very cheap; fines were far greater for knocking down a cow, or even a duck, than for killing a fellow human being.

It seems odd to me but, wherever I travel and however unfamiliar the scenes and situations, I seem to adapt easily to them. I was sitting on a bench inside a ramshackle roadside 'restaurant' consuming the inevitable but always delicious standard Nepalese dish of *dal bhat* (rice and lentils) when a

Gurkha entered on an ear-shattering motorbike. I thought perhaps his brakes had failed and he had overshot his mark but, oh no! He was a man with a purpose: he wanted to reach the hen-clucking courtyard out back and say hello to his granny. In a cloud of reverberating revs and black exhaust, he sent the squawking chickens scuttling as he casually accelerated past our table with a Cheshire-cat grin on his rustic face. And the situation seemed quite normal to me.

On another occasion we were eating the same sort of food in the same sort of place when something caught my eye. Appearing over the big, grease-lined *dal* cauldron was a massive rat, the size of a cat, which impudently stopped to scratch its back, preen its whiskers and sneeze before deftly darting among the pans, pausing momentarily here and there to sample some of the delicacies. Hot on its tail followed another, then another *and* another. 'Oooh aaah, rats!' we exclaimed in horrified unison and then continued with our meal.

Nearing Pokhara, we noticed a scene of wild-winged activity in a terraced field. Huge, hunched, bloodthirsty vultures with crazed looks and evil tempers were feasting on the blood-and-guts gore of a very dead dog, its limbs missing, its skull cracked but its snout still snarling violently in a gruesome, frozen grin. Each bit of the carcass was greedily fought over by these ripping, hissing beats whose steely eyes seemed to burn with hate.

I hop-crawled over to investigate more closely, mimicking their movements. They looked at me and hissed; they squawked and flapped lazy, primaeval wings, but they were never scared and kept hacking ruthlessly at the gory remnants. They were death-seeking monsters — and they smelt. Peter thought me vulture-crazy as I crouched on the ground just out of their spitting distance, grinning ghoulishly while I posed for a picture as if I was at Blackpool Tower.

'Pokhara O km,' said the sign as we entered this happy haven for hippies. Overflowing from Kathmandu, they had 'discovered' Pokhara twenty years ago as word had spread about the free, hash-smoking dreamworld of Nepal. Although the hippie population has diminished since those days, the potent odours of the now illicit smoke still abounded, as did the tie-dyed trousers, and it was said that more muesli was being consumed in this part of Nepal than in Camden and Hampstead put together. Come to that, there must have been more food consumed here than in the whole of Nepal put together. The talk of the town was equally divided between trekking and eating. Trekking gave the appetite and Pokhara provided the food. Attuned to Western gastronomic whims, the locals offered a choice of Chinese stir-fry, Italian pizzas, German frankfurters, Spanish paella, Mexican burritos or — bestseller to the British — Black Forest gâteau. And there was more: cheesecake, banana bread, carrot cake and cinnamon buns in infinite quantity. In a land of severe poverty, scarcity and deprivation, it seemed obscene.

We found a big, airy room in the Garden Resthouse where extravagant pink blooms cascaded through the wide, open windows and jaunty, cocksure mynah birds pilfered bits of breakfast. Walking down the main street, I could look up into the sky and see six of the world's fourteen 8,000-metre mountains including the most prestigious of all peaks — Mount 'Fishtail'.

We walked past the international restaurants, German bakeries and 'swopshop' bookshops, and on past the villagers' thatched red-clay houses which all nestled beside the cool, clean, tranquil and beautiful Lake Phewa, its waters kept continuously clear and freshly topped up by icy mountain streams.

I was treated with suspicion at the Hungry Eye restaurant when I ordered *dal bhat*. The waiter was perplexed: I was a Westerner, so why did I not eat Western food?

'Because I can't get lentil mixtures as tasty as yours at home,' I said. I think he thought I must be ill. In that land of lentils and rice, my *dal* took twice as long to arrive as Peter's pork pie and chips.

The Hungry Eye was packed with 'trippies' — the Nepalese

nickname for the apparently respectable modern generation of budget travellers. These days more people go to Nepal to expand their muscles than their minds. Most were trekkers, chatting with animation about their adventures in the mountains, or novices seeking advice from the experienced, or others laughing about how they would set off for their 'major' expeditions with all the latest high tech and macho garb — heavy boots, garters, goretex, anatomically designed rucksacks — only to have frail but sinewy local women and children nip past them in flip-flops carrying impossible loads from tumplines around their foreheads.

We could not understand Roland, a twenty-nine-year-old lawyer from Tasmania, who said, 'I'm only travelling for three months 'cos I don't want to waste too much of my life.'

'In that case,' I said, 'in your eyes I've wasted nearly half of mine already.' He looked genuinely sorry for me.

Our conversation was interrupted by an angry, fat, acne-faced drugs dealer. He was, as they say in the trade, 'well spaced out, man' and tried brusquely to offload a case of his illicit wares.

'Hey, you want good hash, smack, opium, mushrooms — no? C'me on, man, I have best grass, acid, best price. You want and I can get real good stuff, man.'

What he wanted was hippies, not trippies. No one was buying and he did not like it. He was looking sweaty, mean and frustrated and his sales pitch became forceful and snarling.

'Hey you fuckin' tourist shits, man. You sit and spend poxy rupees on poxy cups of tea — no one buy my fuckin' shit, man. You all crazy tourist bastards — I gonna kill you all.'

He stumbled off, sweating and shaking violently, and went to vent further abuse at a pipal tree across the road. We continued to drink our poxy cups of tea.

It was dark as we ambled back along the lakeside and heard the unmistakable voice of Bob Dylan gently pounding out from a shack near the bakery. Peeping in through the back, we discovered a dimly-lit dope-den run by relics of the true hippy era — obviously the types who still did business with old Acne

Face. Cat Stevens and the Grateful Dead followed Dylan. The place was full of bangles, kaftans, sandals and tie-dye; nettle tea and muesli were being consumed cross-legged on the floor.

A day out of Pokhara I awoke to a misty, moist morning beneath a massive banyan tree which dripped its dangling roots and icy drops on to my sleeping-bag. Camped on a slope, I had lost all contact with my sleeping mat during the night and had slid halfway down a bank, totally unaware in my sleep. Mountain air obviously does great things for sweet dreams. Peter was still aslumber, completely hidden in the murky depths of his sleeping-bag, so I munched my way through some stale chapati and withered carrots in an attempt to warm up.

Two young shepherds stumbled upon us from out of the mist. In a state of bewilderment, not knowing what to make of us, they started jabbering in loud voices. Offering them a carrot, I gesticulated to them to be quiet or else they would wake my friend. My actions only excited them all the more and Peter woke up. In a state of early morning exasperation, he leapt from his bag with unusual energy for such an hour, grabbed the nearest offender and careered around the banyan tree with him at an alarming rate. His hapless victim squealed hysterically before being deposited back beside his surprised friend. Any ideas of further mountain peace were thwarted by the persistent presence of the babbling boys and so we packed up, handed them a consolation banana and headed off into the freezing mist.

Moments later — major mishap. Without prior warning Peter the ornithologist stopped dead in his tracks up ahead, his attention diverted by some lesser-spotted parrot. Cold and bleary-eyed, I rode round the bend and shunted with force into his rear. The impact sent me reeling over my handlebars into nearby shrubbery. Although the speed of impact was far from impressive, I succeeded in giving myself a nasty knee injury for which little could be done until we reached the border of India, seventy miles away.

Meanwhile we had some mega-mountainous descents, all twisting and turning, thumping and bumping this way and that. The race was on — Peter had to reach the border post before his visa expired and I had to get there before my knee exploded. However, with only half an hour of daylight left we had a problem. I had no lights and did not like riding in the dark; Peter had lights and loved night riding. We compromised and kept cycling, neither of us using lights.

It was one of the best rides of the trip. It felt as if we were flying through an endless black void with the inky sky above and death-dark chasms dropping to the distant depths of the roaring river far below. We were cracking and rattling along that deserted mountain road over boulders and rocks, sometimes up to our ankles in freezing water and mud which flooded across the road. Then the enormous full moon rose high and scattered silvery, streaked shadows upon the abyss, ravines and craggy sheer cliffs — and all the time we were falling, spinning on wheel wings.

Passing from Nepal into India was, to our surprise, relatively straightforward. Border formalities were conducted without any of the anticipated and legendary Indian bureaucratic incompetence. The procedure involved a feel of tyres, a twiddle of gears, a cup of *chi* (tea) and questions about my 'mother country' and marital status. When it was discovered that at twenty-two I was not yet married nor had children, the possibility that I was suffering from some serious physical defect was analysed and discussed in earnest with the gathering crowd.

The Customs formalities were so lax and genial that a khaki-clad policeman with shiny black hair and big, heavy boots invited me to record this remarkably swift and uncomplicated border crossing with my camera, an action for which, on other borders in other lands, I might have been arrested or even shot. He stood stiffly, legs astride, face dead-pan, a rifle slung over his shoulder, as I photographed him at his post beside a wall inscribed: 'MEANING OF POLICE'.

POLITE
OBEDIENT
LOYAL
INTELLIGENT
COURAGEOUS
EFFICIENT

By the time we reached Delhi, my knee was burning. Peter's knee had come out in sympathy and was (though I hate to admit it) a lot more serious than mine. For no apparent reason, something in his twiddled and pinged. Whereas I only had to rest my torn ligaments and heal the gash, Peter needed an operation — *operations*, because he also had a kidney stone.

We moved into the East/West Medical Centre in New Delhi and I set up base in the bed beside him. This was home for the next three weeks. We settled in easily and kept referring to it as a hotel rather than a hospital, with its friendly service, lashings of sumptuous spicy food (we gained extra portions when I helped by peeling potatoes and kneading dough), laundry provided and a telephone. There was even a sun-roof where we lay among a sea of flapping washing and the shadows of hundreds of kites that circled and hovered high up in the burning sky.

The East/West was crawling with curious characters, more Western than Eastern. A frail, pallid Danish girl followed me around in a trance, asking bizarre questions and staring forlornly out of the window for hours, the sun shining on her long, golden hair that fell untended in straggly waves down her pale, bony back. We called her the French Lieutenant's Woman. She was only seventeen. She told me that her 'evil' parents had put her in a mental institution in Denmark but she had run away and escaped to India in search of a 'supreme god' who supposedly roamed the beaches of the south.

Then some Americans arrived next door and I went to investigate, curiosity getting the better of me as usual.

'Morning,' I said, 'and what brings you here?'

'Gee,' came the casual reply, 'yesterday we were on a bus

and we just kinda freaked out — but we're okay now.'

I left, perplexed. What did a 'freak out' entail?

Peter's knee operation was painfully successful but his kidney stone proved more of a problem. The Sikh doctor said it was so small that the only way to remove it was to fish it out with a hook, a method which involved feeding a tube (the fishing line) up his privates. I did not question Peter's statement that it was painful: it looked agonizing.

The hospital nurses were vivacious and friendly but basically did not have a clue. They doled out capsules willy-nilly, not knowing what they were for. 'Doctor say take,' they would say, with no further explanation. One of them handed out a pill which the doctor had told Peter he need no longer take: she ran away, giggling, only to return a few hours later to give him the same pill.

One day Peter's fishing line disengaged itself from his tackle and fell out of his rod. For a joke, he placed the end of the tube in his ear and rang the bell for the nurse. Taking her time, she eventually sauntered in.

'Yes, Mr Peter,' she said, 'you called?'

'Yes, nurse, I've got a slight problem with locating my tube.'

'Please Mr Peter, it is I am trusting very good,' she replied and then walked out. She had not even noticed.

We moved out of our East/West 'hotel' and into the home of Naveen, a wealthy, Oxford-educated Indian who owned a biscuit factory and who kindly offered to put us up in his spacious flat near the Red Fort in Old Delhi. Naveen had a garden, sun-roof, stereo, compact discs, television and maid — and a servant whom he referred to as 'the boy'. While he moved from an air-conditioned home to an air-conditioned car to an air-conditioned office, and back again, he passed streets littered with tattered bodies living and sleeping rough in gutters of stinking filth.

One day, driving past them with Naveen, I said, 'It's so terrible, all those poor people.'

'I never notice them,' he said, 'I never worry.' They were of a low, unclean, untouchable caste and, in Naveen's air-conditioned world, they meant nothing.

For Sunday lunch he took us to his club, where we sat outside on huge, immaculate lawns. There was a croquet pitch at one end and a brass band at the other. To the side, long trestle tables sagged beneath piles of food, a lot of which was merely picked at and thrown away. Immaculate waiters in brass-buttoned jackets and great, plumed turbans served the relaxing privileged, some of whom, as Peter remarked, were so gross that whatever privilege these high-caste people possessed was slowly killing them. In the eyes of many rich, an excess of fat was a way of proclaiming their prosperity and Naveen said that it was considered a compliment to be greeted by: 'You are looking very fat and fresh today.' Meanwhile, just down the road in teeming, tin-topped slums, thousands starved.

'East is east and west is west and never the twain shall meet.' Kipling's observation is never truer than in the streets of Delhi.

As I rode up Janpath at the height of the rush-hour, a pink-spotted cow ambled into the middle of a vital intersection and went to sleep. For miles in every direction, the neurotic traffic stopped — horns blaring, fumes and tempers flaring. But no one dared to prod this sacred beast to move it so that tens of thousands of people could get home on time. To Hindus, all cows are holy — even if they do turn the animals out into the grassless, death-defying streets of Delhi by the thousands or leave those knocked down by a hit 'n' run to die slowly in their own blood, carefully guarded to make sure that no one takes the animal's life. At last, someone threw an irresistibly tasty *Times of India* at the spotted cow's muzzle which, to this apathetic object of reverence, was good news. Indian cows are recycling banks: they eat paper, boxes and rubbish, then they defecate it and people trot around scooping up the pats, which they dry and burn for fuel. It is all so simple — and environmentally efficient.

Never could a city be so divided as Delhi. One half is ages old and its narrow, rickety streets were a scene of urban anarchy. They brimmed with filth and crowds, bullock-carts, taxis, beggars, bicycles, black-and-yellow motorized rickshaws swarming like angry wasps with revving engines, bent-backed bearers carrying pack-frames lashed with ridiculous loads. The clamour was overwhelming: horns, hooters, shouts, bells and bangs and clangs and, always, Hindu music blaring in a continuous, distorted wail as every radio was turned up full blast in a futile attempt to override all the others. The crashing noises collided together in a bewildering din, creating an outlandish atmosphere of frantic speed and impatience. In an advertising free-for-all, the choked streets were mushrooming with signs; hoardings pandered to the craving for Western styles by displaying food, insurance, machines, computers, suitings, shirtings, saris and turbans; garish cinema posters flouted pouting heroines and comically leering, mustachioed villains. The air was pungent with the mingled odours of filth, soiled gutters, latrines, dust, exhaust, spice, sandalwood, jasmine and urine, dal and dung.

All this was in such contrast to New Delhi with its wide, spacious avenues and boulevards, grandiose buildings and pretentious, stereotyped houses set back from the road. New Delhi, site of our East/West 'hotel', was a good place to recuperate but the frenetic vortex of Old Delhi was definitely the place to be.

Negotiating Delhi by bike, you take your life in your hands while your heart is in your mouth. The streetlife, teeming with confused chaos, bears down from all directions and at all speeds. Behind the wheel, everyone is a madman. Hurtling through the centre escorted by an Indian friend, I clung to my seat for dear life. Already having a good idea of what the answer would be, I asked him how difficult it was to acquire a driving licence.

'I had no problem,' he said as we swerved erratically from one side of the street to the other. 'The instructor asked, "Can you drive?" I said, "Yes." I got my licence — simple.'

'Yes ... simple,' I replied shakily, wishing I had the little assurance of being strapped in by a seat-belt. Indian vehicles have no such thing.

In Britain we drive on the left, in most other countries they drive on the right, but in India you have a free choice. Vehicles switch like dodgems from one side to the other, depending on how the mood takes them. It is even worse out of the cities. What looks like a two-lane road is actually three-laned: one edge for cars, camel convoys, carts or bicycles, the other edge for those coming in the opposite direction, and the middle for the speeding, horn-blaring, overloaded buses and trucks that only crazed drivers would dare to challenge. And there is no shortage of those in India. Size determines right of way and 'Might is Right,' they say, the only problem being that everyone thinks they are the mightiest. Generally trucks reign supreme, with 'HORN OK PLEASE' painted on their tail boards. On one occasion a bedevilled bus overtook another and managed to push it (along with elephants, camels, bicycles and carts) off the road on to the dirt just as an oil tanker, marked 'HIGHLY INFLAMMABLE', sped past me on a direct collision course with the bus. Each madly challenged the other on the road and they only missed one another by a cat's whisker.

Accidents were common and wrecks of all kinds littered the road. Yet life in all its manifestations was evident on what in Britain might have been the road's hard shoulder where, oblivious to the suicidal drivers, Indians slept, cooked meals, ate, washed, defecated, brought up their children and died.

With knees properly rotated and kidney stones located, we left the grey, noxious haze hanging over industrial Delhi and headed for the countryside and Agra. Our escape was far from peaceful. The spine-shattering roads were a constant blur of bell-ringing cyclists all rattling and rolling and racing their way along beside us. It felt like the motorway as we swerved in and out of a surge of riders with overtaking and undertaking manoeuvres I never would have believed possible on two wheels. Often a plethora of people would perch precariously on a single bike — fragile, veiled old women side-saddling on rear racks; boys balancing in crazy contortions; children strapped to the crossbar along with goats and ducks and carcasses. All this and yet they still managed to accelerate after us in hot pursuit. They were addicted to chasing and racing and no way were they going to let a couple of fancily kitted-out foreigners glide past unnoticed. We sped up, they sped up; we slowed down, they slowed down; we stopped to tend to the call of nature, they stopped to watch. We were constantly the centre of attention — and that is something you are stuck with in India, whether you like it or not.

The Indians could be hair-tearingly infuriating but they were wonderful people, always wanting to help even if they had no idea.

'Which way to Jodhpur?' I asked a camel-man at a fork in the road with no signpost.

'Jodhpur? This way please,' he said with arm outstretched, pointing vaguely in a direction somewhere between the two roads.

'Jodhpur,' I tried again, gesticulating vividly, 'is left or right?'

'Yes,' he said.

'Thank you,' I replied and carried on, none the wiser.

Apart from the roads being a swarming mass of everything

that moved, there were also dangers of the immovable type. The positioning of road hazard signs was decidedly erratic and I often came across gaping chasms in the road, at least six feet deep, without the slightest warning. It was not just people who suffered from a lack of proper road maintenance but also luckless livestock — I once discovered a scrawny goat bleating listlessly as it lay trapped at the bottom of one such ravine.

Another time, as I was merrily flying along with Peter, the road suddenly disintegrated with a fifty-foot drop into a fast-flowing river. There had been no signs, no warnings, and it was only a good pair of brakes that saved us from plunging over the edge (where, we learnt later, two motorcyclists had died the previous night). A little delayed, we heard an urgent shout from a roadside workman busy with a small taskforce of men and camels.

'Hello! Mister — stop please!' he cried as he scrambled up the sandy bank. 'The road — it is washed far away.'

'Yes, thank you,' I replied with bemusement, 'we had noticed.'

As we were riding along one day, a bit of grit lodged in Peter's eye and it puffed up so badly that he could not see out of it.

'What you need is an eye hospital,' I quipped, as if such a thing would exist among such ancient and underdeveloped scenes of paddy fields, stone-breakers, oxen-turned waterwheels, human-pulled carts, sari-clad labourers undertaking backbreaking work and men walking with sacks of goat fodder on their heads. As a cloud of thick, choking dust settled from a passing fleet of swaying camels, I read a sign beside us that said:

EYE-SPECIAL HOSPITAL
PLEASE THIS WAY

Alice in Wonderland? No, this was India — a country which never failed to surprise. We followed a bank in the direction indicated by the sign but could see only a bunch of bangled women chattering in a golden aura of sunlit dust with big brass water-pots on their heads as they walked towards a small cluster of mud huts. We stopped a youth wearing a shabby red shirt with 'Mr India' written on the back.

'Mr India,' I said, 'do you know the way to eye hospital?'

'Eleven minutes walk this way,' he said, pointing in the opposite direction to that of the sign.

'Are you certain?' I asked uncertainly, following his gaze. 'All I can see that way are giant haystacks.'

'Yes, eye hospital certainly this way.'

In India it is not a good idea to ask just one person's opinion, especially as far as directions are concerned. Not wishing to appear discourteous or unhelpful, they will say the first thing that comes into their head rather than honestly and far more usefully admitting that they do not know. It is best to ask as many people as possible and opt for the majority view. This does not necessarily mean that you will then be going in the right direction — it just gives you a slightly better chance of doing so.

We therefore asked as many people as possible but we still ended up lost and it was simply by a stroke of good luck that, exhausted, we stumbled upon a ramshackle hut to replenish our water and discovered that we had finally reached our goal. The eye hospital consisted of two dusty, dingy rooms and a bald, bespectacled little man with a magnifying glass. He looked like Gandhi but he was in fact the eye specialist. Peter was laid out on a board. A dim, flickering torch was shone into his eye and then the doctor produced a syringed needle.

Panic-stricken, Peter sat bolt upright and narrowly missed impaling his eye on it.

'Whoa!' he gasped. 'Where are you going with that? I don't need any needles, all I need is a cotton-bud.'

'You must remain lying. I must anaesthetize the eye.'

The thought of an injection near his eye turned Peter rigid with shock. He lay unflinching as the doctor carried out his delicate manoeuvre and successfully removed the offending article. Peter was pronounced healed, given a bottle of drops and told, 'Please Mr Peter, no charge.'

The Taj Mahal was memorable not only for everything that it is memorable for but also for meeting Aiden, a hairy cyclist from Matlock Bath in Derbyshire, who joined us and amused us with his continual flow of unusual 'slug poems' and reactions to his own case of dire dysentery. We threesomed it out into Rajasthan — a combination which only confused people further.

'Madame!' hailed a tall Rajastani buried beneath a brightly coloured turban. 'I conclude you have two husbands.'

'Well, I'm afraid you conclude wrongly,' I said. 'One's my puncture repairer and the other's my slug-poet.'

'Ah yes, of course,' he replied and turned tail with a flick of his elaborate moustache.

The sun, a blazing ball of fire, set the walls of Jaipur aglow with a deep, flickering, rosy hue as we arrived. It was easy to see why it is renowned as the Pink City but things did not stay rosy for long in the clamorous congestion that followed. Peter, behind me one moment, was gone the next, vanishing into the mêlée. India is like that; it can just swallow you up. Aiden and I spent a fruitless half hour scouring the teeming streets for him but soon gave up. It was a pointless task. We knew we would meet him again somewhere along the way: in a country brimming with nearly 100 million people it is amazing how easily and how often you keep bumping into people you either know of or know.

Peter was located a hundred miles down the road, eating a bowlful of banana porridge beside the Holy Lake of Pushkar, where ash-covered Saddhus with matted hair and loin cloths sat cross-legged in a state of hypnotized spiritualism. The devout wandered with blood-red tika marks on their brows and garlands of marigolds, offering coconuts to the sacred waters where they bathed to wash away years of impurity and to strengthen their good karma in states of rapt reverence.

Pushkar was a wonderful place to hang up my wheels for a while and relax. It was brimming with trippies but it was one of those rare places where an influx of travellers proved an advantage. After weeks of cycling through small rural villages where no bus- or train-travelling sightseer would feel inclined to alight and where we were constantly at the centre of animated and forever curious crowds who unceasingly pummelled us with questions and inane gibbering chit-chat, it was sheer bliss to be able to walk around Pushkar without being hammered or pursued.

The crooked streets were lined with makeshift stalls piled high with pyramids of bananas, papayas, coconuts and peanuts, chickpeas and grapes. Next door to a vendor selling second-hand teeth, I bought some exquisite mangoes and gorged myself silly.

Aiden and I shared a big, airy rooftop room which turned out to be a popular thoroughfare for the local monkeys. These were the sort of thieving, hiss-spitting (possibly rabid) monkeys that you treated with some respect. If they pocketed your bunch of bananas, then you would neither challenge them nor question the act. 'Go ahead,' you would say, keeping a wary distance from their devilishly sharp claws, 'please help yourself — you're very welcome to anything — the choice is yours.' It was better than risking the high possibility of being attacked and bitten.

Sitting on the sun-scorched rooftop overlooking the lake one afternoon, Orwell in one hand, banana in the other, I was dreamily peering down at the pigeons strutting on the water-side steps of the ghats, pecking and drinking, when suddenly the soundtrack from *Jaws* filled my head. Down in the murky depths of the Holy Waters I caught sight of a savage-looking catfish — more a shark than a mere fish — with grotesque, evil eyes and a mouthful of razor-jagged teeth. More of them appeared on the scene — huge, sinister beasts lurking just beneath the surface, scarcely moving but ever watchful of the winged activity on the ghats. The clottish pigeons were quite unaware of the impending danger from the denizens of the deep and continued to peck at the water's edge.

Then came the moment. A pigeon bent down for a thirst-quenching beakful. In a splashing flash, the monster fish leapt from the water, grabbed the pigeon by its neck, decapitated it, retained the head and dived back down into the holy murk.

Every morning at dawn I would pocket a book and a mango and walk beneath reddening skies, out past the stalls, the temples, the curled, skeletal forms of sleeping beggars, to climb a massive, rugged outcrop of rock. At its top was a golden fairytale temple, perched high above the shifting sands of the desert. Parrots with wildly coloured plumage and crests that jutted like ships' prows would flit and swoop like circus clowns; and eagle-like birds of prey would glide gracefully past at eye level. Way down below was Pushkar, a distant shimmer of holy lake and whitewashed roofs gently stirring into life as the sun crept over the sandy horizon. For a couple of hours I would sit, queen of my castle, enjoying the peace, my mango and my aptly titled book, *Far from the Madding Crowd*.

From Pushkar the three of us branched off in different directions. I fancied a while of lone Indian travel and ignored people's warnings, including Naveen's back in Delhi: 'Don't travel alone — the village people are uncivilized and dangerous.' Peter and I arranged to meet for tea several weeks later at the Lake Palace in Udaipur. Aiden, with his slug poems and dire dysentery, was running out of time and jumped on a train. Before doing so, however, he handed me a 'dog stick'.

'I think you might need this,' he said, 'if the dogs of Pushkar are anything to go by.'

He was right. It was not the uncivilized people that would terrorize me but the dogs. India was teeming with pariah hounds. Packs of snarling, salivating canines would surge in my wake, hell-bent on sinking their wolflike fangs into a juicy chunk of blurred, revolving calf. There was no way that I was going to play brave, stand my ground, look them in the eye and ward them off with a few lobbed rocks. They bore down on me from all sides, some of them twice my size — huge, frenzied creatures thirsty for blood. In a state of panic I would reach unbelievable speeds in frantic, lung-bursting attempts to outcycle the ferocious beasts. All the while I would whirl and wield my dog stick, every now and then delivering a direct hit which would send one of my tormentors sprawling with a yelp. This was no dog-loving nation and these were rabid beasts.

As I cycled across the Great Indian Desert, people, places and food and water supplies thinned to a trickle. I would pass the desiccated carcasses of camels and macabre, grinning skulls — a reminder of what could happen if things went wrong. All the time, high above in the burnt white skies, were the ever watchful and ever hungry eyes of circling vultures.

My Indian maps were hopelessly inaccurate and gave little help in discerning what might lie ahead. Villages that I had relied on for food or water or accommodation and which looked quite promising on the map turned out to be dismally small or non-existent. It was no good pointing to the map when seeking directions from a crowd of villagers, either. Most had never travelled further than the neighbouring village, let alone to one fifty miles away. To mention Delhi or Calcutta was like talking of another planet. If I showed them the map a multitude of grappling hands would descend upon it, turning it upside down and back to front in mystification. I gave up trying to extract navigational information from it and wore it on my head as a turban instead, or wrapped myself in it sari-fashion or, when the sea of pressing faces was too over-powering, I used the map to cover my face and disappeared into a glorious but brief respite of crumpled paper where no eyes could meet mine. There I would stand, motionless, among a rabble of hundreds of puzzled people, my features veiled by a 1:1500 000 scale map of India, thinking: is this really happening? I wanted to curl myself up in a dark corner and hide. But the head-shattering din and the treading on my toes made me realize that, yes, it was happening all right. The clamouring crowd would press closer and closer, trying to get a glimpse of this peculiar, map-bedecked alien on a pink bicycle. Then, when I felt they had overstepped their mark and had stood on all my toes, and when a few cheeky types in the front stalls had sneakily tried to peep through the gaps of my mapped disguise, I would suddenly throw it aside and say, 'Boo!' It never failed to amuse.

It is said that India can do strange things to your mind and I can verify that. I would do things in Asia that I would never dream of doing in England. How would commuters on a packed London-bound train react if I suddenly scrambled in through the window, or helped myself, uninvited, to a bagful of someone else's crisps? Imagine, on that same London train, a businessman behind his newspaper — a shield which mutely declares, 'I am holding aloft my barrier, *The Times*, as I have absolutely no desire to make contact with surrounding persons.' What would his reaction be if I rose from my seat opposite and peremptorily removed that protective shield from his suspended hands and, as if it was the most natural thing in the world, started to read it myself? Or what would the office worker beside me do if I were to remove his pen from his busily scribbling hand and study it with a look of intense curiosity? I would be considered at the very least, antisocial, and at worst, mentally ill.

They do that sort of thing in India. The book I was quietly reading would be whipped out of my hands and scrutinized with rapt fascination. Or my biro would be snatched from me as I was writing my diary and the snatcher would say, 'Memsahib, I consider this a very fine pen from your great mother-country England.'

My own behaviour was equally bizarre. I would walk straight into the kitchen quarters of a roadside-shack restaurant and join in the cooking; or I would saunter around wrapped in my sleeping-bag or, to escape the crowds, I would climb a tree and read my book perched like a vulture on the top branch while a sea of dark heads bobbed inquisitively beneath me.

The Indians try your patience — of that there is no doubt. Some foreigners, driven to exasperation, will scream their heads off at them but I saw little point in that. It would only attract yet more attention and turn what had previously been a good-natured and curious crowd into an agitated and possibly hostile mob. And what right was there to burst into a ludicrous fit? It was their country, not ours. They had not invited us, so if we did not like their ways we should go home rather than taking it out on those who were surely right to be curious when an alien appeared in their midst. As an intruder myself, it seemed best just to sit back and accept the situation, no matter how infuriating it might be.

Water supplies were often highly suspect. One night I turned up at a small temple; I asked for water and was directed to a well. I threw down the bucket, hauled it up, added a purifying tablet that tasted of swimming-pools and drank my fill. Refreshed, I went to bed. The next morning I returned to the well and discovered, by the light of day, that a family of fat rats had set up base in its murky depths.

On the road to Jaisalmer I met Philippe, a Belgian bus-driver riding a heavy, single-speed heap of Indian-made Hero bicycle. Fed up with crowded trains and buses, he had bought his bike brand new for £28 up in Rishikesh, a place the Beatles had made famous by staying there during their hippy phase. He would sell it later in Jaisalmer market at only £4 less — not a bad rate of depreciation for a two-month tour covering more than 1,500 miles.

It was a day for meeting cyclists. Down the road I met a white-haired American who had an exquisite brass gear lever. After a collision with a rickshaw in Bombay, he had a new one made up from the shambles of a scrap-metal mechanic's shop. Its precision work surpassed even the like of Campagnolo — and it cost a mere twenty-five pence. Indians are great improviscis; nothing gets wasted and if they do not have it they will make it.

Then out of the heat-haze Peter appeared. That evening we stayed in a small dak bungalow (a government-run rest-house) which we found hidden in a compound in Phalodi. Usually these places provided a degree of escape from the inquisitive locals and this one did too — for about half an hour.

I had a shower in our en suite bathroom — a dark, odorous, cockroach-infested space about five-foot square with a cooking-oil drum full of water and a hole in the floor that acted as both drain and toilet. Then I fell on the bed in a state of sweaty torpor. The whirring ceiling fan had two speeds: slow, which was as beneficial as 'off', and fast, in which it spun in a frenzy with the ferocious noise and speed of helicopter blades gone berserk, stirring up a hot whirlwind of choking dust and threatening to decapitate you every time you stood up. It was better to sweat in silence.

Then we were discovered. Outside the window a small but determined battalion of twelve-year-olds had sneaked up on us unnoticed and then broke into a giggling torrent of: 'Good morning your father name! English is house! What your time!'

We closed the window, closed the door and suffered in stuffiness.

The window was pushed open; a face pushed through. 'Book yes not?' We slammed it shut. It opened again (there was no catch): more faces, more giggles, more screams. Then the door was discovered; it was banged on and pushed open to cries of impish laughter and a retreat of scuffling feet. We wanted some peace, we wanted some sleep, but we were not going to get any. I sat up and started shelling peas. Peter sat up in exasperation. He wanted to sort them out — the boys, that is, not the peas.

'Leave them,' I said, adding hopefully but unrealistically, 'they might get bored and go away.'

I should have known better; Indian staying power is remark-able and the squad outside did not go away. They simply became noisier and more excited. Then they took to hurling missiles.

When Peter exchanged his flip-flops for baseball boots, I knew he was preparing for gang warfare. Then he picked up his bicycle pump. Things were getting serious. He crouched by the door like a tensed tiger ready to pounce before the kill, waiting for an over-confident enemy to fling open the door. I acted as decoy and continued passively podding peas. Peter called me Bait.

THWAACK! The door was kicked open and Peter, emitting a deafening war cry, burst out with such terrifying speed that I dropped a pod in fright. All hell was let loose. He charged into a thick cloud of dust after the panic-stricken stampede. Yells and screams of fear reverberated off the compound walls. The gang leader broke away from the pack and Peter was after him in a flash, accelerating hard as he made a lunge and grabbed him — a blubbering, wailing wreck pleading innocence. The rest of the mob scarpered up the boundary wall and made it to their safe haven, but they were still screaming and leaping up and down like a bunch of berserk baboons.

Peter the Great triumphantly dragged his hysterical, flapping prey into our room. The wide-eyed captive was terrified, certain that he was doomed. Locking him in our cell (the toilet), Peter shouted tauntingly through the door: 'Boy toilet like? Yes not stay? Time now quiet! Not please shout!'

Our victim yowled away, hammering like a mad thing on the door and emitting ear-shattering screams which soon brought the government staff and half the village running. Bursting through the door, they found us both sitting on the bed calmly shelling peas.

'Evening,' said Peter.

'Hello,' I said.

'Aaaargh!' screamed a voice from the toilet. We continued our shelling as if nothing was amiss.

The room became a jam-packed madhouse with everyone shouting and screaming simultaneously. We explained the situation, our wailing captive was rescued and finally the commotion died down. We were left in peace. Bliss.

Later we ventured out to get some dal and chapatis from a small chi house where the owner asked if it was true that Peter had ill-treated a child. Peter relayed the full story.

'That boy,' laughed the owner, 'is my nephew. Always he is very bad boy indeed. Very spoilt. Much needed to be taught a lesson. Thank you.'

Rajasthan: the home of the Great Indian Desert. I had always thought of it as a huge and inhospitably dry place. In one way I was right. Distances were vast and monotonous; it was exhausting to cycle for hours, sometimes days, into heat-blasting headwinds that sapped and drained all moisture and energy away. Yet among all this burning heat, this sand, this dust, thrived a princely state. It was home to the Rajputs who, along with the great fortressed cities, gave the desert its spice, its colour and its pride. Erupting out of the flat, shimmering haze of the desert like a petrified monster was the magnificent spinal-walled fortress city of Jaisalmer.

I found a bed (a string one) on the roof of Hotel Laxmi Nivas and then I went to explore, walking past the ancient sand-gold buildings and into the busy, rickety streets. I passed tall, proud Rajputs with immaculately twirled handlebar moustaches (some a formidable eighteen inches long), their heads wrapped in huge, bulbous turbans of every colour under the sun. There were women in shimmering saris with arms and ankles spiralled with chunky silver bangles. There were trolleys laden with books and magazines; stalls were piled with giant, moulded pyramids of luridly coloured sweets, swarming with flies. In dark, carved doorways gaggles of chattering women crouched as they sifted rice and lentils, shelled peas or cut up carrots. Open-air hairdressers were snipping away with gay abandon in the street, one of them unabashedly shaving another's armpits, while dentists performed painful oral operations with antiquated equipment. Scrawny goats scratched among the vegetable stalls, thieving mouthfuls wherever they could, and I saw a large, silvery, hump-backed cow excreting sacred excrement while its owner caught the pat in mid-flight in a banana leaf and wrapped it away for safe keeping.

From Jaisalmer I went on to Udaipur — the City of Dreams — where every Indian insisted on saying, 'Hello Mr Jamie Bond *Octopussy* filmed here.' On the way I spent a night in the mountains at Ranakpur, the site of a massive, sculptured temple. As in all places of reverence, I removed my shoes and left them with the piles of footwear at the entrance, watched over by an old man.

When I returned, my precious trainers were gone but the old man was still there.

'My shoes,' I said, perturbed, 'where are my shoes?'

'Shoes — yes,' he grinned inanely, pointing towards the pile.

'Yes, I can see those are shoes, but mine are not there.'

'No shoes. In temple no allow shoes,' he said unhelpfully.

'Look! I have no shoes on. I gave you my shoes to look after with everyone else's.' I pointed to the pile.

'Shoes — yes,' he replied, confirming the fact that we were both looking at a pile of shoes.

'Shoes — yes, I know,' I said, feeling like a parrot, 'but my shoes ... no there. Shoes disappear. You see my shoes?' I pointed to my bare feet.

'Yes no shoes in temple,' he said.

Exasperated, I went in search of my missing shoes. With my eyes to the ground, I checked everyone's feet for my shoes; I searched under bushes, behind the huts — everywhere. But no shoes. I knew someone had them. I was concerned. Apart from a pair of broken flip-flops, my trainers were the only shoes I had. It promised to be an uncomfy ride to Udaipur, the nearest place where I could replace them. I kept checking with the shoe-keeper.

'Please, my shoes — you see my shoes yet?'

'Yes no shoe temple allow,' he continued to say.

I called off the search when it grew dark and went to bed dispirited. I was staying in one of the rooms that lined the temple courtyard. It was a tiny, dusty cell, with no bed, no table, no window — nothing. When I lay on the floor I could touch all four walls at once. Outside, the courtyard was over-shadowed by a massive banyan tree with its pendulous roots dripping to the ground; it was full of trapezing monkeys that hissed and chatted and fought among the branches. They clattered noisily across my roof and I had to close the door to avoid them swinging in. I lay in a stuffy, dusty darkness and pondered upon the fate of my shoes.

I arose at first light and flip-flopped over to the toilet block — a tap and a couple of well-soiled holes in the ground. Round the corner I bumped into the shoe-keeper dressed in a shabby, long-tailed shirt which hung floppily over loose, white-stained, baggy trousers held up with a piece of string. Crammed on his feet were my trainers.

'I like your shoes,' I said.

Unabashed, he grinned. 'Yes no shoe allow temple.' He handed them to me without another word and went to perform his early morning ablutions beneath the tap.

After meeting Peter for tea at the Lake Palace Hotel in Udaipur — a palace which floated like an island of dazzling white marble in the perfect reflection of the still waters — I made my way back toward Delhi. The days were a blur of heat. Often I would stop at small, dusty villages to fill up my bottles at the communal water pump where women dripping with jewellery and colours would cluster around, giggling and chatting as they helped me to pump and jestingly splashed me with water.

In India, conversation often seemed to go round in circles. In Chittaurgarh (City of Valour, said my map) the man at the guest house knocked on my door and said, 'Sir. Good evening but your country of origin is what please?'

'You've already written it down five times on five different bits of paper,' I said.

'What is the fine name of your father?'

'You've written that five times as well.'

'In the morning,' he said, 'you are wishing for a breakfast mealing?'

'Yes, that would be very nice. You have porridge?' I enquired hopefully.

'Porridge — yes.'

'How much your porridge?' I asked, surprised.

'Porridge three rupee only.'

'Okay. One bowl porridge in the morning please.'

'Porridge? No, no porridge.'

'But you just said porridge — yes.'

'No. Omelette, chapati.'

'Do you have yoghurt — dahi?'

'Dahi. Yes.'

'Okay, I'll have dahi then.'

'You want omelette?'

'No, just dahi.'

'No problem omelette.'

'No, just dahi.'

'Just dahi?'

'Yes, just dahi.'

In the morning I was presented with a bowl of porridge.

At Bijolia I stayed at a 'hotel' which was half tea-house, half mechanic's shop. My room resembled a scrap-yard. There was a bed — grimy-grey with an oil-stained sheet and surrounded by old tins of grease, rusting wheels, lethal scraps of metal, an assortment of shoddy tools and even an old car engine. Beneath my bed lay a pile of rubbish mingled with an abundance of rat droppings. The floor was stained blood-red from the spit of betel juice. The toilet was the usual filthy hole in the floor and from the door hung a wet pair of brown underpants. It was not a pleasant room but there was nowhere else to go.

I collapsed on the bed in a sweaty heap. Suddenly a man burst into my room (there was no lock on the door), grinned at me and strode straight into the toilet, where he made a lot of very unsavoury sounds. Then he started warbling and sluiced himself with a few cupfuls of water from the oil-drum. I was a bit surprised: I had not realized this was a communal washroom. When he had finished, he walked over to where I was sitting on the bed and pointed to the grimy sheet beneath my sleeping-bag.

'Yes,' I said, 'now what?'

'Bed,' he said.

'Yes, you're right,' I agreed, 'it is a bed.'

'Please excusing me.' With that, he whipped the sheet from beneath me (like a tea-party tablecloth trick) and used it as a towel before wrapping himself in it.

'You British bicycle very good,' he said and walked out.

I was hungry. I would have to head outside to find some food. But in India things were never that easy. It would take a lot to work myself up for a dive into the scrum of horn-blaring trucks, dust, dirt, filth, scavenging mangy animals, incessant noise, and clamouring crowds which, along with the squads of snarling dogs, would pounce upon me as soon as I emerged from my den. I was exhausted as it was from the cycling, the heat, the lack of peace, the suspect food and water — just from India in general, really — and venturing out on a food-finding mission would exhaust me even more. It was not possible simply to walk out, buy some food and return within moments. To head out into the street-anarchy was a major expedition and needed a lot of willpower.

It was half an hour before I even mustered enough energy to sit up, and another ten minutes before I succeeded in putting on my shoes, after which I needed a rest and sat for a while, panting, heat-dazed and sweaty, to contemplate my next move. Finally, my stomach willed me to put one foot in front of the other and I hit the town.

Bijolia was a ramshackle place, the streets and gutters full of rotting rubbish and excrement, the 'shops' full of shoddy goods. It was a small but noisy place — one big, blaring nightmare that resounded in nauseating waves round my head. The people, as always, were curious but friendly. I did not have my bike with me but they all knew who I was.

'Hello English bicycle! Stop! Chapati? Dal? You want very best mealing here?'

I chose one of the many bench-lined food houses whose fronts were adorned with the usual grease-engrimed cauldrons. I peered into each one, rejecting mixtures which had unidentifiable bones protruding from them, and chose the old tasty and (usually) trustworthy dal before retreating to a rickety bench.

The mustachioed chef, wrapped in a tea-towel, was a nice man. He shooed away the encroaching crowds as if dealing with a pack of pestering dogs and left me to eat and write my diary. A few moments later an old-fashioned chauffeur-driven Ambassador car pulled up outside. An immaculately dressed Western couple stepped out and surveyed the squalid surroundings with disdain. I felt quite excited to see them — I had not spoken to anyone other than an Indian for nearly twelve days. I smiled their way and called a chirpy, 'Hello!'

They looked but did not acknowledge me at all.

'Edward,' said the woman in peeved tones, 'I'm just dying of thirst. Tell Narayan to bring us a cup of tea, but only if it looks safe. The place is so frightfully filthy. We'll drink it in the car.'

The chauffeur dutifully obliged and bought the tea, which I noticed cost a lot more rupees than mine had. He did not use one of the tea-house's cups but a special one the woman had given him, presumably for reasons of hygiene. Edward and the woman drank their tea on the back seat of the car, doors shut, window blinds pulled, insulated from the outside world. They had uttered not a word to any of the curious onlookers. Then they drove away.

'Why did you charge them three times more per cup of chi than me?' I asked the owner.

'Tourist,' he said.

'But I'm a tourist.'

'No, you are travelling on bicycle. This I think is very good. I also travelling on bicycle but car I have not.'

When he learnt that I was a cook by trade, he invited me to join in the chapati-making — rolling the dough into putty balls, flattening them with a rapid movement from hand to hand, and slapping them on to the sides of the traditional clay oven, its flames fanned continuously by a skinny boy sitting on his haunches. Making chapatis looked easy but was not. Each time, mine turned out like mottled cow pats, which everyone found very funny — especially when I put one on my head and got on with diary writing. When I left, the owner gave me a going-home present: a day's supply of chapati and dahi.

Back in my luxurious hotel suite, I was sitting on my bed finishing off my Hermann Hesse when something caught my eye. A rat, as big and dark as the shadows, darted under the bed. Had the same thing happened in my bedroom at home, I would promptly have screamed and locked myself in a cupboard. But all things are relative. I would not have expected rats at home but in India I did. I calmly finished my chapter before rounding up the offending rodent (happily gnawing away beneath my bed) and ushered it back down the toilet hole whence it had come. Then I went to bed without giving the matter another thought.

I was awoken in the morning by a couple of men defecating just outside my window. No sooner had they delivered the goods when India's animate version of the Poop Scoop hit the scene with a speed and dexterity which I had always thought was alien to pigs. Greedily they gobbled up their steaming breakfast with a noisy accompaniment of satisfied snuffles and grunts before accelerating away with alacrity to the site of another early morning squatter.

Indians defecate everywhere — like British dogs: streets, parks, gutters, beaches, rivers, hillsides, railway tracks, gardens — anywhere. Unlike Westerners, who always wish to conceal themselves, Indians never look for cover. Defecating is a social activity and whenever I set off early in the morning to beat the heat I would pass scores of squatters with water-pot at hand, clustered in little groups and chatting away happily, quite uninhibited, exchanging news and views and gossip as one might at a WI coffee morning.

For me, though, things were different. Being such a source of curiosity and intrigue, my performance would unfailingly pull in the crowds. Saying things like, 'Don't look — it's rude,' or, 'I'd like to get on with my business alone, thanks,' had absolutely no effect. Quite the opposite; they would edge in that much closer. Personally I found their interest rather unsavoury, not to mention a little off-putting. But what could I do when nature, with all its urgency, was calling? Fortunately I managed to reschedule my body clock so that the predawn darkness covered up my acts of contributing to the laying of night soil.

One day an elephant with big, brightly painted ears pulled up beside me and the driver shouted down: 'Like a ride, luv?' (or words to that effect). I knew better than to turn down an offer of taking an elephant for a spin; I called back and said I would love one.

The driver, by means of some nifty leg-work, executed a three-point turn and old Nelly stopped dead in her massive tracks. Then, instead of jumping down off her side, the driver put himself into reverse and slid down over her tail.

'Memsahib,' he said, 'I am wishing you a travel on my elephant. Please.'

With that, he demonstrated how one sets about mounting such a mammoth. Walking round to the stern, he whacked her awesome leathery behind with a stick, shouted a command and Nelly (I never caught her real name) made a convenient mounting step with her tail — convenient, that is, if you could reach it. As I only came up to Nelly's knees — and that was on tiptoe — it was clear we had an elevation hitch on our hands.

'No problem,' said my undaunted driver. He instructed her to extend a foreleg the size of a tree-trunk and he scuttled up it as easily as a flight of stairs. Now the hard part: my turn. The driver (I did not catch his name, either, but for the sake of argument I shall call him Dumbo) indicated that I should use Nelly's ear to help swing myself up. As just one flap of it could send me flying, I was a little hesitant about using her ear as a handle. Nonetheless, I dutifully obeyed. Dumbo knew best.

Things started well. I stepped carefully past the toenails, shot past the shin, struggled over the kneecap and fell on the thigh. Panicking, I clung frantically to her massive, bough-like leg and hung on for dear life. It was a long way down. Nelly proceeded to do curious things with her trunk, hitting me with force on my behind and sending me plummeting headfirst to earth.

Fortunately I sustained no injury; I was just a little shaken. Undiscouraged, I persevered and this time managed to reach the lower shoulder before coming to grief. On the third attempt I made it to the ear before nearly being flapped into oblivion. Doggedly I held my grip as Dumbo grappled with my flailing limbs and, admirably, managed to hoist me to safety — if being perched precariously on top of a capricious elephant the size of a building can be called 'safe'.

Having established myself up in this lofty driving seat, I cast a complacent and haughty glance towards my cycle before putting Nelly into gear and lurching sedately down the road. Dumbo took the controls and steered Nelly's formidable bulk by doing funny things with his toes and wiggling behind the

ears. Every now and then he would deliver a bracing conk on her head and shout something like 'Eeaigh!' and 'Heia!', sounds which had effects equivalent to those of a car's clutch or brake.

I had been on an elephant once before, when I was eight years old, in Windsor Safari Park. I had been the same size then as I am now, but the mounting procedure had been made that much easier with the aid of a stepladder. As one of a host of screaming children, I had been led about ten paces before my time was up.

This, then, was the real McCoy. Riding an elephant in India was as common as driving a Nissan Cherry in Britain.

I approached Sawai Madhopur on *Holi*, a religious holiday during which Indians enact a bizarre celebration that involves hurling brightly coloured paint over each other. Roadblocks of stones and wood and bodies were constructed by gangs of boys in an attempt to slow down the traffic. Covered in their war paint, they danced around ecstatically, demanding: 'Rupees! Rupees!' Should you refuse, you found yourself a target for a liberal spattering of paint. The same fate awaited you should you oblige. Being bicycle-bound made matters worse and the only hope was to storm the roadblock at speed. A multitude of waving arms, some clutching sticks, would lash out dangerously in a wild attempt to stop me. Usually I managed to fend off the mob — but never the paint. By the time I arrived in Sawai Madhopur I looked like a moving advertisement for Dulux.

It was in Sawai Madhopur that I was directed, redirected and finally became lost when searching for the dak bungalow. My last request to three betel-nut-chewing men at a junction had resulted in being pointed in three different directions. I ended up at a five-star hotel which happened to be on the edge of the Ranthambhore wildlife reserve — part of Project Tiger and home to forty-six of these biggest of cats. Half a century ago there were 40,000 tigers in India; now there are only 2,500.

Contrary to popular belief, their demise was not entirely due to the unrestrained tiger-hunting sport so eagerly pursued by Maharajahs and officers of the British Raj. Agriculture, poaching, deforestation, rising human populations, army stations, tea-growers' plantations, insecticides and industrial development have all conspired to reduce tiger numbers.

I asked the hotel manager for directions to the dak bungalow and he whisked me up into his jeep. We sped to a remote, jungly spot deep into the game reserve and there stood a tent, in a state of severe disrepair: it consisted of a tattered piece of tarpaulin draped breezily over a bough, beneath which lay a string bed which seemed to have been gnawed by tigers.

'Please,' said the manager, 'it is my sincerest pleasure that you come to passing the night here and if you have luck tiger may visit you.'

Personally, I could not see anything lucky about being stuck at night alone in the middle of the jungle with hungry tigers on the prowl. I politely declined his offer, whereupon he invited me to stay in his hotel free of charge, with meals and tea on the veranda included. This offer I could not refuse.

There was more in the bargain. At dawn the next morning, he escorted me in his jeep into the reserve in search of the elusive tiger. Hours passed as our eyes continually scoured the thicket. I saw warthogs, mongeese, monkeys, crocodiles and

many strange species of deer — but no tiger. I was on the point of giving up all hope when suddenly, rippling through the long, dry grasses, was a real-life tiger of heart-stopping magnificence. Dagger-toothed and jagged-clawed, it was a perfectly designed, burning-eyed, striped killing-machine — a mighty vision of pure grace and power.

I was flying home on the Soviet Union's notorious airline — 'Aeroflop'. I arrived at Delhi airport without a bike box and expecting a bit of a fracas at the checking-in desk as my baggage was well over the weight limit.

However, my first confrontation with a Russian went surprisingly smoothly. The laid-back official was not in the least perturbed about my excess luggage and, as for no bike box, he said, 'No problem, leave zee bicycle as goote.' And that was that. My spanner and allen keys lay redundant; the handlebars remained unswivelled; the pedals remained intact. Things were almost too casual for my liking. I walked towards Customs, leaving my bike propped up against the desk amongst the milling hordes of Delhi airport, with a niggling feeling that that was the last I would see of my trusty steed.

At passport control the Indian official, who obviously thought he was 'a bit of all right', wobbled his head in quaint Indian fashion and said, 'No allowing you to passing.'

'Why not?' I said.

'You stay in my country. You are making me fine wife.'

'Sorry,' I told him, 'but you should have thought of that earlier. I have to go home now.'

'No problem.'

'What do you mean, no problem?'

'No problem you staying in India. You making me very fine wife indeed.'

'It's a nice idea, but I'm afraid I'm fully booked. I already have another twenty-seven husbands dotted around. I'd like to fit you in but, you know — you have to put your foot down somewhere.'

'No problem,' (wobble, wobble), 'you fine wife.'

'If you'd like to take a look at my passport, I'll be on my way.'

'Please, first one kiss as you are hurting my heart.'

'Now look here, Sunny Jim, you're supposed to be a sensible passport official. I don't want to hear about your personal emotional upset.'

'One kiss.'

'No one kiss. Passport look.'

'One kiss.'

'Good grief!'

'Good grief?'

'Yes, good grief — you're working your ticket.'

'One kiss.'

'Look! Passport — is good yes?'

'One kiss no problem.'

'Okay. One kiss, but on passport picture, okay?'

'No problem.'

With that, he delivered a wet one on my photograph and, casting a woeful look towards me that would no doubt linger until the next Western female came along, he let me go.

The air-hostess, a dumpy old matron, woke me in mid-flight and told me to raise my seat: we were about to make an unscheduled landing somewhere in the middle of Russia. No explanations were given. We were all forced to pile out into the freezing night and walk in the snow to a shabby air terminal where we were handed a compulsory glass of sickly-sweet apple-juice. Two hours later we all piled back on board. As I meandered drowsily along the aisles, I thought the apple-juice had gone to my head: taking up three seats of its own was my bike.

We arrived in Moscow and I had a twelve-hour wait for the connecting flight to London. I had tried unsuccessfully to get a twenty-four-hour visa in Delhi and it was frustrating to come to Moscow and yet see nothing more than the airport. I decided to try my luck at escaping into the city anyway; the rules might be different here than at the Russian Embassy in Delhi. I left fellow passengers semi-comatose, propped up against back-packs, and tagged myself on to the end of an Intourist party mingling around Customs, where I sneakily changed a few dollars for roubles with an easygoing tourist.

The next I knew, I was standing outside the door of the airport building in a perishing, ice-cutting wind. It had been that easy! One of the advantages of not being tall enough to reach the desk is that no one notices you and I had been whisked through unseen among the crowds. I could not believe it. Before I felt a KGB hand on my shoulder, I jumped on to the nearest bus (destination unknown) and off we went.

Standing on the battered bus, I was surrounded by warmly-clad, white fleshy bodies with dour, insipid faces and sad eyes. Everyone wore a hat (except me), either brown and furry or grey and woolly. I could feel everyone staring at me but they abruptly turned away whenever I caught their eye. What a difference to India, where everything had been colour, clam-ouring chaos, smiles and heat! It was like suddenly entering a monochrome world. The bus was as cold as the inside of a deep-freeze and my face and feet felt like blocks of ice. Every time the bus stopped to pick someone up, a deathly cold wind blasted through the doors and took your breath away.

We passed through miles of grim suburbs, as grey as the skies, with deteriorating blocks of flats and barren wastelands. No one was playing; no one was smiling. I wondered where we were going. I began to feel a little worried, like a mischievous child running away from home and entering a big, alien, unfamiliar world.

Finally the bus stopped. It went no further. I followed the bulk of the passengers and after a short walk we entered an underground station. Down we went and emerged on an immaculate platform with huge, opulent chandeliers hanging from the roof, ornate and elegant tiles on the walls, carvings and sculptures — the decor was more appropriate to some grand country mansion than a tube station and it was all a far cry from the likes of Tottenham Court Road.

With uncharacteristic foresight, I copied down the name of

the station (in its unpronounceable and meaningless script) as a clue for my return journey. After several stops I decided to get off and see where I emerged, which was on the corner of a massively wide and pleasantly traffic-free road. The sun had come out; it was clear, crisp and beautiful.

I walked purposefully, pretending I knew where I was going, but stopping every now and then to ask someone: 'Red Square, please?' Most of my requests were either ignored or received with uncomprehending looks but one man's reply rather surprised me: 'Have you any Marks & Spencer socks?' Later I learnt that M&S smalls were highly desirable commodities as were jeans, tights, Marlboro cigarettes and Johnnie Walker Red. And condoms — curiously these 'play safe' prerequisites were in hot demand. The homegrown variety, by repute, were made of recycled tractor tyres and killed passion stone dead.

I continued to walk past figures covered from head to toe in monotonous 'sensible' wear: fur hats with folded earflaps, thick jackets, greatcoats, scarves, mittens, gloves, boots. However, compared with the bus passengers, people seemed to have warmed with the sun and there was chatter and smiles.

The stuccoed buildings were amazing — huge, aristocratic, neoclassical houses lined the broad streets. Window displays were virtually nonexistent but I passed one which consisted of two torturous bras draped across a dusty and faded pedestal in a half-hearted attempt to say to the passer-by: 'Look! What an eye-catcher! Come and buy me!'

I found myself in Gorky Street and was soon in Red Square — a place named not after communism but after the colour. Red means beautiful in Russian and beautiful it was. The absurdly vivid colours of the twisty domes of St Basil's Cathedral spiralled magnificently into ice-blue skies. I would have paid a visit to Lenin lying in refrigerated splendour but was put off by the interminable queue. I did not have the time.

I sniffed out a cramped self-service coffee bar where the choice of food was either a brown, stewed slurry with mashed potato and sauerkraut, or soup with buoyant gristle. I opted for soup but navigated around the unidentifiable floating objects. It was delicious and so was the dark, heavy rye bread. I stood at a counter as I ate. The man opposite me was shovelling stew into his mouth with unsavoury slurps, most of the meal trickling down his chin and lodging in his ferocious beard. I did not feel like seconds after that.

Without too many wrong turnings, I returned to the right tube station. Time was running short. When unsure which bus I needed to take me to the airport, I approached a bystander and became an airplane; my actions surprised him but he caught on and pointed me to the right one, which turned out to be the wrong one. It deposited me at the internal rather than international airport. Time was now running out. I fluffed around in a flap, finally found a bus to take me to the right airport and jumped on my flight home with, as Tintin would say, not a minute to spare.

6

Veering on the Ridiculous

LAND'S END TO THE OTHER END ON A WHEELCHAIR BICYCLE

I was parked outside Sainsbury's and making steady progress through a bunch of bananas when I noticed that both I and my bike were being scrutinized with interest from across the street. A middle-aged man with a workman's bottom and string vest was waiting for a gap in the traffic before crossing, and then he was upon me. I knew what was coming.

'Blimey!' he said. 'Is that a bike or a wheelchair?' It was a familiar question.

'It's a bicycle wheelchair,' I said, because it was just that: half bicycle and half wheelchair. This simple idea was set to revolutionize the lives of those whose lives were, sadly, anything but simple.

It was called a Duet and at first glance it resembled a conventional bicycle which had nose-dived into the rear of a conventional wheelchair. In fact it was a brilliant invention designed specifically for transporting the disabled or those of limited mobility, allowing them to experience the exhilarating sense of speed and freedom that is the essence of cycling. Made in Germany, the machine was a relatively new idea and very few people in Britain were aware of its existence, while those that were could barely afford it at £2,000.

The Duet, I thought, was one of those awe-inspiring and beneficial inventions that surely could not be ignored and so my Indian expedition had been not only for fun but also to raise money. I wanted to buy some Duets for the Duchenne Muscular Dystrophy Family Support Group run by Gum and Eva Newnham, whose son, Idris, suffered from this tragic disease.

When I saw how much Idris was benefitting from the Duet on family outings, shopping trips and even in the London-to-Brighton bicycle ride, I hit upon the notion of riding one of these contraptions on an elongated version of the well-worn route from Land's End to John O'Groats. By zigzagging across the country and pedalling it right under people's noses, I felt that surely it could not fail to rouse the interest that it so justly deserved. Money raised *en route* would go directly towards buying a Duet for Barnardo's, the children's charity, whose homes I had pinpointed along the way so that I could give the children day-rides.

It was perhaps a foolhardy idea in that, so far, I had merely sat on a Duet and, being something of a last-minute decision, I had given myself precious little time for preparation. I preferred the idea of spontaneity to one of prolonged organization. In other words, I liked to get on and do it. I would think about the disorganized consequences later, by which time it was usually too late.

Only four days before my estimated time of departure, my Duet was delivered to my doorstep by courtesy of Graham Bell, the UK's sole importer. That gave me time enough to get accustomed to it, I reckoned, if not much for practising.

London, like all fast cities where the traffic moves slowly or not at all, was not the best place for familiarizing myself with the Duet's quirky and temperamental handling mechanisms. It called for a lot of weaving in and out of traffic, for a start. Also, I felt a trifle daft riding around with an empty wheelchair and I thought it might be nice to put someone into my wheelchair to look daft with me. Fortunately this was no problem: the summer train and Underground strikes being what they were, I seized the opportunity of springing my rickshaw services upon those commuters who were appalled at the realization that, during this time of crisis, their legs were their only means of ferrying themselves from A to B. I decided to focus my attention on those to whom physical exertion was an alien idea and who would surely jump at the chance of a ride.

The bulk of my business was acquired by patiently queueing up at the local taxi rank — though my 'taxi', apart from being a three-wheeled wheelchair, had no meter or set fares. Instead I had a Barnardo's Appeal collection box dangling from the headrest, leaving it up to the passengers to make a donation of their choice.

Cycling around London with a City gent on board was not quite the sort of training I had envisaged but it gave me a taster as far as transporting a load was concerned ... and what a load! A worryingly large number of my customers were, frankly, very fat. Their bodies, moulded by effortless first-class trains or slobmobiles with every fingertip-controlled gadgets imaginable, were formed around grossly expanded girths. Of course, I had seen tubbies before (after all, I cooked for many and could well be to blame for their shape) but I had never before viewed them from the slightly aerial position that the Duet provided. Poised in the driving seat, I was that much higher and could look down upon the formidable mass I was struggling to transport. All I could see was a head (proportionally small and usually bald) perched incongruously on top of an excessively inflated midriff — and then, far away, looking as though they wanted nothing to do with that body, a pair of lost and diminutive feet.

Once they had overcome the initial shock of being transported in a wheelchair, my passengers would settle in quite nicely, some even pleading for an extra lap around the block before being deposited outside the office. Others would chat away like excited youngsters on a school outing while taking a keen interest in their whereabouts. I liked to get them actively involved if I could. Some excelled themselves as navigators: 'Sharp left! Sharp right! Full steam ahead! Turn... *now*!' or 'Careful! Temperamental Porsche approaching two o'clock.' Others revelled in the role of impersonating a car indicator (erratic arm thrusts — which, on one occasion, nearly brought an overtaking cyclist to grief) or human horn: 'Baaaahhh!' or 'Beep, beep!' or, when neither worked, 'Move over, you lane-hogging bastard.'

It tickled me to think that here I was with maybe a company director who at one moment resembled an outsized schoolboy frantically fending off taxis and orally hooting at the traffic, only to be carrying out some multi-million pound business deal the next.

Generally, the traffic treated us with the respect that such a contraption deserved and gave us a wide berth. But there is always the odd motorized maniac who regards anything else on the road as unimportant. One such whizzkid in his supersonic four-wheeled monstrosity shunted me up the rear. I was not one to let such driving antics get up my backside, literally or metaphorically. I jettisoned my passenger (who felt as angry as I at the driver's behaviour) and quickly caught up with the offender, now firmly lodged in a traffic jam, for a verbal sort-out. The cheeky young whippersnapper was put firmly in his place.

Weight-saving for a cycling tour is a matter I usually take seriously — to an extent. I will take the lightest quality tent, sleeping-bag and sleeping mat that I can find on the market and then go and ruin it all by filling up my panniers with a lorry-load of food. Although I admit to being something of an ounce-counting fanatic in one way, I am a bit of a joke compared with those *Cycling to the Centre of the Earth* Crane cousins, who drilled holes in plastic teaspoons and substituted a forefinger for a front derailleur.

This time, however, since I was attempting to ride a bicycle with the equivalent of an inverted bathtub attached to the front, I decided to treat myself by taking a gas stove (for serious porridge-making), a small radio (to help wile away the time) and an extra pair of undies for . . . well . . . just in case, really.

My original idea had been to carry a disabled passenger all the way to John O'Groats but this would have proved imprac-tical for two reasons. The first was that I would have had to act responsibly (something that has never come naturally) and work out a tightly-kept schedule respecting the needs of my passenger, who would undoubtedly find the journey very diffi-cult, uncomfortable and possibly dangerous. There could be no tearing down the Pennines in a rainstorm with me at the helm nor would it be possible to camp. The second reason was that I would have nowhere to store my porridge supplies: I was strapping a large rucksack full of oats into the wheelchair to act as my 'person'.

The latter was a purely selfish reason but I seriously do not think I would have carried out the challenge had I not been able to camp whenever my legs put their feet down, refusing to take me further, and then been able to make a bowl of revitalizing stodge immediately. It seemed much more practical to ride independently, visiting the various homes for the handicapped and giving them day-rides along the way.

I expected an ugly confrontation with British Rail over transporting such a lump of equipment from Paddington to Penzance — after all, it was often a battle to take a normal bicycle. Unbelievably, the overnight journey passed without incident and, to their credit, the guards were cordial, helpful — and generous: my collection tin was already beginning to rattle most promisingly. The only problem I encountered was that, contrary to what I had been told, the train was nearly full and it was thus impossible for me to catch a good night's snooze by turning horizontal at full stretch on a double-berth seat — usually an easy feat for someone of my size.

The train terminated at Penzance, ten hilly miles from my Land's End starting point. I had no intention whatsoever of riding this distance, which did not count as expedition mileage. Energy conservation was high on the agenda for this ride; after all, I felt that to cycle this contraption nonstop for more than one mile was a feat in itself. I was not going to undertake any superfluous stuff. (As it turned out, my calculations were as usual wildly out and I ended up doing twice as much as originally intended.)

Arriving bleary-eyed on that damp and dismal morning, I discovered that there was a hitch. With uncharacteristic forethought, I had already checked by telephone to make sure that a bus's boot was large enough to house my machine and had been much relieved to be assured that there would be no problem. That had been misleading. It did not fit and it was obvious that no amount of pushing and pummelling and twisting would make it do so.

Time to fret, I thought, as I would now have to pedal and would never arrive at my starting point by the alloted time to meet a local reporter for the all-important snapshot. In fact, it was anybody's guess whether I would reach it at all: so far I had not encountered the slightest slope (apart from the Euston underpass), let alone a hill, and the countryside hereabouts was not flat.

As it happened, the boss busman sensed that I was a damsel in distress and gallantly sprang to my rescue by escorting me in the company van, free of charge. Heart-warming, it was.

Land's End had been given a dramatic face-lift since my previous two-wheeled visit a decade before. Multi-millionaire Peter de Savary now owned it and had turned it into a tourist complex. The writer of the tourist brochure felt that 'nowhere else gives quite the same sensation of oneness with nature'. Hmm. You had the opportunity to be jostled among clamouring coachloads and eat a choice of either 'fast' or 'slow' food, buy 'Cornish' biscuits (made in Devon) or visit exhibitions tantalizingly entitled 'Man against the Sea', 'Spirit of Cornwall' or the sensational 'multi-sensory experience in the last Labyrinth'.

Not in the mood for clambering over models of restored shipwrecks or learning about the past plottings of the pirates of Penzance, I opted to sit on the windswept cliff-top contemplating the coming venture with growing concern. I was joined by my send-off party — all two of them: my brother Dave and my new sister-in-law, none other than Melanie. Not only had they motorbiked all the way from London but also (without any pressure from me) had willingly, albeit foolishly, offered to participate in the first day's activities.

So, out of the wheelchair came my rucksack (full of food) and in went Melanie (full of silliness). A quick cliff-top pose for the photo-call and we were off ... or were we? I was pedalling frantically but getting nowhere. Surely Mel could not be *that* heavy? Scouring my control panel, I discovered that I had forgotten to release the handbrake (all a bit high tech for me, really). A quick flick of the lever and ... ah-ha! That was better. We moved — not particularly fast, I admit, but somewhere was better than nowhere.

After only a hundred yards my legs had already turned to jelly and my temporary passenger was subject to the most uncouth howls of hysteria, which did not help matters much.

Anybody who spotted us weaving and wobbling our way up the road must have doubted the whole pea-brained expedition almost as much as I did myself.

At the first slightest rise in gradient, I was alarmed to realize that it would be both easier and quicker to walk. I pushed my eject button and out shot Mel, who was bitterly disappointed to learn that not only would she be missing out on a free ride to Penzance but also it was necessary for her to become actively involved in pushing the machine.

It was painfully slow going. With the average speed hovering around five mph, I did not dare guess how long the whole trip might take. It was evident by now that it would be a *very* long time. All I knew was that, by the most direct route, John O'Groats was about 840 miles away.

The Duet was something of a 'wide vehicle' and it became evident that we were preventing an agitated bus from over-taking along the winding road. Knowing how infuriating it is to be stuck behind a caravan, I considerately pulled over to the side. As the bus slowly passed its occupants' heads swivelled in our direction, grinning inanely and gesticulating vividly at this decidedly dubious duo. Just up the road the bus stopped in a layby; the spritely driver jumped out, enquired, 'What the devil are you playing at?' and then cheerfully donated some cash to the kitty, saying: 'You'll have a whale of a time. I walked it last year in four weeks and had the time of my life.' A glimmer of hope prevailed: if he could walk it in four, surely I could ride it in five ...

As we crawled to the crest of a hill, St Michael's Mount at last loomed into view. We yelped with delighted triumph — after nearly two and a half hours Penzance was within easy striking distance. With an enthusiastic surge of energy, we found ourselves cruising into town at a fairly respectable speed (in the circumstances) to meet Dave, who had long been awaiting our arrival.

It was an emotional end to the first day, not because I had succeeded in completing the first leg of the ride but because nowhere in Penzance could we find baked potatoes, something my stomach had craved ever since leaving Land's End.

However, we did come across a church hall in which Billy Graham ('LIFE: do you know the meaning?') was beaming down by satellite video live from Earl's Court, rapturously 'spreading the Word'. The place was packed and we wedged ourselves into a pew between a couple of old dears who said, 'Who is this Willy Graham anyroad?' Later one of them noisily unwrapped some strong-smelling meat-paste sandwiches from some recycled bacofoil (Doris: 'You think of everything, Ethel') which they munched, dropping a cascade of crumbs all over their knobbly tweed skirts and the floor of the church hall.

As for Willy Graham, he was impossible to see through the enlarged and distorting grains of the video screen but I did not mind: our surrounding audience proved of far more interest to me. Apart from Ethel and Doris, who polished off their paste sarnies and produced a thermos of tea from their basket as well as some crumbly rockbuns, there were two ten-year-olds in front determined to pull down each other's shorts (unfortunately they failed) and, behind us, a man in a tight white polo-neck listening avidly to Willy Graham's godly pontifications and intermittently rising to his feet to thrust both arms heavenwards and cry, 'Yes! Yes!' with a passionate and holy fervour.

The next day the sun showed its face and from then until I hit the Scottish Highlands I had a British heatwave on my hands. That Sunday morning's ride started promisingly enough and we made it a good ten miles closer to John O'Groats by means of a relay system. When I became weary from pushing Mel's formidable bulk (well, she *seemed* heavy) she took the helm while I sedately reclined up front, acknowledging the curious looks of passers-by with a pompously regal wave. And when Mel flagged (far too quickly) she took the driving seat of the motorbike while Dave pedalled (far too enthusiastically), hitting speeds that almost catapulted me into oblivion whenever we hit a pot-hole, despite my being strapped and superglued into the wheelchair.

We contemplated devising a towing system whereby I

could be hitched to the rear of the motorbike and dragged. It was tempting but I had a niggly feeling that it might be regarded as cheating, as well as dangerous.

With that remarkable ten miles behind us, we stopped to recuperate over a pub lunch. It occurred to me that I had better start acting with embarrassing conspicuousness if I was hoping to raise enough money on this jaunt to give Barnardo's a Duet, and so I pedalled my three-wheeler through the pub and out into the crowded beer garden, parking it to be tripped over by all and sundry. The response was promising and my shaker grew steadily heavier.

Our lunch stop extended far longer than anticipated and it was almost early evening before we summoned enough enthusiasm and energy to continue. To be suffering from such list-lessness on only the second day was not a promising sign.

The next stop was Camborne, where I had the address of Brian Lessiter, an incredible man. A few years previously he had jumped over his neighbour's wall, landed with straight legs and broken his back. In that instant his spine had been compacted — the discs crushed and ruptured — and he found himself confined to a wheelchair for the rest of his life. Whereas I would have withered up and gone to seed, Brian's enthusiastic outlook on life had only escalated. Despite being in constant pain, he was unbelievably good-humoured, optimistic and encouraging — and certainly not one to curl up in the corner with self-pity. He was, as he said, 'a curtain twitcher'; he liked to see what was going on and to become involved. Hence he had become untiringly active in his local groups for the handicapped and disabled and had organized and participated in numerous sporting events. He had even won two Disabled Olympic medals.

Although I had never met him before in my life, after only a few minutes I felt as though I had known him for years — he was that sort of a person. His bravery and his physical and mental strength affected me deeply and made me realize the perseverance and sheer determination that disabled people possess. Brian inspired me greatly and the thought of his dogged audacity would spur me on whenever I hit trying and exhausting times on the ride.

When I left, he gave me a cheque towards the Duet and a foot-long Cornish pasty specially made by his wife, Cecilia, which fuelled me for weeks to come.

Sunday evening. It was time to dispense with Melanie. She clambered from wheelchair to pillion and my support vehicle roared back towards London. From then on I was all on my own but we arranged to rendezvous at suitable weekend locations as I slowly inched my way northwards. Unfortunately, though, my support crew soon realized that they had much better things to do than chase round the countryside in search of their wheelchair-pedalling sister.

On day three I encountered my one and only accident (though there were plenty of near misses). It was a minor spill and came about because I had not yet quite come to grips with the idiosyncracies of the Duet's handling devices. I was on a particularly severe descent amongst the Cornish hills; in fact it was more like a drop than a descent — the road just fell away beneath me, rather like cycling unawares over a cliff. Too late I realized that I was in big trouble and it was not the best time to experiment with my emergency braking techniques. I plummeted downwards and my stomach seemed to shoot out through the roof of my head as I veered across the road out of control. Hitting an inconsiderately placed rock, I jack-knifed and was jettisoned into a clump of roadside nettles. As a result of this incident, the Duet was renamed Vera for its frequent tendency to veer off course.

'I'm sorry, but did you say porridge?' asked the disc jockey, pushing up his baseball cap.

'Yes,' I replied, perplexed as to why he should look so quizzical.

'And you mean to say,' he continued, 'that you think you

would not be able to do this ride without your daily intake of porridge?'

'Well, I'd certainly have severe trouble,' I said.

I had arrived in Exeter minutes earlier, hot and bothered from the severe undulations of Dartmoor which I had crossed in temperatures peaking in the 90s. Peter Tansley, an alternative engineer with alternative ideas and of formidable bulk, had taken me straight into the local Radio Devon studios. My immediate reaction was to panic.

'Don't panic,' they told me, 'the interview won't be live.'

For that reason, I was quite happy to talk about my insatiable porridge-eating capacity in what they told me was the warm-up session. Little did I know that Radio Devon listeners were learning things about oats that they never knew before.

Meeting big Peter Tansley, born and bred in the Shetlands, was one of the most memorable events of my 'End to End' (as they say in the trade). It was easy to see that he was an inventor as soon as I entered his home: by a series of ingenious sliding shunts and tugs, his computer folded itself away and became a guest bed. Then he took me out back for a wobbly spin on his tandem recumbent, which was an astonishing achievement and experience. It felt a bit like 'playing trains', only much better. In his backyard garage ('built without a straight line in it') he had spent ten years building tandem frames with such skill that he had people riding his name all around the world.

Peter was not interested in flaunting his wares; he became bored if he had to make the same thing twice and, instead of churning out a production line of goods, he turned his hand to innovative dabblings. Ingenious experimentation was the name of his game. Dotted around the country are creations which can be credited to the Tansley Touch: a solarmobile car (which he successfully raced in Switzerland's Tour de Sol); a hand-cranked Paratrike (for a paraplegic) which was seven times more energy-efficient than a conventional wheelchair; the Oxtrike, designed specifically for use in the Third World; a car tricycle rack; bicycle trailers; tricycles; and brakes, handle-bars, lights and panniers of all descriptions, jewellery, electric fiddles — oh yes, and tortoise houses. He had even tinkered with remedial cures for Daleks.

Being someone who has trouble reconnecting the links in a bicycle chain, I was truly flabbergasted by Peter's limitless powers of inventiveness.

'So what's next on the agenda?' I asked.

'A degree in geography,' he said in his lyrical Shetland accent. I thought he was joking but he was serious all right. He had shut up shop for a few years and headed back to college to make up for something he felt was missing.

The next day, after his wife Gethyn had refuelled me on an irresistible supply of gastronomic wonders, six-foot two-inch Peter, with arms of steel, escorted me to Taunton on one of his own machines. Every time we reached a hill (which in Devon is often), I no longer came to a standstill and rolled backwards as was my custom. Instead, I shot over one-in-fours at speeds verging on the ridiculous — thanks to the unearthly pushing powers of the Tansley left arm. The secret to such uncanny strength? Scottish oatcakes. Peter loved his oatcakes as much as I loved my porridge and he would scuttle into every store we passed in order to devour their stocks.

Taunton was the first of the Barnardo's homes I visited and my stay went down a treat. The staff were incredibly friendly and encouraging, and Vera was a great success with the children. Despite this, I rode away with a heavy heart. I had never been in such close contact with so many tragically deformed children before. There I was, free and fortunate enough to go gallivanting independently round the world doing what I wanted, while those children, many of whom were confined to a wheelchair for life, were forever dependent on others for their survival and would never be free to venture off on their own down the road, let alone out into the world. The more homes I visited, the more I was amazed at the benevolent determination of the parents, friends, helpers and staff who had dedicated their lives and sacrificed their own independence. Their responsibilities were enormous and my admiration grew not only for the children but also for the sheer strong-mindedness and evident love that the carers put into their work.

Cyclists say that you cannot beat travelling by bicycle — it is neither too fast nor too slow but is just the right speed for noticing things worth noticing. With the bicycle wheelchair, on the other hand, my speed was often so painfully slow that I was able to count the road chippings as I pedalled over them. It was so bad that in the Yorkshire Dales a little old lady laden with shopping overtook me as she walked up the hill.

''Ere, flower,' she said, 'looks to me like yer could do with an 'and like. And all on yer tod too!'

So I strapped on her shopping and together we pushed Vera as we chatted and chuckled all the way to the top of the hill.

With the media full of news about rapes, murders, child molesters, sex offenders and thieves, it is easy to forget just how nice the majority of the people living in Britain are. Before venturing forth on Vera, I had been disillusioned into thinking that the place was full of suspicious characters. It was a pleasant surprise to discover that such undesirables form only a tiny minority; riding through Britain from toe to tip, I found everyone (with one exception) to be chatty, friendly, generous, interesting, hospitable and humorous.

And the countryside, too — I had forgotten just how beautiful it was. When I was seventeen, I cycled round the coast of Britain and Ireland without really appreciating it; although I loved what I saw, I was more wrapped up in the adventure of cycling off alone somewhere. But now, slowly wending my way along narrow and leafy country lanes, I realized not only what a lovely land it was but also how tragically it was being ruined and overrun by the absurd volume of traffic. Cycling over Dartmoor at eight mph, for example, I overtook a continuous line of crawling traffic. The car parks were packed — but not with the vehicles of those who wanted to go for a brisk hike across the rolling moorland. Rather, they 'stretched their legs' with a return trip to Mr Whippy's ice-cream van and then sat encapsulated in their hot metal boxes, eating and licking their lips before rejoining the jams.

In the sizzling sunshine, I passed families cooped up in their cars; the offspring were fighting over a bag of crisps on the back seat, mother was tetchy and in tears, while father steamed and head-butted the steering wheel. I thought: those poor people. Like a fairy godmother I wanted to wave my magic wand (a bicycle pump) and introduce them to the joys of one or two or three wheels. They would have been so much happier mounted on a tandem, the children racing alongside enjoying the wind, the sun and the fresh air. But the majority of people seem to regard bicycles as toys, things for children, certainly not something to take seriously as a 'proper' form of transport. They often say to me, 'When I was your age I used to ride everywhere, I did.'

'So why don't you now?' I ask.

'Oooh! You must be joking! I couldn't — not any more,' they say, 'it would kill me at my age. And it's so dangerous, too.'

It is all a myth. Cycling is easy. There is no race, unless you want one. You go at your own speed, taking your time, and these days there are gears so low that you can ride up a wall — no trouble. As for danger, as long as you ride sensibly and take precautions, I believe cycling is no more dangerous than driving a car.

Today the roads are choking with traffic. I become exasperated when a constant convoy of cars passes me as I cycle along. Where are all those people going? Wherever it is, they do not usually have to go there, or at least not so often. Maybe most of them just drive around in circles.

As a result of my increasing addiction to cycling, I discovered that the more I depended upon my bicycle, the more I disliked cars. I admit they are useful and convenient but it is an overrated convenience which is surreptitiously taking over our lives and making too many people lazy and overweight. Life, it seems, has become too easy and we are paying for that with poor health, stress and dirty air.

Apart from the havoc that cars create in the world at large, they can also do strange things to their drivers. Once inside a car, a perfectly pleasant person seems to undergo a personality transformation and turns into some sort of snarling devil at the mere flick of the ignition key. Normally sane and responsible people can turn nasty the moment they get behind the wheel: they suddenly decide that they are invincible as well as infallible and they let off psychological steam from within the apparent security of their vehicles, releasing pent-up frustration and subconscious aggression in a way they would never do on foot.

Cars have become quiet, cosy cocoons which give drivers a sense of isolation and privacy. How often do you see someone sitting in the car next to you, inches away, quite blatantly cleaning their ears or picking their noses? It is a habit that they would scrupulously avoid in any other public place but, safely ensconced in their comfortable compartment, they feel insulated from the real world outside their glass windows.

Perhaps I am something of an ozone-free, stinging-nettle tea sort of person but I do not wear sandals, nor a beard. I just love cycling, that is all, and hate to see and be threatened by the multiplying swarms of vehicles on the roads — vehicles which kill not only their own occupants but also pedestrians, animals, cyclists and the surroundings. By simply getting 'on yer bike' you can reduce the traffic, help clean the air, improve your health and alleviate your own feelings of stress. At the same time you would be ensuring that fewer new roads carve up the countryside. The billions of pounds could go on something more useful than making another lane for the M25 and the environment as a whole would be healthier and happier.

I admit I have never been fond of the motor car and my immediate reaction once inside one is to get out of it. Such a deep dislike could stem from a nasty little incident which occurred when I was six years old. My mother was driving me and my brothers to school in an old Vauxhall estate; my elder brother was up front in the 'grown-ups' seat', I was in the boot playing happily among some moth-eaten, oil-stained rugs, while somewhere in between was my younger brother, playing the fool. We stopped at Milland crossroads, waited for the road to be clear and then accelerated off up the road. Mum continued to drive schoolwards until, glancing in the rear-view mirror, she suddenly realized something was wrong. In fact, something was very wrong. The door of the boot was no longer visible. More worryingly, nor was her daughter.

Half a mile back down the road, I was found lying spread-eagled and confused bang in the middle of the crossroads, surrounded by remnants of car boot. Thanks to a quick-thinking farmer who scooped me up out of harm's way, I was narrowly saved from being flattened by a fast-approaching car-driver who obviously thought I was nothing more than a cowpat. The outcome was an extremely distressed mother and a severely bruised daughter — but a very welcome day off school.

Back to Vera: Everywhere I went I met people who amazed me with their genuine generosity. Cars would overtake, hooting and tooting, and their drivers would run back to put money in my tin. One woman who read about me in her *Worcester News* spotted me on a country lane south of Newcastle and was ecstatic.

'Oooh! It really is you. I don't believe it,' she yelped. 'I'm so glad I caught you.'

She was on her way to visit friends but she made it sound as though she had spent the past two weeks tracking me down. My head was growing too big for my helmet.

Often farmers would not hear of me sleeping out in their fields: instead they would insist on giving me a bed and enough food to feed the Tour de France. When I parked outside shops, schoolchildren would sacrifice some of their valuable sweet-money and rattle it into my shaker instead. At a small corner store in Durham, the shop assistant would not hear of me paying for my supper supplies. Another woman let me pick from her strawberry fields to my heart's (or stomach's) content. Mr Potter from Cramlington used a defunct toilet named Pink Percy to collect donations from his local social club.

Entering the outskirts of Birmingham, the countryside fizzled out fast before I had a chance to find a camping place. It was dark when I knocked on the door of a nursing home for old women. After the matron's initial surprise, she gave me soap and a shower and allowed me to camp in the rose garden.

'But I must leave a note for the gardener,' she said. 'He is getting on a bit, you know, and to find a tent and your funny bike among his flowers might come as a shock.'

One Saturday afternoon near Leeds, I was surrounded by a bunch of tough-looking, can-slurping football fans. I thought: uh oh, here we go, here we go, here we go . . . and I prepared myself for a dust-up. My fears were unfounded; all they wanted was a test ride and to make a donation.

There was only one unpleasant moment. In a remote part of the Wye Valley a van driver stopped to put money in my tin and asked first for directions and secondly for my undies. I gave him a piece of my mind instead; he returned with a barrage of obscenities and followed me off and on for the next few miles.

Riding Vera all day every day was a tiring business and it did not take me long to realize that I had never done anything quite so strenuous. I was well and truly exhausted and finally thought that I might be slightly overdoing things one day when I was camping in a wheatfield in the Pennines.

I had woken at 5.30AM (my usual time), wolfed down my porridge and then realized I was still feeling weary. I thought: I'll give myself a treat — a half-hour lie-in. The next I knew, I was being shaken awake by a bemused farmer five hours later. I had never slept so late in my life. I felt drugged. As I staggered out of my tent like a zombie, I came face to face with the massive blades of a combine harvester.

'I came to wake you up before beginning work,' the farmer said, 'but you looked so peaceful I thought it best to leave you. I was sure you'd wake up with all the noise; I've been cutting round you for three hours. You must have been dead to the world.'

He had harvested the whole field apart from the small square patch of my camp and I had not heard a thing — a fact I found rather worrying. Had the farmer suffered from myopia, I could have ended up as extra protein in someone's Shredded Wheat.

One of the advantages of riding a wheelchair o'er hill 'n' dale was that at least I was never short of a seat. It seemed a waste to struggle with it for over a thousand miles if I did not make use of the chair. If I was half way up a hill and my legs ceased to be a part of me, I would put on the handbrake, reach for a banana and a book and shunt from saddle to seat for a rest and a read. Thinking about it now, I suppose it is not surprising that I received a few strange looks. At the time, however, I felt it was the most natural thing in the world to pull over and recline in my wheelchair with my feet up.

I arrived in Scotland in style, thanks to Graham 'Bicycle' Bell. He arranged a real live Scotsman kitted out in a kilt and bellowing bagpipes, who marched with me into the Land of Porridge, together with a small procession of Vera supporters which Graham had mustered. Down the road in Coldstream I stayed for a few recuperative nights in his old cobble-floored abode, which he shared with the McGurn brigade. It was also home to *New Cyclist*, the 'happening magazine for bicycle people'.

The miles were flying by and the generosity continued. When I reached Aberdeen, the local muscular dystrophy support group gave me free bed and board in the airport hotel for three days. It was sheer bliss — I lay in a semi-comatose state for most of my stay.

Sea, sheep and a few caber-tossers were all I had for company as I cycled up the east coast of Scotland. The weather deteriorated rapidly but I suppose Scotland would not be Scotland unless you hit misty, wet and windy moments. Near Dornoch the heavens opened impressively with the sort of rain that falls so hard it gives you a headache. People stood watching the downpour from their cottage doorways; others pressed faces against steamy window panes. I was enjoying my battle against the elements but I wondered what these onlookers were making of this saturated, singing blur flying along at the helm of a wheelchair.

It was on the final stretch to John O'Groats that I happened upon a handful of others doing their own thing in their own way on the 'End to End'. Among them was a bunch of businessmen cycling the route in seven days, in aid of leukemia research — the leader's wife had recently died of the disease. In their slipstream were two back-up vehicles and three lurching caravans.

'Where's your support?' they asked, as they glided alongside effortlessly.

'They're on a motorcycling holiday in France,' I said, 'so this ...' (pointing to my porridge-laden rucksack on the front seat) '... has to suffice for now. It's got all I need.'

They appeared a bit stupefied and left me with an EEC mountain of muesli bars before soaring into the distance.

Another fellow was running the route via the highest of Britain's three peaks — Ben Nevis, Scafell and Snowdon. Most bizarre of all was Malcolm Edwards, who was pushing a pram from his home in Yorkshire to Land's End, thence up to John O'Groats and back to Yorkshire again, a total of 1,809 miles. His rather forlorn figure loomed from out of the mist atop the notoriously severe Berriedale Hill. There were no babies inside his pram and all I saw was a motley collection of recycled plastic bags, crumpled and odorous clothes and some sour-smelling milk cartons. Protruding from the pram's starboard bow was a stick with an old duster attached to it.

'To mayke sure them bluudy dravers give me spayce,' he explained.

Malc and I spent a few enjoyable moments comparing contraptions and exchanging news and views, after which I declared him a definite oddball. The fact that he did not agree with me was a sure sign that my diagnosis was correct and I left him to be painfully pram-dragged down Berriedale.

After almost 1,600 miles (twice as many as originally anticipated) and with enough money to donate Vera to Barnardo's, I finally arrived at my goal beneath cold, grey skies. It was an uneventful occasion — just a sign (that I climbed on, sat on and turned upside down on), a souvenir shop (that I gave a wide berth) and a few cold tourists, most of whom remained inside their cars and campers clutching steaming cups of tea and gazing gloomily out to sea.

After five contraption-battling weeks, it was something of an anticlimax to have suddenly reached John O'Groats. The place takes it name from a sixteenth-century Dutch settler, Jan de Groot, who reputedly built the peculiar octagonal house with an octagonal table and eight separate doors so that the eight quarrelling branches of his family would have equal precedence.

It was easy to mistake this uneventful place as the northernmost point of mainland Britain and, standing on the tip, I had presumed just that — until reading some tourist blurb, from which I discovered that this distinction belongs to Dunnet Head ten miles along the coast. I rode westwards until I reached it, and there I thought: Dunnet? Done it. That put me in a higher mood and I rode back to Jan de Groot's, where I ate a banana and then decided to overshoot my mark by paying a visit to the Orkney Islands.

It was the right decision. The Orcadians were unbelievably friendly. On one occasion, emerging from the rolling mists, I met a young family cycling to the fish market.

'Here, lass,' said the father, 'you'll find our wee house top o' hill, the door's open, help yourself to a cup o' tea and make yourself at home.'

Mrs Simpson spotted me riding along Stromness harbour front and, before I had scarce a chance to murmur, she ditched my rucksack, hitched up her skirts and hurled herself into the wheelchair with enthusiasm.

'Ah darling'!' she said. 'Pedal your wee bonny scooter round town and we'll get yee shaker filled in no time.' She was right: we did.

The Orkneys were a collection of wonderfully wild and windswept islands and are now a diver's paradise, due to the disastrous wartime sinking of battleships (mainly in Scapa Flow). Between the islands of Papay and Westray lies the route for the shortest scheduled air service in the world: it lasts a mere 120 seconds and is even shorter if there is a tailwind.

I certainly got the wind up my tail when cycling around Rousay. Having left the bulk of my baggage behind in my tent, I tore around this almost uninhabited island with great gusto. Bounding and bouncing my way among the pot-holes on a bicycle wheelchair (of all daft things) I felt immensely happy. One moment I was soaring along beside the sea-lashed coast, home to a multitude of bobbing seals' heads; the next I was high in the hills being bathed in dazzling streaks of sunlight shining through a momentary break in the unpredictable skies. It was an unforgettable moment but it was a happiness that did not last long.

Back in London there was a message on my answering machine from one of my great cycling friends, Chris Shaw, inviting me to supper. I phoned him up, only to be told the devastating news that Chris had died the previous day as the result of a car careering into him while he was out on his bike.

Suddenly everything seemed so pointless. I felt angry, upset, sickened, deflated and confused. And that was just me — what must his family and really close friends feel like? It seemed such an utter waste. Chris, so young and vibrant, was suddenly gone. There would be no more of his bright and boisterous chatter. Tearing along through the countryside with Chris on mountain bikes while trying desperately to follow in his hair-raisingly navigated wake (which I usually failed to negotiate) would from now on be only a memory. Like that exhilarating and blustery ride on Orkney, it would be an unforgettable one.

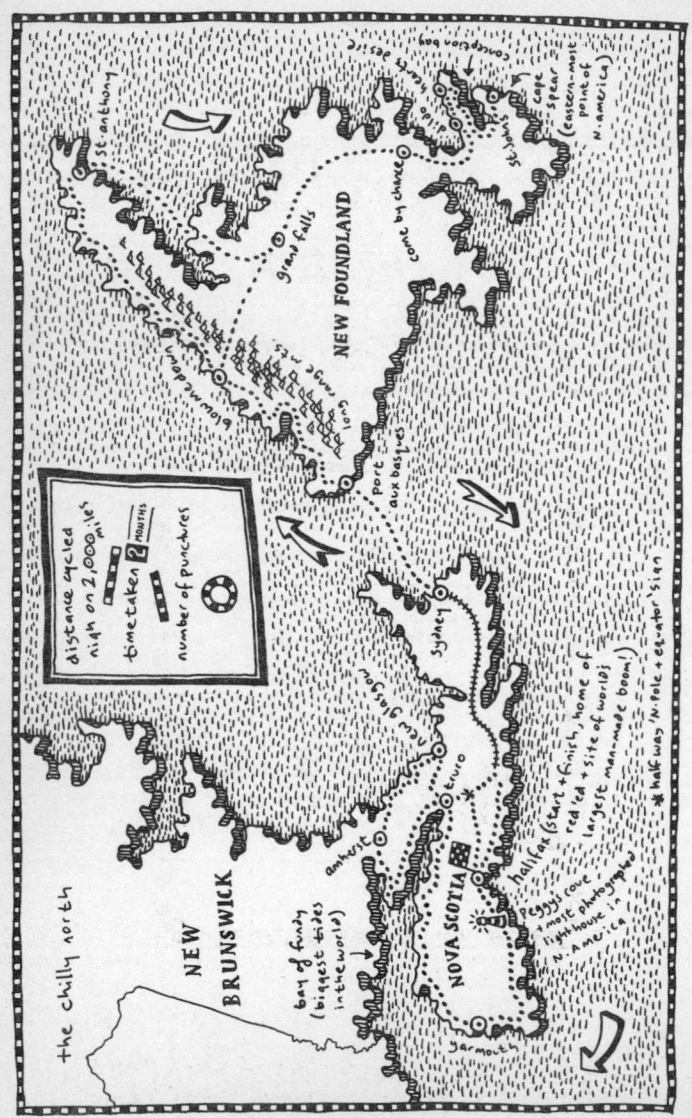

7

The World's Your Lobster

A NOVA SCOTIAN EXCURSION

'When you stop pedalling your bicycle, you fall off.'
SAMUEL LONGHORNE CLEMENS, 'Mark Twain'

'Caution — lobsters crossing,' read the sign. I knew I must be in Nova Scotia, the lobster capital of the world, where in some areas tyre-crushed crustacean carcasses lined the sides of the road. However, they were not the unfortunate jaywalking victims of careless driving. People would buy cooked lobsters, pick at them as they drove along and then fling the inedible remnants out of the car window as if they were apple cores or empty bottles.

I was in this eastern Canadian maritime province for a month's cycling tour. I had started by daring to visit Red'ed: he lived in Halifax where in 1917, he informed me, the largest manmade explosion ever had occurred. (This record was later broken by the detonation of the atomic bomb.) A Belgian relief vessel had collided in mid-harbour with a French munitions ship loaded with 2,500 tons of explosives. In a horrifying split second, the north end of Halifax was demolished. Over 1,600 buildings were levelled, some 2,000 people were killed and another 6,000 injured. Factory workers, sailors, stevedores and children on their way to school along the bustling waterfront were engulfed in a massive blast that killed them instantly. Thousands more were maimed or blinded by flying glass. The explosion was heard in Truro, sixty miles away, and the anchor from the French ship was found in a field more than two miles distant.

I set out alone along the South Shore. My first stop was Peggy's Cove, home to the most photographed lighthouse in North America and one which has the unique distinction of containing a post office. The Nova Scotians seem to have an obsessive pride in their province, claiming the fame of the most mundane building or location as the highest, the first, the only, and so on. I had even passed a bizarre sign stating 'Halfway North Pole Equator' when I was leaving the airport a few days earlier.

After the busy roads of southern England, Nova Scotia seemed a cyclist's paradise. Routes marked on my map as major highways were almost free of traffic. Yet it was certainly no nation of cyclists — everyone drove everywhere and they all treated me as a curiosity because of my preference for two wheels. 'Hell, kid,' the locals would say, 'what d'ya wanna drive a bike for?' (Apparently you drive rather than ride a bicycle there.)

And I could forget about asking anyone the distance to somewhere. Either no one knew or they gave a hugely inaccurate answer, their minds working in motoring time.

'Excuse me,' I would say, 'how far is the town (or campsite or shop)?'

'Only twenty minutes.'

'No, I mean in miles or kilometres.'

'Well, hon,' they would say, 'I haven't a clue.' And it was true.

I wove my way along the rocky, rugged coastline and through many a tiny, picturesque fishing village. There were glorious white, sandy beaches, empty and clean, with not a soul or a piece of litter in sight. Cycling along the banks of the wide La Have river, I frequently spotted herons feeding in the shallow waters at low tide. There were lots of other strange warbling and diving birds that swooped spectacularly from the skies but sadly, being no ornithologist, I was unable to identify them. Herons, blackbirds and blue tits are about my limit.

Having disembarked after the short cable-ferry crossing, I stopped at La Have bakery and asked the owner, Gael, if she knew of a good place to camp.

'If you fancy babysitting for the night,' she said, 'you're very welcome to stay here.'

The bakery was a wonderfully ramshackle, century-old wooden shipping warehouse that reached out over the river, one side being a quay for the many small fishing-boats. Gael and her helpers baked 500 loaves a day.

'In summer we start baking at midnight,' she told me, 'but winter is easy — we begin around 3AM.'

In Gael's family kitchen, which was separate from the bakery, there lived an assortment of animals — a large, bounding dog, a rabbit called Liquorice, the ear-splitting Eric the parrot and soon, promised nine-year-old Sadie, a pet lizard. Amidst this menagerie the son had fixed up a skate-boarding ramp and was colliding with force into every conceivable object, including myself. Gael and her husband, Mike, felt confident enough to leave me in this madhouse while they went off to their country cottage for the night.

'If the fire alarm goes off — run like hell!' they said comfortingly.

Miraculously I had both offspring and livestock under control by midnight and a glorious peace prevailed. But there was a shock in store. The toilet was two flights below, down dark, draughty, attic-like steps with no electricity. I clambered down by the dim beam of my bicycle light. Halfway down, I crashed into something and nearly died of fright: dangling in front of my face was a grinning skeleton. When I told Gael of my hairy nocturnal experience the next morning, she laughed.

'Oh that!' she said. 'It's our ape skeleton. A friend gave it to us as a wedding present.'

The next day I was outside Liverpool's supermarket when an inflated middle-aged man sidled up to me.

'Be careful,' he said, 'Nova Scotia ain't what it used to be.' Then he drifted off.

So far I had met with genuinely kind hospitality and was prepared to cast such words of warning aside. Later that day, however, I was cycling along a lonely wooded way when a man sprang out from behind a spruce and dropped his trousers, revealing all. I told him what I thought and kept pedalling.

A few hours later a white pick-up passed and stopped. A bearded character jumped out and said, 'Have I got something to show you!' Uh-oh, I thought, here we go again. Fortunately he had good intentions and was referring to a ninety-foot schooner he was building just down the road. His name was Kelly Kellog and he gave me a guided tour of the shipyard. When the boat was finished he would be off to sail around the world for five years.

'She's called *Tree of Life*,' he said proudly, 'and she's my dream.'

I had stopped at Goo Goo's Diner to buy a drink when a big, high station-wagon pulled up. A huge canine beast leapt out from the back, snarling and growling at me so pugnaciously that I felt it called for an enthusiastic trial of my new dog-deterrent: a Dog Dazer. As I cowered in the corner preparing to take aim, an ample-girthed lumberjack lolled along. He took one look at my fanged aggressor.

'Shut up, you!' he told it. 'I ain't frightened of no dawgs!'

And shut up it did.

Everywhere there were English names like Yarmouth, Chester, Bridgewater and Liverpool. I came to the River Mersey, which is the oldest documented canoe route in North America (dating back to 1686) and flows into and out of Lake Rossignol, the largest freshwater lake in Nova Scotia. (What famous facts and figures!)

I stopped at the small and empty Sable River campsite. Its owner was a small woman with plastic bags on her feet who tottered around saying, 'I can't walk far, I've had an operation on my bunions.' She lived with her husband and her ninety-four-year-old English stepfather, Maurice Burkett, who came from Stockport in Cheshire. He had left home in 1910 but still had a distinct northern accent.

'Cheshire cats,' he grinned, 'pull their tails and their eyes pop out.'

Later that evening Mrs Plastic Bag-Feet shuffled over to my tent. Suddenly and spectacularly, she sprang high into the air.

'Aaahh!' she screamed. 'There's a bug caught down me blouse!'

I assisted her in its removal. As she turned to go, she said jestingly, 'Miss Doo, I hope there isn't too much of you covering the grass by morning!' I laughed and said I had never heard that one before.

That night the dew might not have troubled me but Canada's 'national bird' (the mosquito) did. It arrived in squadrons, liberally reinforced by a back-up team of smaller but more lethal-biting black flies. By morning I looked as if I had measles.

When camping in some woods on another occasion, I was awoken in the night by some noisy rustling from the bushes. Sincerely hoping it was not another pants-dropper, I gingerly stuck my head out through the tent door. What a relief! It was only a prickly porcupine. I came across many a 'porky' in the province and there were also numerous dead hit 'n' run victims beside the roads — skins of inverted spines that stank like the skunks I never saw, though I met a handful of racoons.

I ventured onwards through the tiny hamlet of Port Saxon, where a local proudly informed me about the marine extraction plant across the road which produced a special glue used in colour television screens. That evening, looking for a place to camp, I came across a farm with a nice grassy paddock and thought: that will do nicely. In the yard a little girl played with Grandpop, who said: 'Inside I've a couple of old Chesterfields; come and sleep there.'

The house looked busy, with friends staying and a tribe of children. Not wanting to be a nuisance, I told him that the paddock would be fine and I set up camp. As dusk drew in, I heard rustling from the wood and looked up to see the base-ball-capped head of a puzzled man.

'Jeeze, kid!' said this portly face. 'That tent sure ain't no place to sleep.'

It transpired that he was the neighbour.

'The name's Don Nelson. Climb up over this here fence and join me for tea.'

Don, a retired Air Canada employee, lived in Ankriston Villa, a grandiose place full of antiquated rooms and one of the few buildings in Nova Scotia not to be made of wood. His friends, Barb and Ron from New Brunswick, were staying with him and told me about the camping hazards of picking up moose ticks which wriggled under the skin and could cause the often fatal Lyme disease. They all insisted that I slept in the villa, though I told them I did not want to offend Grandpop.

'It's dark — he'll never know,' they said as they helped me

stealthily move base by the light of the moon, clambering over the fence with tent and bicycle.

The next morning I caused a considerable stir at breakfast when demonstrating my porridge-eating capacity.

'For one so small,' said Don, 'you hold one helluva lot.'

'That stuff,' said Ron, 'must put a roof on your stomach.'

Many Nova Scotians seemed to clutter their gardens with ornaments. Dotted around the ubiquitous satellite dish would be an array of plastic statuettes, families of garish elves, multi-coloured cardboard cutouts of cows, models of various birds floating on fake ponds. Front paths and steps would be covered with imitation grass carpeting, more at home on a greengrocer's shelve. The only sheep I ever saw in Nova Scotia were of a homemade breed plonked in the middle of an other-wise attractive garden — they were so tasteless that I felt they warranted a photograph.

The owner of the sheep appeared on the scene as I snapped my shot. I could hardly say what an eyesore they were and I managed to string together some favourable comments instead. These were misinterpreted as genuine enthusiasm for the owner's handicraft and she proceeded to describe in detail the method of construction. I feigned fascination while she explained that the wool was the furry lining of an old jacket.

'That's ingenious,' I said. Then she told me she was currently working on a Little Bo-Peep to complement the scene. I said, 'What a lovely idea.'

In three weeks I saw only six cyclists. The first two were a couple of racing cyclists who sped past in a blur of lycra, shouting, 'There's a bike shop in Lunenburg!' The next two were Paul and Pauline from Kent riding Evans' mountain bikes; they had cycled from Toronto in snow and temperatures of −11°C. After that, I did not complain again about my chilly, frosty camping nights.

The last were a racing father, Gayland Goodwin, and his son. On seeing me they skidded to a halt, turned round and said, 'Come and stay with us.' Gayland was a cycle-shop owner, a plumber and a maker of weights for lobsterpots. When I met his wife she told me that she was off to Florida next month for a Tupperware conference (she was a Tupperware party director). I had not known that such events existed.

I followed the red-mud shore of the Bay of Fundy, where the tides are the highest in the world. The record variance between high and low has been measured as fifty-four feet. At Five Islands, where I joined some clam diggers on the massive mudflats, the tide raced in at trotting pace.

Down the road was Parrsboro, where I discovered that the biggest fossil find in North America had been unearthed in 1985. It consisted of more than 100,000 pieces of fossils some 200 million years old. A unique part of the extensive find was a series of dinosaur footprints, each the size of a penny, which are the smallest ever discovered.

May was a glorious time to be touring. The apple orchards of the Annapolis Valley were resplendent with sweet-smelling blossom and the meadows were ablaze with sunny yellow dandelions. For once, I had avoided arriving in a place during its wettest spring on record or its coldest summer for eighty-seven years, or whatever. I was blessed with cloudless skies, although the temperature could change rapidly. In one area it dropped from a sticky 80°F to an icy, snow-flurried freeze within just three hours and I dived from swimming costume to thermals.

Nova Scotia seemed like one big friendly community. Everyone appeared to know everyone else. The store, the gas station and the post office were generally run by an aunt, uncle, mother, son or grandparent and in one village all the mailboxes had the name LeBlanc inscribed on the side. It was certainly a family-friendly place.

When I turned up at the Sweeney's farm, I discovered that Joy Sweeney was a cousin of Mrs Tupperware Party. Joy and

MEANING OF POLICE
- POLITE - - - - - - विनम्र स्वभाव
- OBEDIEINT - - - आज्ञाकारी
- LOYAL - - - - - विश्वशनिय
- INTELLIGENT - बुद्धिमान
- COURAGEOUS - साहसी
- EFFICIENT - - - कार्य कुशल

(आरक्षी निवास)

The meaning of Police in India - though I can't say
I'd entirely agree

India, and still feeling fine after drinking from a well full of rats!

Roadside rat-infested food stop with Peter in India

Dawn in Delhi

An Indian version of
the bicycle horn

India - a river that
washed away the road
and nearly us

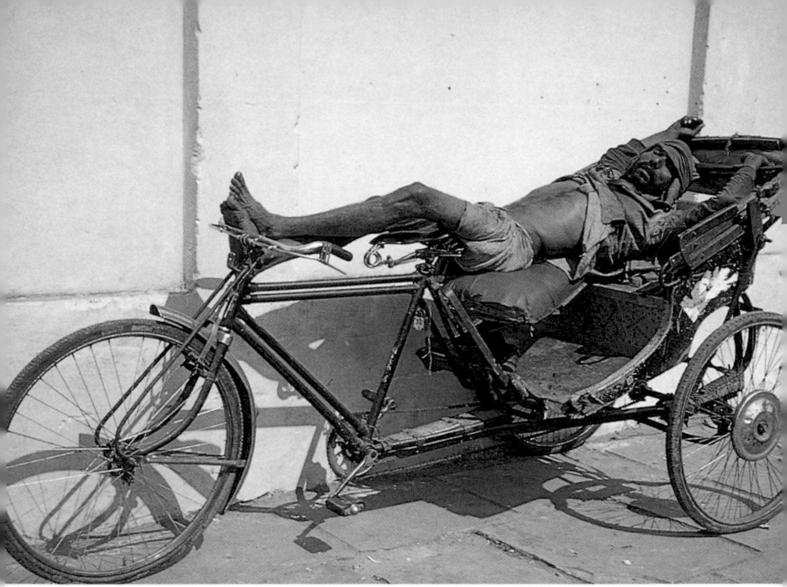

A rickshaw driver at rest in Delhi

The temple of the disappearing shoes in Ranakpur, India

Peter crossing a vulture field in India

Overtaking a camel convoy in Rajasthan, India

Feeling very pleased with myself in front of St Basil's Cathedral in Moscow, after successfully sneaking through customs without a visa

Posing on Vera with Mel at Land's End, just before my legs turned to jelly

A real place in Newfoundland!

Market lady in Sibiu, Romania

Local traffic in Romania. The only hazard to cyclists are the cow pats

A local lady trying my mount for size in Bulgaria

her husband Lloyd had a nine-year-old son, Joel, who was kinda into the word 'kinda'.

'Take a look in the cowshed,' he said, 'you might find something kinda interesting.'

Then he said, 'I think your accent's kinda interesting.' I told him that he was the one with the accent.

Joel was off school, supposedly ill, but he was prancing about energetically, watching television and consuming copious quantities of ice-cream and pop. When I reminded him that he was meant to be ill, he said, 'I know. I kinda feel like a rattin' egg.'

Joy Sweeney, in typically hospitable Nova Scotian style, left me in the house as she went out to work and told me to help myself to anything in the fridge. That, to a hungry cyclist, was kinda tempting — so I did.

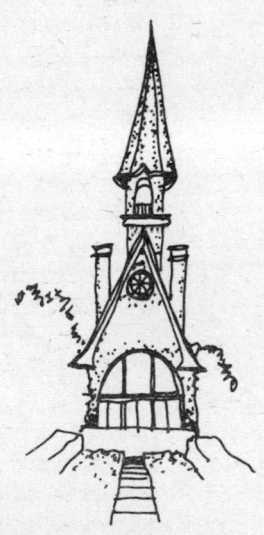

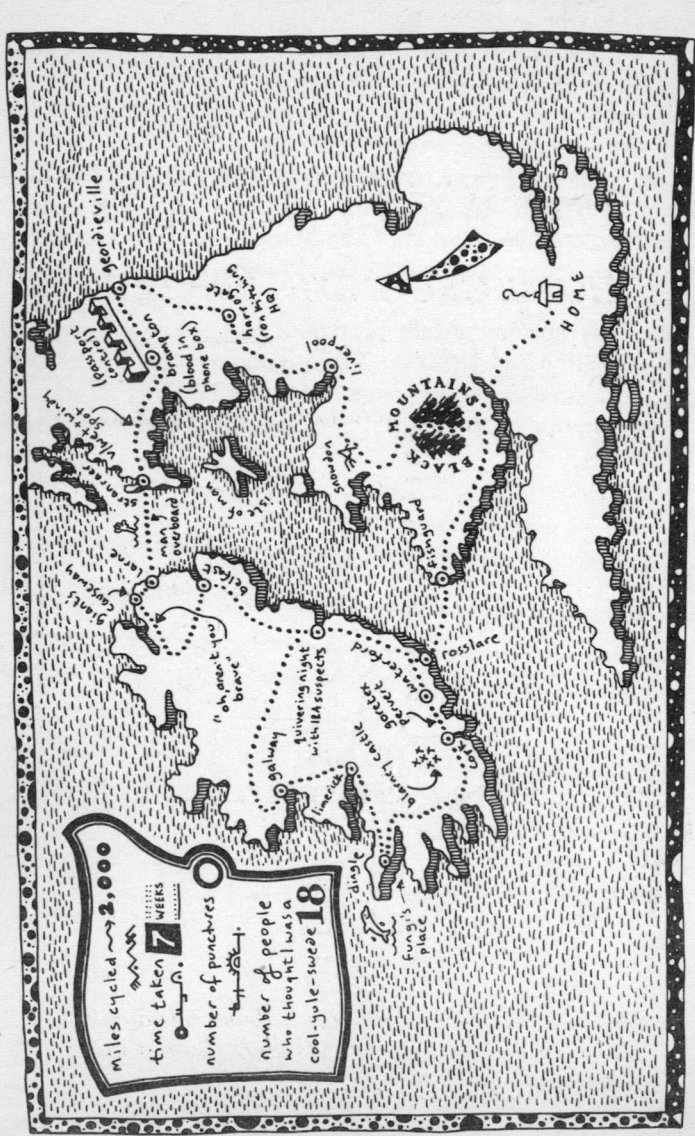

8

The Wall That Was

HOME GROUND IN WINTER

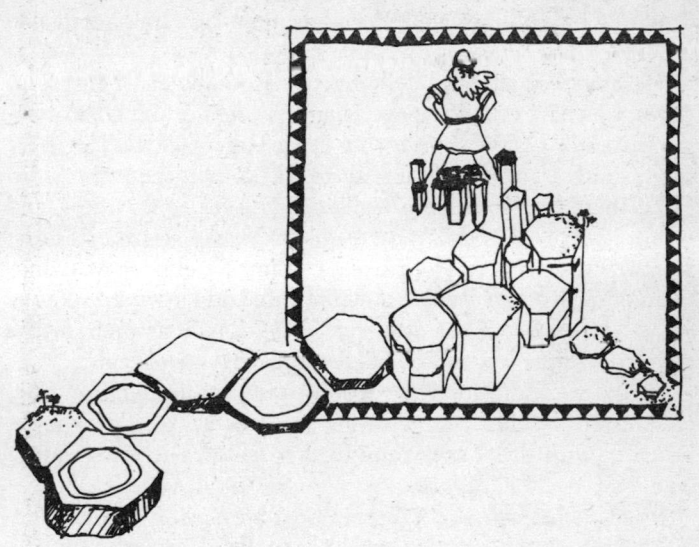

'A tourist is a fellow who drives thousands of miles so he can be photographed standing in front of his car.'

EMILE GANEST

It was New Year's Day and I was cycling in search of Hadrian's Wall. I was sure I was in the right place but I could not find it. Suddenly a farmer appeared at a gate, crook in hand and dog at heel. I pulled on my brakes, skidded on the ice and fell off.

'Excuse me,' I shouted through the howling wind, 'but where's Hadrian's Wall gone?'

The farmer swivelled round 180 degrees and pointed his crook to a small heap of crumbled stones.

'That's part of it,' he said.

I continued to slither on my way. I had always imagined Hadrian's Wall to be a massive construction of awesome proportions — I think I was getting it muddled with the Great Wall of China. I have since been told that there is a noticeable difference and I suspect this to be true.

Hadrian's Wall was built by the Romans in the second century as part of a complex defence system designed to keep the marauding Scottish tribes out of the largely pacified territory to the south. It runs for seventy-three miles across the entire width of northern England, from Wallsend-on-Tyne to Bowness, and was built of the materials most readily to hand — stone in the east and turf in the west. It is said to remain the most impressive monument of the Roman occupation in Britain and I do not doubt the veracity of such claims. However, I never saw it as such: on the day I rode there it was well hidden beneath snowdrifts.

Weather conditions were serious and rapidly deteriorating. Icy westerly winds were blowing in gusts up to ninety mph, bringing with them snow and further gales. The temperature was −8°C and falling fast.

I had cycled across the Pennines to Newcastle for the New Year and would have turned tail to head straight for the warmth and safety of home, had I been made of sensible stuff. Instead, I was overcome by a surge of enthusiasm to cycle the length of Hadrian's Snowdrift. Although the wind blasted head on, its ferocious gusts buffeting me uncontrollably across the road, and although driving sleet stung my cheeks red-raw, I was thoroughly enjoying myself.

The empty road was mine. It followed a high ridge with swooping valleys falling away on either side of me and disappearing towards distant hills. I saw not a soul, except for the occasional cluster of thick-fleeced, spindly-legged sheep, and I thought: this is the way to spend New Year's Day — at the top of the year on top of the world.

But I have to admit that it was chilly. On my feet I wore four pairs of socks, three plastic bags and one pair of shoes and they still felt colder than my deep-freeze. My hands were no better and as for my nose ... well! Rudolph would have been proud of it: red, shiny and frozen solid.

It was a piercing, searching, biting cold and I sallied forth with a stupendous sense of exhilaration. I felt like Scott of the Antarctic battling onwards into blizzards. I thought: where is everyone? Don't they know what they are missing? And then I pictured families sitting around a roaring fire, eating and chatting in various states of merry New Year inebriation. It was only later that I thought: I wish I was there too.

That was when things turned bad. After all, elated emotions do not last long when you have lost all contact with your body mechanisms because of the cold. Life was no longer a pleasure. I hated the wind, I hated the weather, I hated myself. I longed to be round that flame-flickering fireplace, singing, eating and making merry. In fact, I did not care where I was as long as it was under cover and safe from the knifing hostility of the elements.

Finally, as dusk was nigh, in a saturated and shivering state I stumbled through the door of the first sign of occupation I had seen for miles: a pub advertising accommodation. The heat indoors hit me with a force, as did one of the clan of red-eyed, whisky-swigging locals who patted me hard on the back in welcoming northern style. I was bought a drink which helped remarkably towards rekindling my circulation.

But there was no room at the inn. After much raucousness, I was directed up the road to a little B&B. The proprietor, who answered the door, appeared slightly taken aback at the sight of a bedraggled cyclist dripping on her doorstep and told me that she did not open until April. I said that was rather a long time to wait and removed my helmet and multiple reflectors. This apparently worked wonders. I was no longer a luminous space alien who had landed on the wrong planet in the dark. I was welcomed in, given tea and sustenance and shown my room.

During the night the rain slashed against the windows and the wind rattled furiously at the panes. Many times I heard things breaking and banging and crashing outside. Weather conditions had not improved by morning and more gales, storms and snow were forecast. 'Don't go out unless it's essential,' said the radio.

In retrospect I should have headed for Carlisle and taken the train back to London. (Even that would have proved an adventure, as parts of the track were completely blocked by snow. Typically none of British Rail's advanced machinery was capable of clearing the way. 'It's the wrong type of snow,' they said.) Instead, I decided to cross the border into Scotland and head for Stranraer so that I could take the boat to Larne, in Northern Ireland. I had always wanted to go there and now seemed as good an opportunity as any.

I stopped in Brampton to telephone the customers I cooked for in London, letting them know of my latest plans just in case they were wondering where their lunch was. The first phone box I tried was out of order and the receiver in the second was splattered with blood. This gave me a nasty turn. I decided to telephone later, and scuttled out of town.

I struggled westwards along the Solway Firth. The weather, as expected, was appalling. As I wrestled with the wind, it felt at times as if I was riding into the powerful jet-stream of a water canon. I passed fields that had been transformed into choppy lakes, with the tops of trees forming isolated islands. Many times the country lanes were completely flooded — but fording them was fun. I disappeared up to my knees in one.

I stopped in Dumfries at a small corner shop run by a genial Pakistani with a Scottish accent. When I entered, he said, 'Do you feel all right?'

'I feel fine, thanks,' I said. 'How much are your bananas?'

'They're fifty-nine pence a pound,' he replied. Then he said, 'Are you sure you feel all right? Are you really travelling by bicycle? What do you do when it gets wet?'

'It is wet,' I said.

'I know,' he said, 'so what do you do?'

'Get wet,' I replied and promptly ate three bananas.

Then I went into a health-food shop. A little fluffy-haired lady wearing butterfly glasses looked up eagerly as I entered.

'Ah,' she exclaimed, 'you'll be my first customer all day!'

Her clock said 11.05AM.

'Yer surely cannae be cycling on yer tod!'

I said that I was, and thoroughly enjoying it.

'I'm off to Brampton this weekend with my husband,' she continued. 'We're celebrating our Ruby Wedding.'

'That's nice,' I said and told her I had been in Brampton yesterday.

'You were!' she effused excitely. 'What's it like? I've never been.'

I said it seemed like a nice place but I did not tell her about the blood in the telephone box. I thought it might deter her.

I was washed up into Newton Stewart and moored my bike outside The Bobbin B&B. It was closed.

'It shouldn't be,' said a well wrapped-up woman helpfully as she waded past.

Next door was a ladies' hairdresser. When I enquired loudly, above the whirring of hairdryers, if anybody knew of a place to lay my weary head, a head of multicoloured rollers chirped up and said I was most welcome to stay with her. This instant offer of hospitality deeply touched me and I found such invitations to be common among northern folk, as well as those of Ireland.

As I reached Stranraer, it was so windy that people were literally being blown over in the street. Walking was impossible: when the wind came from behind it would thrust you along at a gallop but when it blew head-on you would be bent double, slowly edging forward as if your legs were made of lead. For every one step you took, you would be blown back four.

There was a long delay down at the harbour. The boat from Larne was unable to dock because the tide was too high and the tannoy told us to wait. We waited.

Ten hours later, the ferry chugged out into the inky black Irish sea. It would be the last to leave for two days: all further sailings were cancelled owing to the adverse weather. It was too dangerous, they said.

The crossing was choppy, to put it mildly. I felt dubious at times about our chance of reaching Larne at all. The boat was making heavy work of the voyage, as were the majority of the pallid-faced passengers who staggered around clutching retch-inducing sick bags. I picked up a dog-eared copy of the *Daily Mail* and read how, two days earlier on this very boat, a young man had told his friends he was going out on deck for some fresh air. He was never seen again.

At last the lights of Larne slowly appeared out of the night. Once I was off the ferry, though, the place seemed dark and deserted. Cycling down dimly lit streets, I felt an inkling of trepidation. All the warnings people had given me (and which I had scoffed at and brushed aside) now seemed very realistic. Thoughts of the IRA, bombs and murders filled my head. As I cycled past dark, derelict wastelands and gruesome wall graffiti ('No Surrender', 'Kill the Queen', 'Let Them Die') a shudder of fear ran up my spine. However, it was only on that first night that I experienced such a feeling. I soon discovered that my anxieties about violence and the Troubles (the Ulster euphemism for murder and mayhem) were dispelled in the face of the genuine and open hospitality of Ulster's people.

I stayed that night at Marion Muir's large B&B. It was luxury. In my room I found a kettle, hot water and an electric blanket which I made the most of — until the power-cut. Once again it was dark and very cold.

Marion climbed up to my attic room with a flimsy-flamed candle and invited me downstairs for a chat in front of the fire. All that night the storm raged and the next morning the radio reported that thirteen people had been killed in Ireland alone. The rain still fell in sheets and the wind howled destructively.

In a touchingly maternal manner, Marion expressed her concern at my desire to venture north along the coast. She earnestly debated this matter with a friend and finally they announced: 'We're not letting you go!' They did not want me to be the storm's fourteenth victim.

Instead I decided to take the train to Belfast — a journey which proved quite an excitement in itself. I ran through the rain to the station (narrowly missing being knocked out by a toppling street sign) and made it to the platform just as the guard was announcing: 'Ladies and gents! Your coach approaches!'

We boarded the train and it eased unsteadily southwards beside the wild, white-capped Larne Lough. The wind battered and buffeted the carriages as the waves broke over portside windows. At the most precarious point, with sea on both sides, the train broke down and the lights went out. For a moment there was an anxious silence as the powerful, angry waves exploded over the train, rocking the carriage unnervingly. I felt certain we were going to keel over into the Lough and I wondered how well the electric doors would function under water. Then I got up and closed a small window where the water was coming in. I felt a bit better after that.

We finally got going again and the wind blasted us towards Belfast, where I caught glimpses of Samson and Goliath, two of the world's largest cranes. It was in these docks that Harland & Wolff had built the 'unsinkable' *Titanic.*

Belfast was a city full of fences. The city centre was entirely caged in, the only points of entry being through high-security road barriers. Every building that was worth blowing up was heavily guarded with barbed wire, video cameras, high walls and armed men. Even at those places that were not worth blowing up, there were guards who searched people and checked their bags on entry. The sight of patrolling armoured jeeps with helmeted soldiers crouching in the back behind formidable guns was at first a trifle unsettling — but there were not as many as I had expected and it did not take long to realize that they were as much a part of everyday life as anyone else going about their own business.

I wandered the streets and became caught up in a crowd being evacuated from the large indoor shopping centre. A bomb had been found in Laura Ashley's but people were not so much frightened as frustrated by the inconvenience. 'Always seems to happen in my lunch break,' declared a woman beside me.

I returned to Larne to peruse my new purchase, Dervla Murphy's *A Place Apart*. I wanted to try to understand Ulster.

The ferocious winds continued the next day but the rain had stopped. Marion Muir kindly permitted my departure and I headed north along the Antrim coast. I had no idea it was so beautiful and could not imagine why so many holidaymakers swarmed off to the Spanish Costas when there was something so scenic and empty on their doorstep. And I had never realized that northern Ireland was so small. It covers only six of Ireland's thirty-two counties and is a mere eighty-five miles from top to bottom and 110 miles wide. It became a constitutional part of the United Kingdom some seven decades ago and is not much more than a score of miles from mainland Britain as the seagull flies, but it feels much further away, isolated by the Irish Sea.

The sun appeared for the first time in ten days and I felt immensely happy as I rode along, absorbed in my surroundings. On my right the mighty ocean roared and crashed, its angry foam leaving a white crust on my brow and the tangy taste of salt on my lips.

The previous day's gales had precipitated landslides and I stopped to talk to some road clearers. They told me that parts of the road had been completely submerged by the sea yesterday but I could see that for myself: it was more like a beach than a road and I had to pick my way through seaweed, sand, rocks and driftwood. I almost rode over a dead fish.

I wove my way north around the fascinating nine Glens of Antrim and took an uncharacteristically active interest in the remarkable geology. Within forty miles there were examples of nearly every rock formation and epoch, from schists over 300 million years old to lava fields, glacial deposits, raised beaches and flint beds. Red sandstone tints the beaches and black-and-white boulders are scattered all the way along like thrown dice.

Heading high over the barren, black peat moorland, I looked across the North Channel and could see Mull of Kintyre a dozen miles away. As I plunged down through Bally-patrick Forest, I came to a small expanse of water on either side of the road and a sign which read 'Vanishing Lake'. Intri-gued, I dismounted beside the gently lapping waters and stared quizzically, almost expecting the lake to disappear as I stood there. I felt slightly cheated when it did not.

Near the edge of the forest a car full of young men slowly passed me, heads turning and leering, and stopped just up the road. A door opened and a body was pushed out into my path. The car accelerated away while the body lay slumped and still. A shudder ran down my spine and I thought: IRA. I wanted to turn tail and flee but curiosity got the better of me as usual and I approached cautiously. As I drew level, the body suddenly sprang to life and broke into maniacal laughter. The car re-appeared, reversing at speed; the door was flung open, the occupants guffawing loudly, and the 'body' scrambled back in. The door slammed shut and they tore off down the road.

In Ballycastle I found a B&B overlooking the thunderous sea. I wandered along the beach and suddenly realized it was my birthday. I had never forgotten my birthday before and generally made sure that no one else did either. It was the first birthday when no one had wished me a happy one, yet cycling along the Antrim coast had made it the most enjoyable and memorable ever. When I returned to base after dark, goose-bumped but happy, I found a hot water-bottle down my bed —

a very touching birthday present.

That night I was awoken by loud shouts and shrieks in the street below. I peered out of my window into the gloom and could make out an obstreperous gang of youths in the midst of a fight. Visions of the IRA once again filled my mind until I realized that the missiles they were hurling at each other were snowballs.

The blizzard was still blowing by morning. My landlady told me that one of her customers, from Singapore, was marooned on Rathlin Island and she was concerned that he might be getting a bit cold. This L-shaped island lay eight miles across the Sound — which has whirlpools and harmless sharks — and its tourist brochure boasted that it was the first place to have wireless telegraphy (invented in the late 1890s by the young Marconi, whose mother happened to be Irish). My landlady said its other claim to fame was that there had never been a traffic accident on the island, which was hardly surprising as there was only a handful of cars there.

Through thick, virgin snowdrifts and howling winds I ventured, coming a cropper countless times as I slithered onwards hell-bent on reaching the Giant's Causeway. It took me three-and-a-half hours to cover thirteen miles but I made it. Just as I arrived, the only other tourist turned up — in a car.

'Howdy!' he said (I gathered he was an American). 'Sure ain't no weather to see them rocks.'

With that, he tentatively braved a daring foot into the snow, handed me some advanced and complicated filming device and posed complacently by his car, looking as triumphant as if he had just driven up Everest. With numb fingers, I struggled to manipulate the bleeping digital control panels in order to catch him on film. Mission accomplished, he stepped back into his automobile as I brushed a snowdrift off my head and tried to control my chattering teeth. 'Have a nice day!' he said and then drove away.

The Giant's Causeway is a remarkable natural phenomenon not to be missed, even it if means struggling through Arctic conditions to get there. It is made up of some 37,000 closely packed polygonal columns of basalt and is the unique product of a vast volcanic eruption which affected the landscape of Ireland and Scotland about sixty million years ago. The stone columns, mainly six-sided, were formed by the cooling and shrinking of molten lava that created the Antrim plateau. Today the column tops form 'stepping stones' leading from the foot of the cliff and disappearing into the sea; they match similar formations on the Isle of Staffa in the Hebrides. Legend has it that the giant Finn Macool, an ancient Gaelic warrior, built the Causeway as a road to Scotland in order to wage war upon his enemies. The columns have descriptive and fanciful names like the Giant's Granny, Lord Antrim's Parlour, the King and his Nobles, the Harp, the Honeycomb, the Chimney Pots and the Giant's Organ (the musical instrument, that is).

For the next few days the snows continued as I slid my way south.

'Ooh, aren't you brave!' said a middle-aged market lady in Coleraine. 'Travelling all alone in this weather and so far from home too!'

She told me that she had not yet ventured 'across the water' (the Irish Sea); she had always wanted to but never had the time or the money.

I arrived in Dublin in a snowstorm and a scene of rush-hour chaos. Buses were taking two hours to travel a mile (much the same as in London on a good day) and frustrated commuters were abandoning their cars in the middle of the road, which did nothing to help the flow of traffic. It was dark and conditions had become so bad that I was unable to complete the twelve mile ride to my friend Maeve McGuiness's house. When I phoned her, I found that she had booked me into a hotel at her own expense. Sometimes such genuine Irish hospitality can be embarrassing.

I headed into the Knockmealdown mountains and thus into Dervla Murphy territory, where I met this intriguing and remarkable woman. In 1941, at the age of ten, she was given an atlas and a bicycle and from then on possessed a longing to travel. However, it was not until twenty-one years later, finally freed from looking after her invalid mother, that she embarked upon her secret ambition to cycle to India. She set off across frozen Europe in one of the worst winters in memory. As she had experienced such hardships, it surprised me that she expressed concern about my cycling in such cold conditions.

'I'm sure this is nothing to what you must have endured in that winter of '63,' I said gallantly. 'Just how cold was it?'

'It was so cold that when I arrived in one place I had an icicle on the end of my nose!' she replied.

We sat in her writing room, warmed by a sturdy, log-burning stove and surrounded by typewriter, piles of manuscripts, three cats and a dog. She was writing a book about her hike around Romania. Her trekking had not lasted long: one morning in Moldavia, staying in a small hotel, she had walked down a dark staircase wearing her heavy rucksack when she had slipped on 'some pile of vomit that someone had thoughtfully left there' and had broken her foot. Apparently there were no crutches in Romania and she had to send a telegram to her daughter, Rachel, to bring some from Yugoslavia.

Such a mishap had been a blow but being immobile had its advantages. By living in one place for so long, rather than being peripatetic, she was able to build up the friendship and trust of local folk so that they confided in her.

'So how is your foot now?' I asked.

'No longer good for trekking,' she told me, 'but fine for cycling.'

Would she be returning to Romania on Roz, her tried and trusty steed of Dunkirk-to-Delhi fame?

'No,' she chuckled, 'Roz is now in retirement in Dublin.'

I carefully removed a slumbering bundle of curled cat from my lap, thanked Dervla for the coffee and cakes, and wheeled my bike across the cobbled courtyard.

'Happy cycling!' she called as I set off towards the snow.

And happy cycling I had until a white transit van overtook me and pulled into a layby up the road. A flat-capped man jumped out and cowered behind his vehicle until I approached. With an accompaniment of leers and lewd gestures, he sprang out at me to drop his trousers and flaunt his wares, such as they were.

Until then, I had thought that the more flesh a cycling woman revealed the more harassment she would receive; previous flashers had always struck when I had been cycling in T-shirts and shorts. But this latest indecent encounter disproved that theory. In order to battle through the wintry conditions I had been wrapped up in multiple layers of winter-woolly warmers, swathed from tip to toe in goretex (hood, jacket, bottoms) and with the usual assortment of plastic bags wrapped round my feet and hands. It was hardly passion-pulling stuff, yet I was still subjected to the usual unsavoury exposure. I was amazed. I had heard about the eroticism of leather and rubber — but goretex?

By now such sordid behaviour was old hat to me but I was determined not to let this specimen get away with it. I executed a swift U-turn and extracted pad and pencil to take down his licence number before high-tailing it to Waterford, where I reported him to the police. I was asked for a detailed description of the man — length of hair, colour of eyes, type of shoes, whether he had rings on his fingers, any distinctive

features and size (height, that is . . .). I did my best but said it was very difficult to be so detailed as it had all been over so quickly.

'Is that the complaint?' quipped the rather rumbustious officer.

Two weeks later, back home, I received a phone call from Waterford police station informing me that they had caught the offending individual. They thanked me for my vigilance and I replaced the receiver feeling well satisfied that I had — at last — taught one clever dick a lesson.

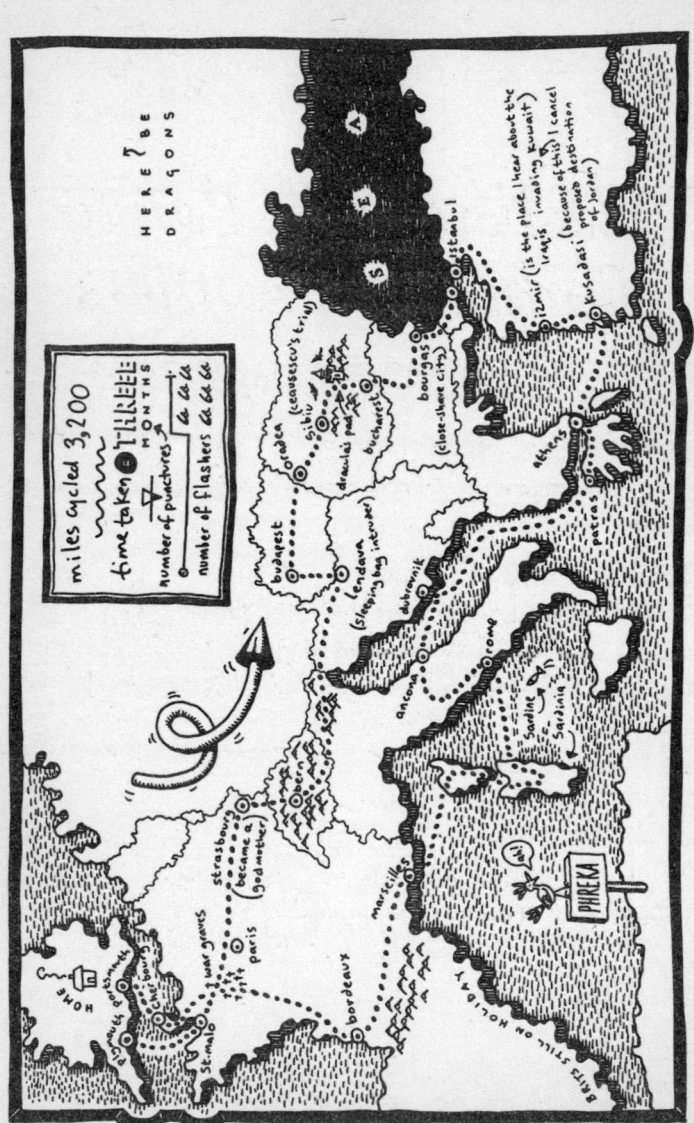

9

Flashers in the Pan to Forbidden Frontiers

ROAMING IN ROMANIA

'Holidays are an expensive trial of strength. The only satisfaction comes from survival.'

JONATHAN MILLER

I had been cycling in Romania for three days on an empty stomach before I discovered, the hungry way, that the *alimentara* (grocery shops) were not the places to obtain food. The few that I came across in the countryside were invariably padlocked and looked as though they had been for years, while those in towns offered little more than dusty, dented, unlabelled tins and jars containing forlorn, unidentifiable objects floating in murky grey solutions of brine. Instead I stocked up on supplies at the *piata* (market), which offered sheep's cheese, fruit, vegetables and bread. Fifty years ago, Romania had produced such fine wheat that its flour was exported to France for use in the lightest of Parisian pâtisseries; today the only bread available in Romania is heavy, hard and grey, even when fresh.

One day in Tirgovişte, on my eternal quest for food, I stopped to ask a bulbous little woman (laden down with a string bag of chilli peppers) to direct me to the market. She said something, grunted and pointed to her armpit. That's odd, I thought. So far my abysmally limited Romanian had been sufficient for the locals to get the gist but obviously not for this woman. Perplexed, I tried again, and again she gestured towards her armpit. Only when she started to gesticulate vividly did I gather that she was asking me for anti-perspirant, an unobtainable commodity in Romania. Sorry, I said, I was a smelly cyclist and did not have any — it was too heavy. She grinned and nodded and finally directed me to the market.

I wheeled my way among a plethora of potatoes and people. A commotion erupted when they spotted me: I was poked and pointed at and heavily patted on my back in welcoming Romanian style. Everyone was friendly, eager to help, to know my country, to know my name and to know what on earth I was doing on a bicycle. I said I was English, on a cycling holiday and looking for some carrots. A boisterous man in a bright orange shirt and big, dusty trousers helpfully attempted to wheel my bike and led me to a meagre mound of carrots. Despite my protests, he insisted on buying some for me along with bread, tomatoes, onions and apples, before opening a bottle of beer and wishing me well on my way.

This experience was no exception. People all over Romania would shower me with gifts (most of which, fortuitously, were edible) and it made me sad to think that it was generally those who had so little who gave so much.

Whenever my father learnt of my intentions to cycle somewhere he did not consider to be 'a good idea', his usual ploy was to scour the newspapers and cut out off-putting articles about the places I intended to visit: murders, riots, disorder, uprising — that sort of thing. When he had accumulated a considerable wodge, he would present them to me and say, 'I think you should read these before you make any further plans.' The amount of off-putting cuttings for Scandinavia, for example, had been minimal; for Eastern Europe and Turkey, however, he had a considerable pile.

As for my mother, whenever I returned in one piece from an excursion she would give vent to a large sigh and then ask optimistically, 'Have you got this travelling bug out of your system yet?' as if she was referring to a severe bout of amoebic dysentery. She did not worry nearly so much when I went off with a companion. Although I enjoyed travelling with a friend (when I could find one) and although it was not nice to go away and leave Mum in jitters, I generally preferred to be by myself. It was more exciting, more of an adventure, and I always met more people, noticed more and ... well, it was far less complicated. I could stop for something to eat without the kind of major drama that usually went something like this:

Me: When do you want lunch?

Companion: Oh not yet — I'm not hungry.

Me: Aren't you? You're usually hungry. What's wrong? Are you ill? I'm hungry.

Companion: Well, you're constantly hungry and just because I usually am doesn't mean to say that I always am and now is one of those rare moments when I'm not. So no, I'm not ill — I just don't want lunch yet.

Me: I do.

Companion: Yes, but you always do.

Me: No, I don't. There are times when I'd far rather have breakfast than lunch, or supper than breakfast.

Companion: Now you're trying to be clever.

Me: No, just getting the facts straight, that's all. Anyway, do you think we could have a rough approximation of when you might be requiring an intake of sustenance so that I could send word down to my stomach, as I know it appreciates being kept informed?

[*Major altercation ensues over timing of lunch* ...]

Later. Selecting a suitable picnicking spot:

Me: That looks like a nice field — how about there?

Companion: Too exposed — be far too windy.

Me: We could sit behind that bush.

Companion: It's in the shade.

Me: Okay, how about there by that tree?

Companion: Too near the road. Anyway, I'd prefer to be by the sea.

Me: But the sea's at least ten miles away.

Companion: Well, by then we'll have a better appetite.

Me: I couldn't have a better one than now if I tried.

Companion: It'll be worth it in the end. Mark my words.

Me: I'd rather not.

On arrival at sea-spot:

Companion: Perfect! Right on the beach and out of the wind.

Me: I don't feel hungry any more. I've got beyond that stage. My stomach must have shrivelled. Let's keep cycling.

When I was riding with Ward, he even forbade me to stop for a pee as it upset his rhythm. My only solution was to accelerate up the road at speed. By the time my mission had been accomplished, His Serene Highness would be passing — momentum undisturbed.

Reading *The Old Patagonian Express*, I decided that Paul Theroux had the right idea when he said: 'Travel is at its best a solitary enterprise: to see, to examine, to assess, you have to be alone and unencumbered ... It is hard to see clearly or to think straight in the company of other people ... Travel is not a vacation, and it is often the opposite of rest. "Have a nice time," people say to me at my send-off. It was not precisely what I hoped for. I craved a little risk, an experience of my own company, and in a modest way the romance of solitude.'

When Mum started fretting at my imminent departure for Eastern Europe, I decided I would take her with me — or at least some of the way. My ploy worked a treat: her reactions were then reversed. She was exuberant. She could not wait for departure day! As a birthday treat, I had bought her a boat ticket to Guernsey (hers was a return, mine was a single) and off we went together for an energetically enjoyable cycle-camping-walking tour round the Channel Islands. Not bad going for an old bag.

After seeing her off on the ferry back to Plymouth, I took the hydrofoil to St Malo, where I made sure of giving the Airborne Stove campsite a wide berth. It was not a memory I cherished.

I rode across the green, rolling hills of northern France, past fields of death where vast and immaculate war cemeteries lay amid Monet landscapes of fiery-red poppies. I arrived at Didier's home in Alsace just in time to become godmother to Colin during a ceremony which lasted about twice as long as an English wedding. I remember my own christening at the age of eleven: Mum took me to church, where I received a token dunk in the font and that was it — over in five minutes. Then I went back to school.

Colin, on the other hand, had the full works. Gift-clutching friends and relations in jovial spirits and elegant dress filled the aisles. Video cameras whirred, instamatics clicked. Various guests stepped forth from the congregation to recite with feeling a selection of prayers — prayers which sounded so much more pious and romantic in French. A beautifully embroidered lace handkerchief was laid on Colin's head as the priest delicately wetted his brow from the font. Candles of all shapes and sizes were lit and I was summoned to sign an elaborately calligraphic scroll beside the altar. The rest of the day was spent feasting and merrymaking and playing football with the boys.

I continued up and over the spectacular Swiss Alps. Nearing the top of the Susten Pass, I was engulfed by a thick, blanketing mist which just seemed to appear from nowhere (as most people say when caught unawares up mountains). My handlebars became something I could feel but not see. All that lay between me and the possibility of plummeting a few thousand feet down the mountainside were some intermittent whitewashed stones lining the roadside. Luckily I collided into an old workman's hut before anything more serious happened to me. I prised open its boarded window, clambered through with bags and bicycle and slept on the table as a howling storm raged outside. During the night I kept dreaming that the hut was rocking.

The mist had lifted by morning. It was cold but perfectly clear and then I noticed that I had not been dreaming after all. The hut was perched right on the edge of a precipice. Three of its four anchoring stays had broken and my future had depended on the one remaining frayed wire that prevented the hut from toppling over the edge.

Riding through France, Switzerland, Italy and Austria, I had the misfortune to be plagued by a series of pants-droppers — men who seemed to glean considerable satisfaction from the mere prospect of dropping their trousers and giving a full-frontal. Nor was it just a certain breed of male. The suspect types ranged from teenagers to workmen to BMW-driving businessmen in three-piece suits.

I had been sixteen when I encountered my first flasher. Cycling alone in the Lake District, I was riding up a steep hill when I saw a man ahead of me, walking a dog beside the road. When I drew level, he turned round to face me and, with a manic grin, exposed all. I got such a fright that I shot up the hill as if attached to a turbo-boost.

As I continued to cycle regularly, I discovered that the biggest problem about being a girl on a bicycle was men. There seemed to be an alarming proportion of the male species who would apparently have preferred to have been born a bicycle saddle. "Ere! Lucky saddle!' (and far worse) were cries with which female pedallers were all too familiar. Groups of workmen or carloads of likely lads were the main culprits, although once a taxi driver leant out of his window and patted me on the posterior as he drove past.

Bottom-patting was fairly rare in Britain but appeared to be all the rage in Mediterranean countries like Italy, Greece and Spain. Maybe it was because the majority of the hot-blooded population rode around on mopeds, thus giving themselves both easy access and adjustment of speed to carry out their cheeky raids on suspecting lone female cyclists. I emphasize the word 'lone'. My rump has always been left well alone when I am accompanied by a man.

It is hard to know how to react when you are confronted by a dickhead who is gesturing and shouting obscenities. Do you shout obscenities back? Do you try to ignore him and pretend you do not care? Do you adopt the role of Agony Aunt and tell him you would be quite happy to lend an ear to his problem, on condition that he pulls up his trousers? Do you inform the police (as I had in Waterford), an experience which can be almost as intimidating as the original confrontation? Do you deliver his equipment a hefty blow with your equipment (a bicycle pump)? Do you calmly deliver belittling comments like: 'I don't know what you're showing me that for. You've got nothing to be proud of — it's the size of a bean'? Or do you just put your foot down and make yourself scarce without further ado?

Every situation is different but it always gives you a shock and a scare, especially when it occurs in lonely places. And then you never know whether he might be some crazed psychopath — whether he will turn violent, rip you from your bike, rape you, stab you or simply blow your head off.

The more it happens, the more frustrated and angry it makes me. He may get hot down his pants but I get hot under my collar. What right do these men think they have to intimidate females? They may see themselves as the domineering sex and as big and strong (which, in comparison with me, they usually are) but there is absolutely nothing big and strong about them. They are all cowards who, whenever I face up to them with aggression, ignominiously turn tail and run.

When I had a series of three flashers in a row as I headed for Eastern Europe, they each elicited different reactions from me. Cycling down the Rhine, I was overtaken by a van driver who crawled along just in front, constantly leering in his rear-view mirror. Finally he stopped up the road, pretending to pee. I knew better but was determined to show that I could not care less. I broke into a chirpy whistle as I approached, breaking off only to greet my *français* flasher with a merry '*Bonjour, Monsieur! Ça va?*' as I passed. My unruffled air seemed to do the trick. Moments later he roared past in a humiliated burst of speed and vanished into the distance.

The next day, in mid-descent, I completely ignored a suave businessman who dropped his pin-striped bottoms.

A short time later, in Austria, it was one of those days when nothing goes right. I had burnt my porridge and lost a sock; a fat *Fräulein* had burst into inexplicable rage when I leant my bike against the wall of her campsite office because, she said, I would damage it (the wall, that is); and I had a head-on collision with an escaped cow. All these misfortunes were during a freezing, headwind downpour. It was the last straw when a lorry driver jumped out of his cab, looking ready for action with tool in hand, as it were. Exasperated, I battle-charged straight for him, wielding my trusty bicycle pump with which I delivered a direct hit. Before he could gather his senses or his underpants, I had retreated triumphantly down the road at speed.

*

I stopped at a Reisach campsite just as a violent thunderstorm burst forth. I did not have a tent with me, only my bivi-bag — which feels like sleeping in a glorified dustbin liner and in which you can do nothing except lie horizontally. It was the first time I had taken one on tour, preferring to forfeit comfort and privacy for extra food space in the panniers.

In drier climes, these body bags really do come into their own. They are more adaptable and better camouflaged — that is, of course, if you have a shrubbery-coloured one rather than something in vivid, eye-catching, red and yellow stripes. Mine was a dark bottle-green which blended very nicely indeed with the foliage — so well, in fact, that I frequently had trouble finding it when I camped out in the wilds and came back from a forage in the forest.

Being so well camouflaged could be a dangerous disadvantage on official campsites. Bivi-bags were a rarity among the seas of brightly coloured tents and motor homes as big as buses and, unless you positioned yourself with caution, your motorized neighbour could quite easily mistake your slumbering form for a 'sleeping policeman' road-hump, which is exactly what happened to my bag in Colmar. Fortunately I was brushing my teeth in the toilet block at the time.

I loved my bivi-bag. Weary after a day's cycling, I would arrive at my camping spot, throw my bag on the ground and that was that: I was set up for the night. Fellow campsite 'campers' thought me mad. As I stretched myself comfortably beside some monstrous motor home, I would look up to see a row of uncomprehending faces pressed against steamed-up windows. I would give a jolly 'hello-in-there-it's-much-nicer-out-here' wave and continue to enjoy lying bivouacked in the blustery wind. Even if it did get chilly at times, I would far rather sleep beneath the stars than in some of those massive home-from-homes, their lockers brimming with food bought in a mad frenzy from their local supermarket before leaving home, the wardrobes full of clothes and clobber, and the 'home' itself fully equipped with electricity, fridge, cooker, television, telephone, video, heating, air-conditioning, upper deck, master bedroom, en suite bathroom, wine cellars, built-in swimming pool and sauna. I saw motor homes in Canada resembling gargantuan space capsules with cars tethered to their rears like dinghies.

It seemed that the occupants' idea of camping was not to expose themselves to a moment's discomfort or inconvenience and above all to avoid fresh air. How strange. They could have stayed at home instead of lumbering around the countryside blocking the roads, jamming villages and ruining views with their house-sized beasts.

Caught in the rain in Reisach, I was insistently invited to join a German couple in their motor home and we all had supper together as the rain drummed on the roof. I have to admit that motor homes are wonderful places for a quick pamper but I could not accept the Germans' invitation to stay the night — it was too claustrophobic for a fresh-air freak. I said I would sleep in the shelter of the laundry block's overhang. They said I would freeze. I said it was June and I would be fine. Then I left.

I was lying contentedly bivouacked watching the storm when a Dutchman suddenly appeared, holding his children's tent.

'We have heard you prefer to sleep outside but in this weather I do not believe it good. Please use my children tent. My wife says you must really.'

It was no use arguing. I packed up and followed him through the rain. The tent had no flysheet and I knew I would get far wetter than had I remained 'bagged' beneath my over-hang. But after I was installed within, a large plastic sheet with which to cover the tent appeared anonymously outside the entrance. The Dutchman told me later that a little old Austrian woman had put it there but she could not speak English and had crept shyly away.

The border into Yugoslavia was the first place where my

passport had made an appearance since leaving home some five countries away. After squeaky-clean Austria, it seemed strange to plunge into a communist land full of staring people and soaring inflation where four noughts had to be ignored on the banknotes to give a more realistic value.

Slovenia was a curious place. One road was littered with millions of black-and-white butterfly corpses. Instead of seagulls swooping in the wake of ploughing tractors, there were huge white storks which set up base in the most precarious and windswept places: their giant nests adorned chimneys, streetlights and telegraph poles and from these they placidly watched the world go by.

In Lendava I cycled right past the campsite, mistaking it for a building site. There were no tourists or tents — only rubbish and cement mixers. I did not want to sleep out in the wilds and so, for the extortionate price of £5, I had the pleasure of sleeping on the floor of an exposed, half-built toilet block. I would have been both richer and safer had I slept in a field. Two beer-clutching workmen appeared, Niko and Svetko, who told me that my name in their tongue was Džosetina. They scoffed at Romania's defeat by Ireland in the World Cup and then said, 'Our country have much trouble. You want sleep with us in log cabin?'

'No thanks,' I said, sensing it was time to retreat. They lingered around for a while, whistling and drinking, before disappearing.

During the night I was awoken by a toothless, crooked-mouthed man trying to clamber into my sleeping-bag. In a state of fright I hit him over the head with my indispensible bicycle pump and he slunk away into the shadows.

Hungary was heaven in comparison — cheap, cheerful and full of well-stocked ABC supermarkets — but Lake Balaton, the biggest lake in Europe, was like one big Butlins camp, brimming with Germans and Hungarians and prefabricated holiday bungalows.

Cyclists were forbidden on roads with single numbers (the main highways) and even on smaller roads I came across the ubiquitous round sign depicting the forbidden use of bicycles, tractors and horsedrawn carts. I ignored them; often there was no alternative and no one ever stopped me.

With the collapse of the Cold War, I was expecting Eastern Europe to be overrun with Westerners but, except in Budapest, I was generally regarded as a very rare species. The only cycle tourist I saw was a Hungarian boy with a sack on his back, heading towards Lake Balaton.

Long ago it was said that if Eastern Europe is a prison block, then Hungary is the luxury cell. With Budapest as the most westernized of all the capitals, this seems very true, but it was still definitely eastern as far as the efficiency of its monolithic tourist organization, Ibusz, was concerned. In search of accommodation in the capital, I cycled to the main tourist office at the central railway station. Three of its five windows were shut and the two that were open did not look promising. A sallow-faced youth lay slumped across the desk of one, either asleep or dead — I never once saw him move. At the other a glowering woman read her book. I stood opposite her on the other side of the glass partition, waiting to be served. Eventually I said, 'Excuse me.' She did not look up. I rapped on the glass.

'Hullo,' I called, 'is anybody in there?'

Still no response. This was silly.

'I can see you,' I called, 'and you could see me too if you looked up. I don't know if you are purposefully ignoring me or whether this is how your system works, but either way, when you've got a moment, could I possibly trouble you for some information?'

Not a glimmer of acknowledgement flicked across her features.

'But don't rush yourself,' I added, 'I've got all d. . .'

'Wait!' she hollered, with such ferocity that I almost knocked myself out on the ceiling. I even found myself apologizing.

'Whoops! Sorry,' I said.

I waited. Nothing happened. Confidence regained and patience well ebbed, I said in the dogmatic tones of a peeved English holidaymaker: 'I would like a map of the city and some addresses of cheap places to stay — now!'

I had made contact! There was movement, albeit sluggish, and a map appeared.

'There is *no* accommodation Budapest,' she said. 'All full.'

When I pressed her, she marked on my map with a perfunctory, messy squiggle the site of another Ibusz office where I might get help. I rode across the city towards the location of the squiggle, stopping off at small, dilapidated hotels on the way — all full. When I finally found the place, it was closed — and had been all day. I rode back to inform the book-woman so that she would not send other tourists on a wild-goose chase. Naturally she was unmoved and unapologetic.

As I failed to extract any further useless information from her, I sauntered dejectedly out on to the streets to contemplate my next move. Looking down the street I saw a McDonald's and my spirits rose. If ever there was a place to restock on diminished toilet-paper supplies, then the Home of the Hamburger was the one.

The 'Ladies' proved a lot more promising than Ibusz for finding accommodation, too. Waiting in the toilet queue were two excessively fat American girls who told me they had heard of a boys' school in Pest, on the other side of the Danube, which acted as a hostel during the holidays. I cycled there and found a bed.

Visiting a city to traipse around churches, museums and galleries teeming with tourists is not my idea of fun but to meander down quiet backstreets sniffing out the markets is. Any market — food, flea, book antique or just rubbish — will keep me happy for hours, indeed days. I never come away disappointed. They are always fascinating places of action and interest with true local colour and character.

Food markets are always a highlight — the smell, the produce, the colours, the variety — and the markets of

Budapest did not disappoint me. There were the small, dishevelled ones in the suburbs where little old women with sun-wrinkled faces, clad in traditional garb of black scarves, skirts and tight-button tops with puff-pleated shoulders, stood stiffly by meagre offerings of herbs, onions and nettles which they had pulled from their village gardens that morning. And then there were the big, bustling, well-stocked markets of the centre.

On the Pest side of the Liberty bridge, I found a great, black, Gothic building inside which was Vásárcsarnok — the magnificent central market. Stepping into this oasis from the polluted chaos of Budapest's streets, it was as if the countryside had invaded the city. There was a panoply of paprikas — nearly every Hungarian dish uses this little capsicum and they came in countless varieties, from the mildest and sweetest to the head-blowing hottest and spiciest, in shades from fiery red to crimson to dark grass-green and insipid, mottled yellow. Stalls were festooned with garlands of the red-brown dried pods dangling with strings of fresh, plump, potent garlic. Beneath them the trestle tables groaned under the weight of dried fruit, nuts, seeds, spices, honey and jam. Other stalls were piled high with pumpkins, peaches, quinces, pears, giant radishes and earthy carrots. There were cheeses, yoghurts, salamis, livers, breads and pâtisseries; downstairs there were pink-plucked, goose-pimpled chickens hanging upside down in lines and coming face to face with bowls of staring sheep's eyes. Next door, packed into blue fishtanks, there were trout, carp, pike, perch, sturgeon, eel and catfish, all fresh and still very much alive from Lake Balaton and the Danube and Tisza rivers.

There was even a mushroom-identification stall manned by a wiry professor with the obligatory electric-wild hair and clinical white coat. He could distinguish between the edible and the poisonous so that people who had been foraging for fungi in the forests could have them expertly identified instead of inadvertently ending up dead. Pharmacies provided the same service; instead of the usual displays of antiseptics, plasters and potions, their windows were alive with knobbled fungal forms.

From Budapest, I headed across the Great Hungarian Plain

through shimmering fields full of golden wheat, burnt stubble and maize. I slept in a field of head-bowed sunflowers and lay with my ear glued to my 'trannie' as I listened avidly to the BBC World Service coverage of the World Cup and became completely absorbed in the football commentary. Had anyone walked past me that night, they would have heard faint cheers of jubilance and anguish rising from the sea of sunflowers as England lost to Germany in the penalty shootout.

The following night, in Jászberény, I met ninety-one-year-old Cscysa Gynbane whose kindly face was furiously furrowed with wrinkles. She plucked me handfuls of dark, sweet plums and tiny, juicy pears from her garden and invited me to stay in her dilapidated cottage. In the wall beside my bed was a hole so large that it served as a window.

We sat on rickety wooden chairs and drank tea together from chipped china teacups. Cscysa spoke no English and my Hungarian phrases were limited to Hello, Goodbye, Yes, No, Which way to? and Have you got a toilet? But we smiled and laughed and made strange communicating sounds. Every now and then she would hitch up her embroidered apron and skirt, lean forward, pat my legs and point to my bike, emitting small, frail gasps of admiration. By arriving on bicycle, I think she thought I was strong — or stupid.

As I approached the border with Romania, I passed the occasional straggler heading along the road towards me, looking tired and dishevelled. They were Romanians. Because it took so long to cross into Hungary by car (maybe twelve hours in a two-mile queue for petrol and then another twelve hours or more waiting in line at the border), many Romanians chose to walk anything up to twenty miles to the Hungarian towns to stock up on basic food supplies that were impossible to obtain in their own country.

The border officials, casually fingering Kalashnikovs, treated me as something of a joke. This came as a surprise, for I had constantly been warned and told many tales of ruthless guards at Customs taking you aside for lengthy interrogations and searches. Often they would steal. I met one Western traveller who, entering Romania by train four months earlier, had had photographic and camping equipment worth over £1,000 confiscated — never to be seen again.

For me, it was almost too easy. The officials stopped turning out the contents of the patiently queueing Romanian and Hungarian cars, leaving open suitcases, cardboard boxes and plastic bags with their contents strewn everywhere in a sea of bric-à-brac, and focused their attention on me. They were good-natured and jocular. They felt my tyres, counted my gears and marvelled at my milometer. Only as an afterthought did they ask for my passport. Then they shook my hand and waved me into their country with a high-spirited '*Drum Bun!*' ('*Bon Voyage*') before returning to strip the waiting cars, removing doors and turning out seats. I was glad I was on a bike.

It was nine miles into the town of Oradea. Beside the road snaked a huge, rusting pipeline which wormed its way ever deeper towards the grey, industrial skyline where monstrous factory chimneys belched out thick, stinking smoke. It was easy to see how much of Romania (and other parts of Eastern Europe) still suffered from the type of air pollution which had caused the infamous London smogs of the 1940s and 1950s. As a result, thousands of people were dying prematurely from breathing the noxious air, while many more suffered chronic lung damage which left them ill and disabled.

I propped my bike against the pipeline in a field of sickly-looking maize — the leaves were yellow and brittle and covered with soot. Hot and tired, I took out my lunch: a melon from Hungary that tasted of cotton-wool. It was late afternoon and the flies were everywhere. They buzzed in my face and landed on my spoon, though I tried to slap them in frustration. They were too quick for me and escaped every time. Then two swarthy boys with grubby faces and shabby trousers saw me from the road. They stopped and stared. One pointed to my bicycle and then they ran up the road, inexplicably laughing.

Entering Oradea, I jockeyed for road space with horses and wooden wagons, oxen and carts, juggernauts, tractors pulling battered coachloads of workers and even a motorbike with a sidecar full of squealing piglets. I had the address of Rodica, a sultry Romanian woman whom I had met in the Budapest hostel. When I had told her that I planned to pass through Oradea (her home town), she had given me some Romanian currency and told me to contact her. I telephoned her from the railway station and then waited for her.

As I waited a big, swarthy gypsy with fleshy hands approached. He grinned from cheek to cheek.

'Ha! Inn-glish!' he chortled. 'Scholar?'

'Scholar? No, I'm a cook,' I said.

'Ha! Ha! Scholar!'

'No,' I repeated, 'me ... cook, and you ... scholar? You are a student?'

'You! You! Scholar. Ha! Ha!'

'No, not me. Are *you* a scholar?'

'Scholar. Yes! You! You!' he said, pointing to himself.

'No! No!' I said. 'You is you and me is me.' I was pointing vividly to emphasize the difference but it was no good. My attempts at an elementary English lesson were futile. He insisted on pointing at me as he guffawed, 'Me — scholar. Ha! Ha!' Then he took my hand and kissed it.

Rodica arrived and saved me. I chased after her battered, windscreenless car over the excrutiating cobbles and into the suburbs where she lived high up in a bleak and dingy tower block with Raul, her ten-year-old son. Her husband had recently been posted to Philadelphia to work as a mechanic in his uncle's garage. Rodica was not sure when she would see him again — maybe in a year if things went well.

Raul was watching a *Carry On* film on a television set so full of static that it hurt my eyes. It was impossible to see what was going on and the subtitles were completely obliterated. All I could hear were the distorted voices of Sid James and Hattie Jaques talking as if from the bowels of a toilet. Raul seemed to be hypnotized. Rodica said that he watched television all day; there was nothing else for him to do.

Over a cup of 'special tea' (special because it was from

Germany and bought on the black market), she told me a little
about life in Romania.

'Ceausescu was shot nineteen times,' she said, 'as everyone
wanted a go. Had he still been alive today, it would not have
been possible for you to stay with me. Talking to foreigners, let
alone inviting them into our homes, was strictly forbidden.
The Securitate were everywhere. If someone was caught, they
were taken away for questioning; they were beaten and heavily
fined — a year's wages — or jailed. Sometimes people just
disappeared altogether. We never knew who to trust. We say
here in Romania that half the population are part-time Securitate and the other half are full-time.'

I asked Rodica if life had improved since the revolution.

'No, not really,' she said, 'a lot of things are worse and
finding food is a big problem. The queues are about as bad as
before the revolution, only now we can complain about it.
Things will get worse, too, before they get better. And this will
take time — possibly years.'

I had come to Romania six months after the revolution in
which the tyrannical communist dictator, Nicolae Ceausescu,
was finally and triumphantly toppled after twenty-four years of
totalitarianism. For a while things had looked promising. The
despot was dead; so too was his sidekick and driving force,
Elena, shot in the head along with her husband. Hardships
appeared to lessen. People no longer worked the seven days a
week of exhaustive and relentless toil that had been part of a
national drive to increase production from which none of the
workers had benefited. It was no wonder that food was scarce:
seventy per cent of it was exported to the Soviet Union as part of
Ceausescu's plan for paying off Romania's rocketing foreign
debt.

Now the people were freer to vent their feelings and opin-
ions and to speak to foreigners without the constant fear of
one citizen betraying another by informing the omnipresent
Securitate. As soon as someone had fallen target to the
Securitate, they would be followed wherever they went and
would often be forced to leave their job or home — they could

even lose their right to live in a particular town. Their friends would be harassed, followed and questioned to such a degree that it was both easier and safer to ostracize themselves. They became outcasts.

But then, as Rodica had told me, life since the revolution had changed little except to become more expensive. The Romanians were constantly struggling to come to terms with their 'liberation'. It appeared that the Securitate were as rife as ever (they had simply acquired a new name) and the communists were still in power. Just as I was entering Romania in June, on the other side of the country President Iliescu's suspect government deployed thousands of club-wielding miners on the streets of Bucharest, where they brutally battered opposition movements into submission. The president justified his actions by saying the democracy had to be defended.

Despite all I had read and heard, I had very little idea just what to expect from Romania. I was even unsure about the water, though I did not go to such precautionary extremes as a strapping Swede whom I met. His name was Max and he was indeed mad. He was lumbering around Eastern Europe with a rucksack full of bottled Swedish tap water.

Travelling in Romania was like travelling back into another century. Life was slow, ponderous and traditional. I passed fields of villagers scything and raking and tossing hay high on to rough wooden wagons, using wooden pitchforks, while their horses dozily swished their tails in the shade of a tree. The menfolk wore peasant clothes and conical black felt hats perched comically on their heads, while the women, their hair tied back in kerchiefs, wore voluminous gathered skirts with printed pinafores and resembled romantic figures in a scene from *Tess of the D'Urbervilles*.

The villages sprawled across the dusty road where children played with stones and puddles among the pecking chickens and gaggles of white, waddling geese. Women's shrill voices rose from beside the rivers and streams as they sang and chatted while they beat and scrubbed their washing upon the rocks. When they saw me, they would wave and call and then burst into fits of giggles.

The houses were old, wooden and decorative, some with elaborately carved gables and delicately painted with friezes of flowers and intricate patterns. The doorways were shaded beneath pots of flowering and trailing vines and drying ears of golden corn. Each cottage had a well, a small vegetable plot and a fenced compound for livestock — they were self-sufficient or shared and swopped produce with their neighbours, as growing their own food was the only chance of survival. Those who were fortunate kept a cow and I would pass women along the road walking their beasts on the lead like family dogs.

Many of the houses were concealed behind magnificent carved gateways, wide and high enough to allow a hay-piled horse-drawn cart to pass. Beside the bordering fences, crude wooden benches lined the dusty road and here little groups of women would sit huddled together, chatting, doing embroidery (which they would hang on lines, like washing, to sell to passers-by) and calling good-naturedly to neighbours across the way. Men in black hats gathered in clusters, playing cards and smoking.

These active communities were the villages that Ceausescu had planned to demolish under his notorious systematisation scheme. He believed that the main opposition to Communism in this predominantly agricultural country lay in the villages, so that by destroying their age-old customs and by equalizing people's living conditions he could (he believed) convert antagonistic Romanians to his own beliefs.

Almost half the 13,000 villages were due to be razed and their inhabitants, whose families had lived on the land for centuries, would be resettled in centralized agro-industrial complexes — massive grey blocks of hideous flats so shabbily constructed that they were in states of severe disrepair even before the villagers had moved in. Walls were cracked and damp, heating did not work, door handles were missing (the workmen had sold them on the black market) and there was a total lack of privacy. Bathrooms and kitchens had to be shared, making the threat of eavesdropping informers stronger than ever.

My first Romanian hotel was … an experience. As I rolled up at dusk after a weary day bouncing around in the saddle on road surfaces that varied from smoothish to crater-like, the hotel was locked and apparently deserted. I knocked and called and snooped round the back until finally a little gingery man opened up. It took over an hour to go through the bureaucratic procedure of filling out meaningless pieces of paper in duplicate. They were meaningless to him as well as to me and he would stare forlornly at each form as if he had never seen it before. Maybe he had not, or maybe he was just making it all up for want of something to do. Romania could surprise you like that.

Eventually I was bundled into my room with my bike — and here the fun really started. There was a vintage television but no electricity. There were light-fittings but no bulbs, a window but no glass, a toilet (draped across its lid like a Miss World sash was a printed paper band stating 'Sanitized for your convenience') but no plumbing — the contents ended up on the floor. When I opened the door to the cramped balcony, it fell off its hinges and nearly knocked me out. When I collapsed on the bed in bemused despair, the whole thing caved in. But what could you expect for twenty-five pence a night?

I tried only one official campsite, near Alba Iulia, and it resembled more an open sewage plant than a place to pitch tents. The ground was covered in rotting litter and human excrement; there were no toilets and there were no campers. By then it was dark, as I had already spent more than two hours looking for a place to sleep. There had been nowhere suitable to camp in the open and both the hotels in Alba Iulia had said they were full, although both appeared dead quiet. Later I was told that, as hotels were state-owned, the management had no interest in vying for custom and indeed life was far easier for them if no one stayed.

As a last resort, I went instead to a trucker's café to see if I could hire one of their campsite bungalows, which looked like chicken hutches and smelt as bad. I sauntered past the stares of the beer-swigging truck drivers and poked my head through a dirty food hatch. From the greasy heat-haze the lard-white form of a corpulent women emerged who, after finally understanding me said all the chicken hutches were full. It was the same old story — but I knew otherwise. I had already been on a reconnaissance mission and had peeped through the pitifully small windows: they were all empty. I stood my ground but so did that meaty matron. With her elevated cleavage, she remained stony-faced and chose to ignore me. By then I was so tired that I was quite happy to stand there all night, and did in fact momentarily fall asleep as I stood, like a horse. One of the oily truckers woke me up by drunkenly grabbing hold of my arm and, with breath that smelt like an old brewery, he asked me to marry him.

'Not now,' I said, 'I'm not in the mood.'

There was a tap on my shoulder and I turned to find a shy young girl offering me a key. She smiled with diffidence and wrote the number '7' on her hand, pointing up the hill to the chicken run. I got the message, thanked her and left.

The hutch, as expected, was no sumptuous suite. It was about the size of a coffin, with the temperature of an oven. Of course there was no electricity or water (the cracked basin, like the floor, was used for storing rubbish) but there was a bed — though my bike-light revealed unappetizing blood stains and numerous 'short 'n' curlies' on it. I smothered the lot with my groundsheet, collapsed on top and suddenly realized how hungry I was. Apart from a bag of tiny, sour apples, I had not eaten anything since the previous day. Nor, apparently, had the mosquitoes who flocked to my flesh with whining relish. No matter how tired I am, I cannot stand being sucked to death by blood-thirsty mosquitoes. I thrashed frantically around my coffin, creating a scene of squidged mass murder, and did not stop until the majority had been slain.

My troubles were not yet over. A tribe of teenage likely lads had tracked me down and now burst through the door (the lock did not work from the inside), falling over my bike. Good grief, I thought, whatever next? The roistering posse picked themselves up and flapped around excitedly.

'Quiet, boys,' I said, in tones reminiscent of a school teacher, 'I'd quite like to go to sleep.'

Words had no effect. They touched my bike in awe, refusing to believe that my panniers were not full of 'ceeg-er-ette', 'shock-er-lart' or 'gummi' (sweets). All I could offer them were some bendy carrots and shrivelled onions — my supper. They were not amused. Nor was I: it was a dismal selection for a hungry cyclist.

I managed to manhandle them back outside but these troublemakers refused to leave me in peace. They kept shouting and laughing and pushing the door open. Then they bombarded my wooden hovel with stones and banged on the walls with sticks. I thought: I'm going to ignore them, they'll get bored, they'll go away. It was wishful thinking. Their noise and numbers increased. I felt imprisoned. The hutch was infernally hot, like a putrid sauna; I had a pounding headache; mosquitoes had regrouped and were attacking with whine-diving force; I was trying to eat my supper of bendy carrots and a quarter bottle of warm water; and I was desperate to relieve myself but could not get out. My patience was being tested to exploding point. There is only a certain amount you can take before an overpowering force overcomes you. It overcame me. Was this what the American girls in the East/West Medical Centre had called a freak-out? Grabbing my cable lock, I burst through the door and charged in full yell after my tormentors, whirling my lock around my head like a lassooing cowboy gone berserk. The mob scattered, scared witless, and I did not give up the attack until the last lingering lad had receded into the night.

I returned to base, confidently triumphant. I had gone into

battle single-handed and disbanded a mob of ruffians, most of them twice my size. My freak-out had done the trick. I felt good about that.

After travelling alone for weeks and having come to terms with talking to yourself, freak-outs and a deluge of pants-droppers, it can be very exciting to come into contact with your fellow countrymen again.

In a hotel in Sibiu I met Brian and Aminge Dale-Thomas, the first Britons I had met since France. They were friendly from the start, although I noticed they were giving me curious glances. I soon realized why when I caught a glimpse of myself in the mirror — the first I had seen for a fortnight. I had been cycling close to Copşa Mică, Europe's most polluted town, where spewing stacks belched forth industrial poisons that coated the whole area, the people, the trees, the washing and the vegetable patches with black carbon. I looked like a chimney sweep.

Brian and Aminge were a wonderfully lively pair of youthful grandparents who were driving a jeep from Belgium to Bucharest. It was full of toys and equipment which were being donated to the Colentina hospital for children suffering from Aids and infectious diseases. They were a spritely and cheerful couple: I warmed to them immediately — and not just because they spoilt me rotten by treating me to supper for three nights in a row.

Being given a five-page menu to drool over proved to be an unnecessary and unkind gesture. The first dish that caught my eye sounded fishily unappetizing: it was 'crap', Romanian for 'carp'. The rest was much more promising but when we had finally selected some tantalizing dish we were told that the only food available was an unidentifiable slither of meat or a tinned-pea omelette. Even these were delicious after living for weeks on little more than stale bread, squidged tomatoes and tired carrots.

Bullet holes in buildings and general signs of destruction in

Sibiu were grim reminders of the December uprising. It was by chance that I arrived during the trial of Nicu Ceausescu, the thirty-nine-year-old son of Nicolae, who was renowned for his hedonistic lifestyle and his reckless indulgence in heavy drinking, gambling and womanizing.

The trial was too good an opportunity to miss. Taking my most official-looking document (a student card) I crudely obliterated the word 'student' with the word 'journalist' in big capital letters. Then I clambered into my most respectable garments (stripy longjohns and inside-out Dennis the Menace T-shirt) and strode purposefully to the courthouse, past army and tanks, trying to look as though I knew what I was doing. When I was stopped by the Militia, I flashed my 'Press' card and chirped that I was a freelance British journalist who had just flown straight from London for the trial. Standing no higher than the Militia man's hip-slung gun-holster, I gazed upwards and said authoritatively that it was imperative I be allowed to pass.

Quite rightly, I was searched and taken away for intensive questioning. That gave me a nasty turn. I thought: now I've really put my foot in it. Then an army commander appeared, dressed in a rather dashing camouflage outfit and built like a tank. He looked like trouble to me — and he was, for a while. He did a lot of shouting and heavy-booted striding around; he kept punching his right fist into his left palm for emphasis; but he did not frighten me as much as he could have done had I been able to understand what he was saying. It took a while for one of his minions to interject and explain that I did not speak the lingo. That was when he almost caught me out. He demanded, via the interpreter, to know how I could report on the trial if I could not understand Romanian.

By now, I was getting a little worried. I thought: quick, I need an excuse! But my brain was not co-operating. The best it could come up with was to suggest that I act like a simpleton and blurt out in wide-eyed surprise something like: 'Look, there seems to be some sort of misunderstanding — I thought this was the tourist office.' You know, make it sound as if I was a dim-witted tourist who had taken the wrong turning. I decided that I was in too deep and old Fearsome Features would not fall for it. Instead, I heard myself saying that I had a colleague inside who was acting as translator for me — which was partially true. The previous night I had met Rupert, who worked for a Scottish newspaper. I knew he was in the court but he did not know I was out here.

More palm-punching followed, more boot-clomping, more shouts. Then, as luck would have it, he was called away on another assignment. Now was my chance, but I had to move fast. I managed to befriend an armed guard who sneaked me downstairs where, in exchange for my passport, I was issued (almost too easily) with a high-security pass and then whisked back upstairs to the courtroom.

I had made it just in time. The trial was about to begin. Then my chances were almost ruined when I bumped into Rupert in the doorway. Naturally surprised to see me, he exclaimed to his companion, in front of a wall of frosty-faced militia men and far too loudly, 'Hey! This is Josie. She's just cycled from England.'

Before anyone caught on, I dived into the nearest seat and submerged myself among flapping notepads and pencils. I was joined by one of Rupert's friends, a Romanian who worked on the local newspaper. She spoke perfect English and explained everything to me as the trial began.

Nicu, I learnt, was not the hated man I had presumed he would be. Suffering from a terminal illness (acute cirrhosis of the liver), he had won sympathy from many Romanians, including the majority of the population of Sibiu — the town he had controlled as Communist party chief. The man many thought had been groomed as his father's successor was accused of ordering the killing of more than eighty civilians in this Transylvanian town during the early days of the revolution.

Nicu sat under the dazzling lights of the courtroom looking gaunt. With the swarthy, fine features of an Italian and wearing dark glasses, he could have been a character straight out of the Mafia. Armed militia in white helmets like upturned pudding-basins lined the side wall nearest him. The trial, being shown live on television, took place before the eyes of millions of Romanians.

It was only on my return home that I discovered the outcome. The trial was adjourned for a month when, in a surprise move, the Bucharest tribunal dropped a charge of genocide which would have carried a life sentence. Instead, Nicu Ceausescu was found guilty of 'instigating aggravated murder' and jailed for twenty years.

I cycled on across the Transylvanian plateau towards the Făgăras mountains, which appeared through the heat-haze sudden and blue. The haymakers were working in earnest. Women raked and turned the swathes of sun-soaked hay, while the men loaded the carts which I often passed on the road.

One of these yellow, wooden carts, its paintwork as tattered as the clothes of the driver, decided to give chase. The helmsman stood enthusiastically whip-thrashing and yee-harring, his wide-brimmed hat flapping behind him in the wind, so that he resembled a combination of Wild West cowboy and Roman charioteer. The race was on.

I glanced behind me. He was right on my tail. I changed into top gear and accelerated away. The road was flat, the wind (for once) was at my back and I tore along with all ideas of sight-seeing or map-reading instantly gone. As we stormed through a small village like a couple of maniacs, he drew broadside, neck and neck, his steed at full canter. In a cloud of dust we sent children and chickens scuttling for cover — two mad speed-fiends racing through regardless. As he broke in front, he turned and gave me a conquistador grin, believing he had the better of me. That look gave me an extra surge of energy. Lungs fit to burst, I edged up — nose to nose, and then ... a downhill! My advantage. His poor piebald was on its last legs and he pulled back into a trot, accepting defeat. As I shot forward, I looked back and smiled. He touched his hat and waved.

Tales of vampires, werewolves and alcoholism run rife in Romania. Judging from the number of inanimate bodies I passed at the side of the road, I fancifully suspected that Dracula had been on the prowl again. But I was letting my mind run wild in this land of cloaked vampirism. The road-side corpses were inebriated Romanians, out for the count. The local liquor, especially *tuica* (plum brandy), was potent stuff.

Up in the Carpathian Mountains I stopped to visit Bran Castle, the legendary home of Count Dracula. High on the rocks it loomed, dark and menacingly dominant. I arrived in a thunderstorm and beneath the blackened skies it was easy to imagine that the circling rooks were devil-fanged bats.

No one was about and I climbed up to the castle with eager anticipation of a good spook and a scare — but I came away disappointed. Since an American tourist had dropped dead of a heart attack, the staff had stopped hiding in coffins and suddenly swinging them open.

Time seemed to have stood still in Romania and indeed, most of the church clocks either had no faces or their hands had stopped dead. Because of this, the people were much more approachable than those in the West: they actually had time for you. Life may have been hard but it was slow; it was also lived mainly outside. The majority of the people were not cooped up in offices or rushing from one place to another in the confines of fast cars, without a moment to spare. They were out working the land or riding in horse-drawn carts at a sedate pace (apart from those who decided to give chase). They were curious, uninhibited and friendly. I would ride alongside a trotting cart as the peasants called and joked and laughed. Sometimes they would lean out and hand me some bread or fruit or smelly goat's cheese. Once I was passed a pork-fat sandwich (their staple diet, which probably explained why the majority of Romanians were hefty blubber-balls despite the lack of food). This was something I would have spurned at home but I ate it with relish and found it delicious. I was that hungry.

Out of a population of twenty-three million, nearly two million are gypsies. People constantly told me to be on my guard and never to trust a gypsy as they were notorious for sly and mischievous deeds, theft and murder. But I found them intriguing, dressed in their flamboyant, brightly coloured clothes, with wild waves of jet-black hair and big silver rings in their ears. Travelling in prairie-style covered wagons, they struck me as the romantic epitome of a vagabond life.

Often I would stop to sit among them in the shade of a tree and I found them just as captivating to watch as they seemed to find me. They would give me water and we would exchange what little food we had; they would scrutinize my bike and I their wagon. Maybe I was just fortunate, but they did not seem to me a race to be wary of. The only trouble I had was from the boys who would occasionally use me as a moving target for their catapults and pea-shooters.

With its lingering reputation as the Paris of the East (dating from before the Second World War), Bucharest came as a shock. There was nothing remotely Parisian about the place. It was a gruesome conglomeration of depressing grey Empire State-style buildings in crumbling concrete.

Despite its rundown and sobering air, I enjoyed my few days in the capital. I stayed with Rupert's landlady, Geta, a jocular and rolypoly woman who lived with her eighteen-year-old daughter, Katalin. Since being burgled a couple of years back, they had fitted two front doors. The inner one boasted an assortment of locks and chains that would have put any locksmith's shop to shame, while the outer, a colossal affair of armour-plate steel, looked thoroughly tankproof. The flat had never been left empty since: one of them always remained behind to guard this miniature fortress.

Many a convoy of humanitarian aid vehicles from Germany, France, Switzerland and Britain had passed me as I cycled through Romania and I decided to visit Bucharest's Colentina hospital to see for myself what a wonderful job the British nurses were doing by helping children suffering from Aids and infectious diseases. I found that I had only missed Brian and Aminge by a day. They had delivered their jeep — but not all the toys, as it had been broken into on the last night.

After all the publicity about the atrocious state of orphanages and hospitals that came to light after the revolution, I felt like just another Westerner taking a snoop. But the inexhaustible Anne McNicholas, who was in charge of her Health Aid team, could not have been more welcoming. She took me round the wards and explained in detail the appalling conditions in which the children had been kept. Later, in her cramped HQ room downstairs, she showed me a video of the hospital taken when they had first arrived: screaming children being hosed down with ice-cold water; filthy beds and bandages (cotton had been so rare that thread and bandages, like needles, had been re-used); shared beds and bedbugs; no laundry facilities or sterilized bottles or toys or pictures or cots.

Now the children lay in brand-new cots, though the old, soiled mattresses were still piled high on the stairs. The authorities had forbidden their removal until the ministry had issued a certificate. Anne said that they should have been burnt and disposed of immediately; instead they had been there for months and were likely to remain on the stairs for just as long again.

The wards had been repainted with cartoon characters and bright colours; there were toys and pictures and new medical equipment — but the most important gift to the children was affection. For the first time in their lives, they had learnt not to be scared at the approach of an adult.

I stayed a day in the hospital and spent half of it with three Romanian women, sorting through boxes of towels that had been sent from Britain. The women were sewing on hanging-loops, using old Singer sewing-machines. Anne told me it was imperative that I never left the room because a bundle of towels would disappear as soon as I was out of the door. She said that it was impossible to trust the Romanian hospital staff: there was so much corruption and cheating and stealing among them, and they were more concerned about themselves than about the helpless children. Huge amounts of donated medicines, equipment and toys had been stolen and taken back to their own families.

Aid was of course an enormous help, when it actually reached the intended beneficiaries, but it was not the whole answer in a country that had for so long been under such a repressive regime. As one nurse told me, the real response from the West should not be pouring aid into the country at random but should be in helping the Romanian people to reconstruct their own society. Unless that changed, they would continue to behave as they had when Ceausescu ruled.

Downstairs in the Aids ward, Anne handed me a two-year-old baby. As I rocked it gently, it felt like nothing more than a tiny bag of bones. Its skeletal, hollow eyes stared out with a pitiful, wasted look.

In the next bed lay a little boy who had just died (four or five died each week). As hairy as a monkey, he lay peaceful at last, eyes closed, clutching a red carnation that had been placed in his bony hands. Although the British nurses could certify him as dead, the Romanian nurses were unqualified (Ceausescu had forbidden training of any kind) and his body could only be removed from the ward after two hours — on the assumption that if he had not stirred in the meantime he must indeed be dead.

The number of abandoned children was truly tragic. In order to build up Romania's workforce, Ceausescu had made contraception and abortion illegal — his outrageous propaganda went to the extreme of saying that all methods of contraception caused cancer. He lowered the marriageable age to fifteen and made prostitution legal. Abortion was only permitted if a woman had produced five children by the time she was forty-four years old. Many mothers abandoned their children as soon as they were born, simply because they could not afford to keep them. Others would sell their babies so that they could buy something that they considered more useful, like a television or a car.

Before I left Bucharest, I cycled down the vast Victory of Socialism Boulevard, leading up to Ceausescu's monstrously awesome Presidential Palace. It was one of the biggest buildings in the world but was still unfinished at the time of his death, although construction work by forced labour had continued unceasingly for twenty-four hours in every day. To make way for this hideous pretentiousness, huge areas of ancient Bucharest had been demolished, including centuries-old churches, old cobbled streets and intricately carved vernacular architecture. One church had been so dear to the people that anarchy would have prevailed if Ceausescu had openly bulldozed it. Instead, it perished during the night in a 'gas' explosion.

As I cycled out of the city, I passed the ubiquitous lines of people waiting outside shops. Queueing was a way of life in every town and city I had seen in Romania. Whatever they wanted, from a loaf of bread to a pair of tights, they would resolutely wait in line. The queues for petrol could stretch for miles. People would rise before dawn, or take time off work (time which had to be made up later) to stand in line for food that we in the West would never consider buying — things like chicken feet or pork bones. There was no guarantee that they would be rewarded for their efforts; often, after waiting for hours in all weathers, they would find that there was nothing left for them. The day I met Adriana, a local newspaper journalist, she told me she had been queueing for five hours for a Chinese toothbrush (the only type available) which disintegrated in her mouth the first time she used it.

Entering Bulgaria through Ruse entailed crossing the Danube

by way of the three-kilometre span of the ugly yet impressive Friendship Bridge. The queues of cars and juggernauts stretched as far as the eye could see. This was even worse than waiting in line for up to twelve hours for petrol. It could take as much as three days for a car to cross the bridge and five days for a truck.

It would have taken me little more than ten minutes had I not been continuously stopped by holidaying Czechs, Poles and Russians (on their way to and from the Black Sea coast) who eagerly invited me to participate in their kerbside picnics. I was amazed at the good nature of the people in such chaotic circumstances. Had this been a bank holiday traffic jam in Britain, tempers would have been boiling over like the radiators. If it had been in America, people would no doubt have been shooting each other. Here, however, everyone calmly resigned themselves to continuous problems and the atmosphere in this stationary and endless traffic was almost that of a carnival.

I had been led to believe that Bulgaria had a far higher standard of living than Romania. Generally I think this was true but the country was on its knees when I was there. Parliament was in turmoil, in the process of electing a new government.

Food was frighteningly scarce for a ravenous cyclist, even more so than in Romania. I once managed to find some rancid sheep's cheese and a rusty tin of sardines, which I succeeded in rationing out for nearly a week. Water was in short supply as well: it was usually turned on for only two hours a day at the most — sometimes not at all — and I would invariably arrive to fill up my water-bottles just after it had been turned off.

The people, although slightly more solemn-faced and reserved than the Romanians, were nearly all most generous and fun. One hot afternoon I rode past a group of full-skirted women who were hoeing a field by hand. They glanced up, spotted me and charged across the road to offer me their water. Then they sat on my bike, sang me songs and jigged in the road.

It was shortly after passing a massive billboard which paradoxically proclaimed TOURISM IS THE PASSPORT TO PEACE that things began to go wrong for me. I had not eaten properly for two weeks, nor had I drunk nearly enough to replace the fluid I sweated out daily as I rode in the mountains. On this unfortunate day, I realized I was in a bad way. The sun beat down inexorably and my head ached and thumped in pain. I was hungry and thirsty but I could not stop to rest as I was desperate to find some water.

At intervals I came across small, rusty pipes from which mountain spring-water should have flowed but they were all dry. At last I came to one that dribbled pathetically but a queue of cars, snaking for ever down the mountainside, was as long as the Romanian queues for petrol as people waited to fill up their giant plastic containers, beakers, buckets, bottles, jars — any receptacle they could find.

One man had almost finished loading his containers into his boot when he saw me and insisted on filling up one of my bottles. I gulped it down. He wanted to refill it but I would not let him: I already felt guilty, having deprived him of even half a litre of the water for which he had probably queued all day. I thanked him and went on my way, hoping to find water in a village fifteen miles further on.

When I arrived, the water was off. The café was closed; dirty plates and glasses were piled high on the tables. I looked at my map — it was about another twelve miles to the next village. Maybe I would strike lucky there.

Just as I was about to leave, a fisherman in a blue van pulled alongside. In disjointed French, he said he was heading back to Bourgas and asked if I would like a lift. He saw that I was not very well and said I was welcome to come back to his apartment for a rest, to meet his family and to have as much water as I wanted.

In every country through which I cycled, people would stop to offer me a lift — they could not seem to understand that I was cycling for fun (nor could I, sometimes). I always refused, never wanting to take the risk, but the fisherman's offer was very tempting. I had never felt so much in need of a lift and I almost accepted. Instead I thanked him and lied that I was fine.

Feeling on my last legs after riding into a strong, oven-hot headwind, I arrived in the next village to the same old story. No water. I knocked on a door and an old woman gave me half a bottle of water from an urn on the floor. When I pointed to her tap, asking when the water would next be turned on, she just shrugged in resignation and looked heavenwards. Like the man in the mountains, she wanted to give me more water but my guilt prevented me from accepting and I said I had enough.

As I wilted on a bench in the shade, feeling sorry for myself and wondering how I was going to muster the energy for the final twenty-mile burst to Bourgas, the blue-vanned fisherman appeared again and repeated his offer. I was hesitant, but desperate. When I saw a photograph of his wife and two children on the dashboard, I felt that he would be a safe bet. I decided to take the chance.

We bundled my bike into the back; I climbed into the tattered passenger seat and, with a splutter of the engine, we were off. At my feet was a big bagful of tiny grey lobster-like creatures. Their eyes flopped around on stalks and their serrated pincers, although small, looked as ferocious as sharks' teeth. The fisherman said they were delicious.

'Yes, I'm sure,' I said, not at all confident, and kept a very wary eye on the bag in case any decided to use my legs as a handy escape route. I had been apprehensive about the cunning powers of crustaceans since a nasty little incident in a London kitchen when I had to cook a live lobster. Being a softy at heart, I had not felt good about the thought of plunging it into a bubbling cauldron of boiling water. I knew lobsters were supposed to taste much better when boiled alive but I tried putting myself into its feelers and the prospect of being scalded to death was not an attractive one. In a fit of compassion I thought: never mind the customer's tastebuds (not a good motto for a chef). With rolling-pin in hand, I prepared for battle by stunning the creature before the crime.

At the crucial moment, as I murmured my profuse apologies to the crustacean concerned and lifted the pin to strike, the telephone rang. Leaving the lobster on the counter with a few prolonged minutes of life, I went to answer it. When I returned, the lobster was not there. This gave me a shock. Where had it gone? Suspecting it might have taken its own life by falling into the cauldron, I took a look. But no — the pot was bare. It was not altogether a pleasant feeling to be in a kitchen with a wild, pincer-snapping lobster on the loose. My first precaution was to put on a pair of thick, stout walking boots to protect my toes. Then I started to look in silly places — in the fridge, the oven, on the ceiling (I did not like the idea of a lobster falling on my head), in the Magimix, in the bread bin. There was no sign, not even a clue. Where *had* it gone?

I started to quiver, to shake, to panic, to think irrationally. Maybe it was seizing its opportunity to get its own back on mankind and had radioed for back-up in support of a *coup*. Maybe if I opened the front door I would be besieged by an armoured lobster army ready to attack. I prepared myself accordingly and stood on a chair, broom in hand, clad in combat gear (boots, rubber gloves and cycling helmet). I was ready for action. But nothing happened.

It was the window cleaner who brought me back to my senses when he tapped on the glass. I think he thought I was practising for the local village pantomime. Sheepishly, I stepped back down to earth (and reality) and explained to him that I had lost my lobster. I thought he would laugh but, bless him, he took the whole thing very seriously. I helped to pull him through the window and he gallantly joined in the search for the elusive crustacean. Together we scoured the kitchen, but to no avail. Lobsters, I discovered, were fast movers and we finally tracked it down to the bathroom, where it was trying to get into the toilet.

'This lobster is a lobster to be proud of,' I proclaimed and dutifully returned it to the source whence it had come. My customer had the tinned stuff instead.

*

Fortunately the fisherman's catch remained well behaved and the blue van arrived in Bourgas without incident. He lived in the suburbs, five storeys up in a grey and shoddy block of concrete flats. I helped him upstairs with his bags to his apartment, where be brought me a big jug of cool water — the best I had ever tasted. But my head still pounded; I felt shaky and exhausted. The fisherman told me to sit down and have a rest; his wife and children would be home soon, he said, as he showed me photographs of them on the mantelpiece. Then he left me alone while he had a shower and busied himself in the kitchen.

A little later he appeared with more food than I had seen in weeks. There were the miniature lobsters (dead), cold liver, hard-boiled eggs, bread, peaches and sour milk. He had gone to a lot of trouble and I said he was a *chef magnifique*. We ate together, communicating with the help of a French/Bulgarian dictionary, while the television in the background droned on about the presidential elections. He poured himself beer from a container that looked like a petrol can and I promptly declined when he offered me some. It did not look like a good remedy for my thumping headache.

Having been fed and watered, I felt much revived and far more like myself. For the first time in days, I could actually think about things other than water or food and I started to take stock of the situation with a clear head. I thought: what *am* I doing? At last it had dawned on me that I was taking a bit of a risk. It was only a passing thought, though. I trusted the fisherman. He seemed a good-humoured and generous man, and anyway his family would soon be home. When the time had ticked well past the hour he had expected them back, I was not in the least concerned — I just started getting a bit itchy to move on. His cigarette smoke was not improving my headache and I wanted to find a place to camp before dark.

The fisherman said I was welcome to stay the night. I thanked him but said I wanted to cycle down the coast to make Turkey by tomorrow. I cleared the table and took the plates out to the kitchen. When I returned, he was standing in the doorway and I remember thinking how big he looked. He repeated his invitation for me to stay the night and meet his family — they would be home soon. Again I thanked him but said I must be going.

'*Non!*' he bellowed suddenly, so fiercely that his angry eyes almost popped out of his head.

It was an awful moment. My stomach dropped a mile. I felt very frightened, but also cross.

'What do you mean, no?' I said in English. 'Yes! I'm going, thanks.'

As I stepped forward to push past him, he thrust me backwards forcefully, kicked me to the ground and jumped on top of my sprawled form. As I was pinned to the ground beneath his massive hulk, he tried to burn my face with his cigarette. I managed to protect my face and fend it off so that he only burnt my wrist.

I wriggled my other arm free and hit the cigarette aside. Then he grabbed my wrist and pushed it back so far that I thought it was going to snap. I screamed at him, calling him every name under the sun, and thrashed around wildly trying to push him off.

I had been pinned on the ground in that position many times before but usually laughing my head off beneath Mel in our self-defence classes. Any movements I had been taught, however, now went to pot. Reality was different and I just kicked out willy-nilly, desperate to escape.

I managed to squirm myself from beneath him and made a hasty dash for the front door which, of course, had no handle and needed a key to open it. Luckily I had previously noticed the key on the table and I swept it up as I shot past. I plunged it into the lock. But this was a Bulgarian lock. When I turned the key, it just kept turning. Nothing happened. I tried frantically. The door would not open. It was like a bad dream, or a scene from the movies — so nearly free but not near enough.

Within moments he had lunged upon me and hurled me back across the floor. He kicked me viciously, dragged me and yelled at me, then threw me on to his bed, trying to rip off my clothes. Struggling wildly, I lashed out for all I was worth, but he was bigger and he was stronger and he picked me up and threw me around the room like a ragdoll. He punched and whacked me in the face and kicked me in the back and stomach.

I had always wondered what it felt like to be beaten up — and now I knew. It did not hurt at all. I did not feel that I was part of my own body. It was an unreal experience; I was very aware of what was going on and yet I felt alienated from it. Through an intangible haze, all I could feel were dull thuds as he hit me about the head. I remember thinking: I mustn't get knocked out, I mustn't get knocked out. I knew that anything might happen if I lost consciousness.

My only advantage seemed to be that, being fairly supple from cycling, I managed to keep bouncing back up on my feet again whenever he hurled me to the ground, instead of lying in a crumpled heap of broken bones. Locked into the flat, with nowhere to run, the only thing I could try to do was immobilize him, knock him out or even kill him. I was desperate enough to do that.

At one stage he grabbed me from behind and, with all my might, I thrust my head back into his face. The noise of our two heads crashing together was awful. He howled, and let me go — but I had only succeeded in making him more furious. With bloodshot eyes bulging like those of an enraged bull, he picked up something hard and heavy and whacked it over my head. I saw stars and things went black momentarily, but it did not knock me flat.

Dazed, I found myself flung into the kitchen. I managed to kick him where it hurt most but it was not hard enough. Like a crazed psychopath, he grabbed a carving knife, pressed it to my throat and dragged me across the floor to the balcony.

Well, I thought that was it. My time had come. I could not believe this was happening, but thoughts like that were not particularly useful for self-preservation. I did not want to die — or be hurled over a balcony five storeys up. I had to do something. I had about five seconds to devise a plan.

The more I had retaliated with hits and kicks, the wilder he became. So I tried the opposite. I went limp, floppy, defenceless, to calm him down. It worked. He dropped the knife and let me go. I started doing stupid things; I started laughing, trying to make him believe that a nasty joke had just got out of hand. I tried to make a joke about our injuries by comparing wounds — bloody gashes, bumps and bruises. We were both in a terrible state, with ripped clothes, blood and sweat. I made an effort to clean his wounds and he started to relax. I was desperate to keep busy. I did silly things like straightening the rugs and the furniture and washing up the dishes.

Then he pulled me on to the sofa with him. I sat in the corner, rigid, legs tightly together but half-heartedly smiling. I was terrified of making him angry again because I knew it would be curtains for me if I did. He poured himself more beer from the petrol can and tried to force me to drink some. He was now pretty jubilant; he thought I had resigned myself to being his, that he had me for the night.

I realized that I would be safe as long as I did what he wanted. On the outside, I gave the appearance of being completely calm and relaxed, slapping his hand playfully (though I would have gladly shot a bullet through it) as it started to work its way up my thigh. But on the inside my head was in turmoil, I was petrified, screaming in my head and frantically repeating to myself, 'What can I *do*?' What can I *do*?'

He was practically sitting on top of me now, one arm around me, the other trying to feel all over. Drunkenly, he kept trying to kiss me. I kept my mouth tightly shut. But he did not like that; he started to get agitated and annoyed. With a gruesome grin, he indicated the balcony. I knew only too well what he meant: if I did not comply with his wishes, then over I would go. I knew I was playing a dangerous game; he appeared relaxed but he was hovering on the brink of anger and violence. I had to be careful — one wrong move from me and his brutal rage would be triggered off again. I had to bide my time. I had to be careful. The television flickered on in the background.

He forced his slimy tongue into my mouth. I felt sick, disgusted. I wanted to bite it off, like in *Midnight Express*, but that idea was even more revolting. Anyway, it would not knock him flat. He tried to push me down to his nether region. I managed to distract him: there was a documentary on the television showing a pig giving birth. He thought this very funny. I did not care what he thought, as long as his focus was not on me.

The position did not look promising. I was trapped in a locked flat five floors up with a drunken, sex-crazed madman. No one knew where I was. I could not believe I had got myself into such a ridiculous mess. I became very aware of the shouts and laughter of children playing in the street below; of the women hanging out their washing and happily chattering in the block of flats across the road; of the airplane going over, its passengers sipping drinks or reading newspapers. I was deeply envious of all these people. I wanted desperately to be in their shoes; to be free; to be away from this hell-hole. I wanted to run out on to the balcony and scream to them all — the people opposite — the people in the street. I wanted *help*. I longed to yell to the world for help.

But what good would it do? They would just see a girl having a fit and before anything could be done I would be tossed over the balcony. If I wanted to survive, I could not act rashly.

Most of all, I wanted to be safe — I wanted to be home. Instead, I sat squashed up on the corner of that horrible sofa, fending off sexual advances as good-humouredly as possible, and racking my brains as to what I could do.

Communication with him was not easy. Not only was he drunk but he had also given up all attempts at French. It was down to murmuring the odd Bulgarian word and gesticulating — something that was made even more difficult by the fact that the custom of shaking and nodding one's head has quite the opposite interpretation in Bulgaria. A nod means no, a shake means yes. This is muddling at the best of times but many Bulgarians have adopted the more familiar connotation when talking to foreigners: nod — yes; shake — no. The result was utter confusion all round which, under any other circumstances, could have been decidedly comical. Now it was deadly serious. I did not know if my head was inadvertently saying yes! yes! when he was asking if he should throw me over the balcony. To play safe, I neither shook nor nodded but went round in circles.

The sun started to set. I had been imprisoned for over five hours. He was now completely and drunkenly relaxed. He kept hold of me, stroked my legs and occasionally kissed me, but he was in no hurry. He knew he had me for the night. He knew he could do whatever he wanted to do to me. And I knew that if I remained his captive for the night I would be raped. And that, even if I survived, there was no guarantee he would then let me go. He had proved he was violent and for all I knew he would have his fun, use me and abuse me, and dispose of me. That way there would be no way I could report him to the police.

There was one thing of which I was certain: I would never let him rape me. I would rather jump off the balcony than submit to his repugnant desires. And I can now understand how, when desperate, people will do rash things. The thought of falling five flights did not scare me in the least — quite the opposite, in fact: the idea of flying free through the air away from him was preferable by far to remaining in the rapist's den.

And I almost did it. I almost jumped. But I stopped myself. I thought of Mum — how her worst fears would come true; how her regular supply of postcards would dry up; I thought of her ever growing and sickening worry. Then I thought of the money I was raising for the Guide Dogs for the Blind Association and I felt a surge of determination that I was going to buy that guide dog, no matter what. And I thought of my cycling, how important it was to me, how much I loved it and how much more I wanted to do. All these thoughts combined to stop me from taking a death-leap over the balcony. I was not going to kill myself for this one lunatic. There had to be another way and I had to find it. But soon.

Sweating profusely, I suddenly realized how thirsty I was. I said I wanted a drink and walked into the kitchen. He was like a limpet — he did not leave my side for a moment. I gulped down glassfuls of water, which he found most amusing and patted my stomach as though it was about to explode. I smiled and chuckled back, but all the time I was scanning the kitchen for potential weapons. There were empty wine bottles by the sink; there was a heavy pot; and there were knives. But trying to knock someone out or launch a life-or-death attack is incredibly difficult when they are constantly on top of you. If I had lunged for the wine bottle, his arm would be upon mine and his fury roused. That would be it — my chances ruined. If only he had turned his back for a second, it might have given me the opportunity to knock a pot on his head. But he never turned away and I was too frightened to risk my attack back-firing. I could end up with a bottle in my face, or worse.

The kitchen had a tiny balcony and I sauntered out, pretending to admire the sunset but really to see if it offered any possible means of escape. There was nothing – just a dead drop to the street down below.

There was a small bar across the road and he pointed towards it. He kept repeating, 'Whisky? Whisky?' He seemed to be suggesting that we go down there together for a drink. Had he run out of beer, or was he too drunk to realize that if we did go down there I would be free and he would not? A fantastic surge of hope flooded through me but I tried not to look too enthusiastic. We went back inside, where he made it clear that if we were to go for a drink I had first to have a shower and change from my cycling shorts and ripped, bloody T-shirt into a dress. A dress! I did not have one. Pedalling around with a party frock in my panniers was not something I did. I had a clean pair of longjohns and a fairly respectable shirt, but that was all.

That would not do, he said. It had to be a dress. I thought of his wife, but of course there was no wife. No, he said, we were not going to the bar. Maybe he had not intended to go at all — the whole thing was just a cruel ploy to raise and then crush my spirits. I felt desperately depressed. But there was one last chance: the balcony off the living room.

Standing out there, I could just glimpse the sea through a gap between the flats opposite. I managed to get him to ramble on about something to do with the sea while I took the opportunity to size up my chances of escape. I saw a crowbar propped up on the corner and I toyed with the idea of attacking him with it. But all I could envisage was an ugly struggle and me being the one to end up over the balcony.

Then I saw that there was a neighbouring balcony on the other side of a thick concrete partition. The only way I could get into it was to jump a good four feet up on to the front of his balcony, balance there and, without toppling off, swing out and over to the other side. And I would have to do it quickly, before he realized what was happening and pushed me off. It looked practically impossible and I doubted whether I was even tall enough to jump on to the front rail. I did not think I had the guts. But the more I cast furtive glances at it, the more I knew that it was my only chance of escape.

He gestured for me to move back inside — it was now almost dark and he wanted to close the door to stop the insects from getting into the room. If I was going to make my jump, I had to make sure he went inside first. As we moved towards the door, I suddenly lost my courage.

There was a flowering plant just by the door and I stopped him, exclaiming some rubbish about how lovely it was. He moved towards it and was now in front of me. I had given myself one last chance. While he drunkenly drivelled on about the plant, I knew it was now or never. Inwardly I was worked up into a frenzy — my mouth was dry, my heart was pounding, my head was exploding with 'I've got to do it! I've got to do it!'

We could not gabble on about a flowering plant all night and I gestured that I was ready to head in. He took one step inside and as soon as I saw his back turn on me my head screamed 'NOW!' I hurled my water glass at him and sprang up on to the balcony railing.

I felt some dangling wires, which I grabbed with my left hand and then kicked myself off and swung round the wall, landing on the floor of the neighbouring balcony. I had done it — I was free! It was the most incredible feeling I have ever had. I screamed for help and crashed my hand against the window of the flat.

But there was no one in. Suddenly I was terrified that he was going to come round after me. With the adrenalin pumping furiously, I swung myself out like a demented Tarzan and round another three balconies. At last a woman saw me and rushed out. I have never been so relieved to see anyone in all my life. I then knew for sure that I was safe.

My immediate reaction was to hug her. The family looked rather shocked, which was hardly surprising — they were probably not used to having a blabbering, bruised and bloodied alien landing on their balcony halfway through supper. I tried to explain that there was a madman on their floor who had beaten me up and I scampered to the telephone, crying, 'Militsia! Militsia!' They did nothing, for which afterwards I was grateful. Everything would have got too complicated if the police had become involved — I could not speak the language and how could I explain my case? For a start, most people could not understand how a girl could want to travel alone in foreign countries. For all they knew, maybe I had been looking for a good time which had gone a bit wrong.

Men and boys from the street had seen me leaping from balcony to balcony and now raced up the stairs. Some were armed with rough cuts of wood. I felt as if I had an army on my side. One boy, Yancho, the only one who could speak English, said, 'Please, please — what has happened?'

Briefly I told him, but while we were all clustered in commotion round the stairs the door of the fisherman's flat opened. He had groomed himself, put on a shirt and then entered into a heated argument with the crowd. The sight of him sickened me and I was filled with nothing more than contemptuous hate. Had someone handed me a gun at that moment, I could quite easily have shot him in the goolies.

I ran past him down the stairs. Yancho followed and I told him that my money, my shoes and my belongings were still in the flat. With reinforcements, Yancho went and retrieved everything for me and then we all went outside.

They led me to some wooden tables where men were drinking, smoking and playing cards. Yancho, concerned and caring, was beside me all the time. For a moment I just sat with my head in my hands as the clamouring crowds gathered. I wanted to get away from everything — to wake up in my own bed knowing that the whole thing had been a hideous nightmare. Then I felt Yancho gently touching my arm.

'Please,' he said, 'what are you going to do?'

'I don't know,' I said, 'just get away from here as far as possible — find a hotel or somewhere to camp.'

'You cannot,' he said. 'It is late — all hotels expensive and full in Bourgas. And you have many hurts. This man, he says you are very welcome to stay with him.'

'Whoa!' I said, and cowered into the corner.

'It's no problem,' said Yancho, 'he has family.'

'I've heard that one before!' I replied with a teetering smile.

'No, it is okay. He is my friend.'

I said I would only trust that man if I saw his family on parade in front of me. A few minutes later the man, Valcho, appeared with his wife, Rilka, who spoke excellent English and worked for Balkan Airlines, and two lovely young daughters, Jenia and Polina (who was clutching a hamster). When I discovered that they lived on the ground floor, I decided they were a safe bet and said I would love to stay with them. Yancho came with me and helped me with my bike. As we walked, he told me the fisherman was renowned for getting drunk.

'No one really knows him,' he said. 'He was married once, but he had much problem.'

Rilka tenderly administered first aid to me as I sat on the toilet seat. That was when I started shaking — the most uncontrollable jitters I have ever had. I went into a spasm of violently quivering trembles. But my hands were the worst: they were jumping and bouncing all over the place in such a ridiculous fashion that we both burst out laughing. I was not really in a laughing mood — I felt terribly sick; my head, with a protruding lump like a unicorn's horn, ached more than ever and my whole body felt an agonized wreck. All I wanted to do was to curl up in a dark room and go to sleep. I was totally shattered.

Rilka had other plans. Although it was well after midnight, she had whipped up a meal and said how honoured she felt to have me to stay — she had never had a foreigner in her home before. How then could I say I would rather go to bed?

At last Rilka made up a bed for me on the sofa and left me to lie in the dark with only the insane wheel-spinning hamster and blood-whining mosquitoes for company. As I shut my eyes, the room spun and my head whirred and I was back in 'his' flat — back in the nightmare.

In one way I wanted desperately to catch the first flight home and forget this lark of gallivanting round countries alone. People had always told me that the world was a dangerous place and I now realized that perhaps they were right. But the more I thought about it, the more I thought no, why should I give up what I loved doing most just because of one drunken goofhead? Through all the years I had spent saddle-bound, all the wonderful places I had seen and people I had met, this was my only bad experience. I may have escaped his clutches but if I gave in, went home, found a sensible job and threw my bike in the shed, it would be like surrendering, and he would have won in the long run.

After a restless few hours, I arose at dawn and crept out of the house with Rilka, who was going to work. We walked along the back streets together and met Yancho. They joined the bus queue and then both gave me a huge hug and told me to write. Then I cycled south out of the city and kept going, riding in a sort of frenzied daze, ignoring the pain and noticing nothing around me. I was just intent on putting as large a distance as possible between me and Bourgas. The further I left that doomed city behind, the more my spirits rose.

After escaping alive from a car crash in China, Paul Theroux had said: 'There is something about the very fact of survival that produces a greater vitality.' I now know exactly what he meant. As I soared south along the coast I felt as though I was bursting with a sense of elated energy and I did not stop riding until I reached the patrolled watch-towers and grim, high barbed-wire fences which heralded the border with Turkey. I was back in the saddle again, grateful to be still alive, and with the reassuring and familiar sound of the wind in my wheels.

Appendix

EQUIPMENT DEPARTMENT

The following is a list of equipment I take or have taken over the years:

SLEEPING ARRANGEMENTS
Tents:
Ultimate Pea Pod 1 Superlight. Apart from pinged-poles, performed very well for two people. Good ventilation openings at either end.

Saunders Jet Packer (2lb 15oz). Performed faultlessly, even standing up to Iceland's notoriously relentless and severe storm-whipping winds. Takes too many pegs, though, and zips could be stronger. Admittedly Red'ed was right — feels a bit like sleeping in a coffin. To save weight I took single pole instead of 'A' poles so kept head-butting it in the night and having to pirouette round it to get in or out or just to move. A normal-sized person would find this tent a bit of a squeeze.

Moss Solet (3lb 2oz). Hooped, single pole. Inner tent walls made entirely of mosquito netting. In dry weather it is like sleeping outside only better as biting insects keep their distance. No bell-end, which I miss when it is wet and not too good in high winds, but I have not blown away yet. Takes only six–ten pegs and can be erected in less than two minutes: a definite bonus.

Pegs:
North Face Super Tent Peg
Chouinard T-stakes (indestructible)
I also take small spare aluminium inner sleeve in case of pole breakage.

Ground Sheet:
Cheap plastic sheet cut to size or woven fabric all-weather original American space blanket.

Bivi-bag:
Mountain Range, goretex (1lb 3oz). Very adaptable and no messing with poles or uneven ground, but there is precious little hope of privacy. If you do not mind being stared at and looking stupid (and the impractical aspect of occasionally getting wet) then this bivi-bag is well recommended.

Sleeping-bags:
Mountain Equipment — Lightline (2lb). This was my first down sleeping-bag and is now fourteen years old but is still going strong, although it has developed rather too many bald, cold spots.

RAB — Micro 300 (1lb 5oz). Goose down, no zip, packs down into nothing. Excellent, but can get a bit chilly in really cold weather.

North Face — Blue Kazoo (2lb 2oz). Best all-rounder.

Sheet sleeping-bag (6oz).

Mosquito net (11oz) for use in countries where malaria threatens.

Sleeping-mats:
Therm-a-Rest Ultralite ¾ length — inflatable sleeping-mat (1lb). Lightweight luxury.

Karrimat — insular foam cell (10oz). I always take this with me now as it is lighter than the Ultralite, puncture-proof, more adaptable and only marginally less comfortable.

MSR (Mountain Safety Research) X-GK — (also take fuel bottle, spare washer and valve, small stove spanner and pricker). Travelling alone I had never taken a stove and had always shunned them for one person (too much weight and clobber), but when porridge withdrawal symptoms struck I decided to treat myself. X-GKs can burn ferociously and I had been told they were unreliable and unable to simmer: I have not let mine within sight of Ward and it has performed faultlessly — it also simmers. I do not take it to hot, cheap countries.

COOKING / EATING UTENSILS

1 × 6oz stainless steel pan and lid.
1 × small plastic food container — use as a bowl and lid doubles up as chopping board.
1 × plastic mug.
1 × plastic snap-top container for honey.
1 × Kitchen Devil small, serrated sharp knife with homemade blade protector.
1 × vegetable peeler (in countries of suspect hygiene it is important to peel all fruit and veg as human excrement is often used as fertilizer).
1 × aluminium spoon.
1 × aluminium knife.
1 × pot scourer (cut in half).
1 × 10cm sq tea towel.
Plastic bags — all shapes and sizes including zip-locks.
Katadyn pocket water filter (1lb 7oz) — after picking up some intestine-destroying amoebas in India I now plan to use this in countries with suspect water supplies.
3 × water-bottles (for bike) and lightweight collapsible water container that can be hung from trees etc.
1 × lightweight collapsible rucksack.

CLOTHING

Cycling cape — apart from its Port-a-loo convenience (and

occasional ground sheet) I cannot get to grips with these flappy things at all.

North Face Velo Goretex cycling jacket — a fairly recent acquisition, but I now never leave home without it and do not know how I ever managed without. Have also made a customized hood for it which helps immensely with retaining heat. Could do with pockets on the outside though. In really cold, wet conditions I now take over-trousers too.

Rubber overshoes (found in a gardening shop for 30p) are good in saturating conditions. But a few layers of plastic bags are just as good if slightly more inconvenient and unsightly.

Berghaus Polarlite Activity Sweater (i.e. fleecy top) — far better than draughty and heavy old school tracksuit tops which I used to take.

Mittens — Helly Hansen Polvot.

Cheap waterproof(ish) over-mittens.

Thermal inner gloves or silk liners.

Leather, padded fingerless cycling mitts (helps to avoid numb hands).

Silk balaclava.

Neck tube.

Woolly hat — bought from stall in Iceland and made from real Icelandic sheep's wool (heats your head in seconds).

Sam Browne Reflective belt and ankle bands.

Helmet — Bell V1 Pro — taken mainly to keep Mum happy, but which spends most of the time bungied to my bicycle rack. I am not a great advocate for helmets — I get too hot-headed and claustrophobic, but I think they are a good idea. I wear them occasionally but generally not in hot Third World countries — I do not like to look more alien than I do already. I wear them at night, in fog or on fast main roads.

1 or 2 pairs cotton-lycra longjohns (leggings).

2 pairs custom-made stripy cotton-lycra cycling shorts.

2 pairs Andiamo Short Liners from Smuggled Goods (true bottom savers).

Undies — never seem to take enough as when I hang them out to dry on my panniers dogs-in-chase tend to get their teeth stuck into them but . . . rather my undies than my shins.

2 pairs Marks & Spencer or Berwick Market white ankle socks (wear one, wash one). In colder weather take more.

1 pair thermal longjohns.

1 × swimming costume.

2 × T-shirt vests.

1 × T-shirt.

1 × bandana.

1 × thin cotton spotty scarf — good not only for blocking out neck draughts but also for make shift slings, bikini tops, blindfold (when trying to sleep in brightly lit places) and emergency towel.

1 × pair Nike (stiff-bottomed) trainers.

1 × pair flip-flops (always use in showers).

WASHBAG / FIRST AID AND OTHER BITS AND PIECES

Washbag (small, lightweight stuff-sack) with toothbrush, toothpaste, shampoo, soap etc.

Dental floss (not only good for teeth, but for making washing lines, tying up parcels / panniers / bits of bicycle back together, making trip-wires round the tent to forewarn of unwanted nightime prowlers and lots of other uses).

Lip-block sun cream.

DIY insect repellent (neutral cream base with lemon grass essential oil added — works a treat and avoids smothering body with harmful chemicals).

Tiger Balm — good for sprains, headaches etc. Insects do not seem to like this either.

Toilet paper (would be lost without it).

Calendula cream — good for everything (saddle sores, cuts, dry lips etc). Arsen Alb (for food poisoning), Arnica (injuries).

Washable foam ear-plugs — for those really noisy nights (also good for when camping in the wilds to block out too-close-to-the-tent-for-comfort scary noise; I prefer to remain oblivious rather than lie awake trembling with fright all night).

Small pack of Quest multi-vitamins and minerals — useful for when I cannot find anything else to eat.

Small 6in length of cut-your-own plasters.

Small bandage.

Mini tube Savlon antiseptic cream.

Safety pins, needles, extra strong 100 per cent polyester thread (good for all repairs).

Mini nail clippers.

Cloves — good to chew on if toothache strikes.

Syringes, drips and needles.

Card clearly stating bloodgroup.

Pencil, rubber bands, airmail paper, envelopes, permanent marker pen, Pritt Stick, Sellotape, diary.

Credit card-sized solar powered calculator (maths is not my strong point and good for currency calculations).

Oxford Minidictionary — to help those all-too-frequent blanks when I cannot spell (or speak) — also provides something to read if I have run out of reading material.

Book(s) — I always strive to carry a reading book with me.

Maps.

Mini thermometer to dangle off handlebar-bag.

Swiss Army knife with tin opener, tweezers and scissors.

Mini (50p-sized) mirror for hoicking flying insects out of eyes.

Mini address book.

Money belt.

Passport, money (American Express traveller's cheques — can have letters sent to their offices, like a safer method of Post Restante — dollars, local currency, credit card), insurance, E111 form (for Europe), Camping Carnet (for Europe), plane or boat tickets, international driving permit, driving licence, YHA card, student card (for discounts), spare passport photos. Photocopied details of passport, traveller's cheques etc stored in another place.

Dog Dazer — battery operated dog deterrent.

Small padlock for cheap hotel rooms.

Petzl Micro head torch.

Spare batteries for camera, cycle computer, watch.
Cheap digital watch with alarm.
Sony mini shortwave radio.
Sunglasses.

CAMERA
Canon idiot-proof Sureshot. Highly recommended.
Last two tours have taken Canon AE1 Programme with
Tamron 70-210 lens (and padded case).
Minox mini tripod.
Slide film:
Kodachrome ISO 64
Ektachrome ISO 100 or ISO 200.
Fujichrome ISO 100

BICYCLE TOOLS

Small adjustable spanner.
Allen keys — to fit all sizes on bike.
Mini Philips screwdriver, spoke key, chainlink tool, few spare
chain links, TA crank remover, TA crank spanner, block
remover, cone spanners (for removing pedals), few spare
nuts and allen screws, oil, grease, picture wire, rag, surgical
gloves, gaffa tape, insulating tape, short length of 4mm rock
climbing cord, 3 × bungies.
Spare tyre — Michelin Hi-Lite Expresss 26 × 1.50.
Spare inner tube(s).
Plastic tyre levers, puncture repair kit, spare spokes, brake,
gear and straddle cables.
Pump — stored in rolled-up sleeping-mat to prevent theft.
Mini pump — Barbieri (Italian) as back-up pump, and pump
adaptor.
1 × cable lock.

ADDITIONS FOR FORTHCOMING TOUR TO
MEXICO
Compact binoculars; Rohan clothing; hammock; bodyguard.

BICYCLES
The following bike I used for my early years of touring as well as for Harwich to the Sahara and St Malo to Malaga:

FRAME: 19½″ cheap unknown dark blue sport touring.
WHEELS: Mavic rims, stainless steel spokes impressively handbuilt by Mick Perry of Wielersport.
HUBS: Campagnolo Gran Sport.
TYRES: Panaracer Touring 700c.
HEADSET: Campagnolo Gran Sport.
HANDLEBARS & STEM: Cinelli.
BRAKES: Campagnolo Gran Sport.
CRANKS: Campagnolo Gran Sport.
CHAINRINGS: Campagnolo double 42 / 52.
CHAIN: Sedisport.
FREEWHEEL: Maillard 13 - 34.
DERAILLEURS (front & rear): Campagnolo Gran Sport.
GEAR LEVERS: Campagnolo Gran Sport.
PEDALS: Campagnolo Gran Sport.
BOTTOM BRACKET: Campagnolo Gran Sport.
SEAT POST: Campagnolo Gran Sport.
SADDLE: Rolls (black).
TOE CLIPS: Christophe.
WATER BOTTLE CAGES: cheap, bendy metal ones.
COMPUTER: Cateye mate.

For Iceland and Morocco the following components were changed:

CRANKS: Campagnolo Victory 170s.
CHAINRINGS: Campagnolo 35 / 50.
WHEELS: Mavic rims, stainless steel spokes with Campagnolo Nuovo Record hubs.
FRONT DERAILLEUR: Shimano 600.
REAR DERAILLEUR: Campagnolo Rally.

For Newfoundland the following components were changed:

CRANKS: TA 155s.
CHAINRINGS: TA - 26 / 36/ 40.
SADDLE: Regal (white).

The following bike I used for India and Romania and all UK riding:

FRAME: 18" Roberts bronze-brazed pink touring bike.
WHEELS: Mavic 26" rims oxygen M6CD, stainless steel spokes.
HUBS: Campagnolo Nuovo Record.
TYRES: Specialized Nimbus 1.4.
HEADSET: Campagnolo Nuovo Record.
HANDLEBARS & STEM: Cinelli.
BRAKES: Deore XT Cantilever.
BRAKE LEVERS: Campagnolo Super Record.
CRANKS: TA 150mm.
CHAINRINGS: TA 26 / 36/ 40.
CHAIN: Sedisport.
FREEWHEEL: Suntour 13 - 32.
DERAILLEUR (front & rear): Deore XT.
GEAR LEVERS: Campagnolo Nuovo Record.
PEDALS: Campagnolo Gran Sport.
BOTTOM BRACKET: Specialized S1.
SEAT POST: Strong.
SADDLE: Regal (white).
RACKS (front & rear): Blackburn.
COMPUTER: Cateye mate.
WATERBOTTLE CAGES: Specialized.
TOE CLIPS: Cateye nylon.

For Nova Scotia I used the following bike:

FRAME: 18" Tamarack custom expedition purple and chrome

touring bike designed and made by Red'ed from Columbus SP and Reynold 531 ST tubing.

WHEELS: Saturae H × 22 rims. DT stainless steel spokes.

HUBS: Campagnolo Nuovo Record thirty-six-hole large flange.

TYRES: IRC All Terrain 1.75.

HEADSET: Campagnolo Nuovo Record.

HANDLEBARS & STEM: Cinelli.

BRAKES: Deore XT.

BRAKE BLOCKS: Scott Matthauser mounted on Moot Mounts.

BRAKE LEVERS: Campagnolo Super Record.

CRANKS: TA 150mm.

CHAINRINGS: Chris Bell's precision-made Egg-Ring inner and outer. Mavic middle - 24 / 36 / 40.

CHAIN: Sedisport.

FREEWHEEL: Shimano 600 13 - 34.

REAR DERAILLEUR: Huret Duopar titanium.

FRONT DERAILLEUR: Shimano 600.

GEAR LEVERS: Campagnolo Nuovo Record.

PEDALS: Campagnolo Nuovo Record road/strada.

TOE CLIPS: Cateye nylon.

TOE STRAPS: Binda extra reinforced.

BOTTOM BRACKET: Camagnolo Nuovo Record cups; Dura Ace lockring; Specialized S1 spindle.

SEATPOST: Campagnolo Nuovo Record.

SADDLE: Regal leather.

RACKS (front & rear): Blackburn.

HANDLEBAR COVERING: Kryptogrips (no longer made).

MUDGUARDS: Petijean.

COMPUTER: Cateye ATB.

WATERBOTTLE CAGES: Blackburn.

PUMP: Silva with primus end-chromed lugs.

Index of People and
Places

A GLORIFIED GLOSSARY

RIDING THE DESERT TRAIL

TRAIL

Bettina Selby

Armed with a sun hat, insect repellant, a Swiss army knife and an 'all terrain' bicycle, Bettina Selby set off. 4,500 miles later she reached her destination – the source of the Nile. Her journey took her from the sites of one of the most ancient civilizations to some of the last discovered places on the planet.

From the Mediterranean to the mysterious Mountains of the Moon; from the Pyramids, the great temples of Luxor, the Valley of the Kings and all the magnificence of Egypt to the empty burning sands of the Nubian Desert, war torn southern Sudan and Uganda. She endured endless miles of yielding sand, swamps, deserts and jungles, was arrested and nearly killed – and emerged at her journey's end to tell the fascinating tale of the encounters that befall a solitary traveller in remote and often dangerous lands.

'A satisfying blend of physical and mental adventure, diverting vignettes, fascinating insights and shrewd reflections'
Dervla Murphy, *Irish Independent*

THE LOST CONTINENT

Travels in Small Town America

Bill Bryson

And, as soon as Bill Bryson was old enough, he left. Des Moines couldn't hold him, but it did lure him back. After ten years in England he returned to the land of his youth, and drove almost 14,000 miles in search of a mythical small town called Amalgam, the kind of smiling village where the films of his youth were set. Instead he drove through a series of horrific burgs which he renamed Smellville, Fartville, Coleslaw, Dead Squaw, Coma, Doldrum. At best his search led him to Anywhere, USA; a lookalike strip of gas stations, motels and hamburger outlets populated by obese and slow-witted hicks with a partiality for synthetic fibres. He found a continent that was doubly lost; lost to itself because blighted by greed, pollution, mobile homes and television; lost to him because he had become a foreigner in his own country.

'Both a brilliant piece of travel writing and a wonderfully funny, perceptive view of small town America'
Publishing News

'A very funny performance, littered with wonderful lines and memorable images'
Literary Review

'Funny as this wonderful book is, it is also a serious indictment of the American way of life and the direction in which it is going . . . he is genuinely shocked, as we are, by the statistics of affluence, poverty, crime and culture that he drops in hither and thither'
Irish Times

'High-spirited . . . hilarious'
Observer

Warner now offers an exciting range of quality titles by both established and new authors. All of the books in this series are available from:
Little, Brown and Company (UK) Limited,
Cash Sales Department,
P.O. Box 11,
Falmouth,
Cornwall TR10 9EN.

Alternatively you may fax your order to the above address. Fax No. 0326 376423.

Payments can be made as follows: Cheque, postal order (payable to Little, Brown and Company) or by credit cards, Visa/Access. Do not send cash or currency. UK customers: and B.F.P.O.: please send a cheque or postal order (no currency) and allow £1.00 for postage and packing for the first book, plus 50p for the second book, plus 30p for each additional book up to a maximum charge of £3.00 (7 books plus).

Overseas customers including Ireland, please allow £2.00 for postage and packing for the first book, plus £1.00 for the second book, plus 50p for each additional book.

NAME (Block Letters) ....

ADDRESS...

....

☐ I enclose my remittance for _____

☐ I wish to pay by Access/Visa Card

Number ☐☐☐☐☐☐☐☐☐☐☐☐☐☐☐☐

Card Expiry Date ☐☐☐☐

Riding the Desert Trail
by: B. Selby